THE REAL FIGARO

*The Extraordinary Career of
Caron de Beaumarchais*

Cynthia Cox

THE REAL FIGARO

The Extraordinary Career of
Caron de Beaumarchais

Coward-McCann, Inc.
New York

CONTENTS

Illustrations follow page 54.

FOREWORD

How many of those for whom the adventures of Figaro have been immortalized by the music of Mozart and Rossini yet know the strange life-story of the barber's original creator? For while Figaro is undoubtedly the mirror of his author's own personality, the career of Pierre-Augustin Caron de Beaumarchais, watch-maker, musician, playwright, business-man and secret diplomatic envoy, is far more extraordinary than any adventures of the characters he created.

The story of his life begins in the middle of the eighteenth century, in the Paris of Louis XV, where hardly anything was too fantastic to happen. For in what other setting, we may well ask, would a man convicted—even though unjustly—by the Parlement of Paris on a charge implying forgery and under sentence of civil degradation, have yet been employed by King and Government on highly confidential missions entailing in every case the handling of large sums of money, have continued this work in the succeeding reign, and, in addition, have acted as adviser to King and Ministers in matters not only of internal administration but even of foreign policy? But these were the years before the Deluge, when the French monarchy, like a ship whose steering gear has broken down, was drifting into the path of the hurricane which at the end of the century would sweep away for ever the candlelit world of elegant frivolity satirized with merciless wit by Beaumarchais. Yet the story of his life is above all one of struggle, a struggle sustained with obstinate courage, often in face of the heaviest odds, on the part of a single individual against injustice, whether at the hands of the old régime, or, later, of the Revolutionary Government (when he confronted the formidable Danton in person), and in which survival often required the exercise of all the Spanish barber's wit and ingenuity.

The career of this real-life Figaro, who was presently to take the name of Beaumarchais (which he borrowed, as it was said, from one of his wives), was largely moulded in its beginning by a chain of events which his own versatile gifts linked together. For if the young Pierre-Augustin Caron had not gained access to the highest circles of Louis XV's Court through his talents as watchmaker and musician, he would not have been in the position to enlist royal support for a project of Pâris-Duverney, an action which gained him the great financier's friendship and gratitude. Although his association with Duverney was later to involve him in the lawsuits which were the bane of his career, it gave him experience of large-scale financial operations which was to be of great value to him in later life in building up his own fortune. Moreover, had he not in the first place made himself so opportunely useful to the old financier, the latter might never have deputed him to visit Spain. For it was the furtherance of Duverney's business in that country which was the real purpose of

Beaumarchais' visit to Madrid, rather than that of chivvying his sister's reluctant Spanish fiancé to the altar—an incident which his exuberantly fertile pen was later to clothe with all the trappings of drama. But without the encouragement and powerful support of Duverney, it is possible that Beaumarchais might not have made the long journey to Spain, much less have remained twelve months in Madrid 'in a whirl of business and pleasure'. And without this first-hand experience of eighteenth-century Spanish society, the world might never have made the acquaintance—at least in their actual guise—of the characters who were to bring their author his most enduring fame: the Count and Countess Almaviva and their faithful henchman Figaro.

In writing this book, intended for the general reader, my aim has been simply to tell the story of Beaumarchais' astonishing career, set against the background of his times, and to show something of the character of this original Figaro. I have not attempted any detailed study of his polemic and dramatic writings, since that lies rather within the specialist field of French literature. Nor have I dealt at more length with his law suits than was necessary to explain the part they played in his career. Apart from the grim light they throw on the judicial methods of the time, their only interest for us today is that they provided the occasion for some of Beaumarchais' most brilliant writing, in the *mémoires* by which he undertook his own defence and which carried his name all over Europe before either of his two great comedies had been publicly performed. I have, however, tried to give some account of the translation of these comedies on to the operatic stage, a phase of their career which has been almost entirely ignored by previous biographers of their author. Yet it is precisely the operas made from *The Barber of Seville* and *The Marriage of Figaro* which have done most to extend the fame of Beaumarchais' characters over the whole civilized world.

C. C.

ACKNOWLEDGMENTS

The extracts quoted from the despatches of Lord Stormont, British Ambassador in Paris, 1772-8, being unpublished Crown Copyright material in the Public Record Office, are reproduced by kind permission of the Controller of H.M. Stationery Office. I am also indebted to Messrs. Routledge and Kegan Paul Ltd. for permission to quote from pp. 130 and 131 of their *Memoirs of Lorenzo da Ponte*; to Professor A. Carey Taylor, of the Department of French, Birkbeck College, University of London, for his helpful advice over an English rendering of Beaumarchais' scathing description of his enemy Marin; and finally, to the late Mr. George Kamm for his work in preparing the book for publication.

C. C.

Chapter 1

THE CARON FAMILY

EIGHTEENTH-CENTURY Paris was far from being the fine city bequeathed to succeeding generations by Napoleon III. In 1700 its extent was still limited to the area enclosed by the medieval walls; although these and some of their gates were already beginning to be demolished, and their sites transformed into a chain of tree-lined boulevards which by the middle of the century had become the most popular and fashionable promenade of Paris. But beyond the western end of the enclosure terminated by the Porte Saint Honoré and the palace of the Tuileries, the future Place de la Concorde was as yet only waste land flanked by ditches; while the site of the Champs-Élysées was occupied by thick groves of elm trees planted in alleys alongside the rough, dusty road leading up towards the hill where stood the little village of Chaillot. To the north of this road lay a region of kitchen gardens and bowling-greens which, as the city began to spill out westwards, was presently to develop into the Faubourg Saint Honoré.

But inside the area which had been enclosed by the walls, Paris remained a medieval labyrinth of narrow, winding streets flanked by high, stone-built houses; the streets being all without sidewalks and sloping towards a central drain which in wet weather could be relied upon to provide the luckless pedestrian with a mud-bath from passing vehicles. It was a city of sharp and startling contrasts, where, in the words of Rousseau, 'flaunting wealth and the most appalling poverty dwell together'. On the one hand was a scene of great splendour in what Voltaire describes as the arts of social life, and that not only among the great nobles: 'I do not hesitate to declare', he says, 'that there is five times as much silver plate in the houses of the bourgeoisie of Paris as in those of London.' (He had lived in London.) 'Your notary, your lawyer, your tailor, is far better lodged, has far better furniture, and is far better waited on, than any magistrate in the capital of England. More poultry and game is eaten in Paris in one day than in a week in London.' It was indeed a period of extravagant living and reckless gambling (was it not the time of Manon Lescaut?) in which the Government had taken its share by the Regent's encouragement of John Law and his ill-fated schemes for the replenishment of the national coffers. Yet it was also the period when the life of the *salon*, which had become the common meeting-ground of noble and intellectual, reached the height of its brilliance under the guidance of such presiding queens as Mme Geoffrin, the blind Marquise du Deffand – with her extraordinary passion, at the age of seventy, for the fifty-year-old Horace Walpole – and Julie de Lespinasse.

But, on the other side of the picture, the contemporary writer Sébastien Mercier notes that 'in front of the splendid colonnade of the Louvre, old-clothes men openly display rags and tatters in the square. Grandeur and indigence side by side!' The plain truth was that a sea of the most appalling slums lapped the very walls of the royal palace, and was to continue doing so until the middle of the following century. Louis XIV had removed the Court to Versailles, where – except for a brief period of seven years at the beginning of the following reign – it had remained ever since, a self-contained community with its own preposterously artificial pattern of life. But here in the capital, adjoining the Louvre, was one of the chief breeding-grounds of the mob which was to figure so hideously in the worst excesses of the Revolution.

Between the Louvre and the eastern boundary of the city, guarded by the grim fortress of the Bastille and the adjoining Porte Saint-Antoine (entrance to the Faubourg of sinister revolutionary fame), lay a maze of old streets dating back to the thirteenth century and even earlier. Among these was the Rue Saint-Denis, street of jewellers and clock-makers, whose fame in the eighteenth century was so great that visitors came from all over Europe to see and admire their work. It was in this street, at a point almost opposite the Rue de la Ferronnerie that there came to live, in the first quarter of the eighteenth century, one André-Charles Caron, who, like his father before him, was to prove himself a clock-maker of some talent.

André-Charles, a native of the old province of Brie (now the department of Seine-et-Marne), was, however, no ordinary clock-maker. He was a man whose interests were of a variety and width unusual for his station in life, for they ranged over literature, the arts and science; which was all the more remarkable since he was largely self-educated. It is no small tribute both to his knowledge and his intelligence that in 1746 the Governor of Madrid, to whom he was personally known, should have turned to Caron for advice on methods of dredging ports and rivers, and that the clock-maker of the Rue Saint-Denis should have sent a lengthy memorandum on the subject to the Governor. André-Charles also possessed the musical talent and the zest for life which he was to pass on to his children. After serving as a soldier in the Rochepierre Dragoons, he obtained his discharge in 1721 and then came to Paris to study and perfect himself in his father's profession. He was at this time a Calvinist like his parents, but only a month after his arrival in Paris he reverted to the faith of his more remote ancestors. Whether, as some have suggested, he found that being a member of the reformed religion was an impediment to his career, and decided, like the first Bourbon monarch, that Paris was well worth a Mass, we do not know; but it is not unlikely. For since the revocation of the Edict of Nantes, Protestants had had no legal existence in the state; even marriages celebrated by their pastors were declared illegal, and the children of such marriages illegitimate. By this time, also, certificates of Catholicism had become necessary for admission into artisan corporations. Thus, when a year later Caron made application to be received as a master clock-maker, he was able to make mention of his recent abjuration of Calvinism.

A few months afterwards, on 13 July 1722, André-Charles took to himself a wife, Marie-Louise Pichon. We do not know very much about her, except that she was the daughter of a Parisian bourgeois; however, she provided her husband with nine children, four sons and five daughters. But three of these sons died in infancy; the fourth, Pierre-Augustin, made his entry into the world on 24 January 1732, in a room over the little clock-maker's shop in the Rue Saint-Denis. He was thus to be the only boy in a family of five adoring sisters. The eldest sister, Marie-Josèphe, married an architect named Guilbert, and went to live with him in Madrid, where he was architect to the King of Spain. There she was joined by the next sister, Marie-Louise, known as Lisette, and the two set up a fashion shop in the Spanish capital. We shall hear a good deal more of them presently. The third sister, Madeleine-Françoise, was married in 1756 to Lepine, a celebrated watch-maker; but it is the fourth sister, Marie-Julie, who is the most interesting of all the five. She was not, it appears, a great beauty (her nose was too long, though she had fine eyes), but she had both charm and gaiety, and a brilliant mind which was more like that of her brother than any of the other sisters. Julie and her brother were in fact devoted to each other, and remained so to the end of their lives. Julie was accomplished,

3

too, as well as charming: she had a knowledge of both Italian and Spanish, played the harp and 'cello, and composed songs. But more than all this, she possessed great courage; as we shall see later on, not even the Terror would be able to break her dauntless spirit, or quench her irrepressible sense of humour. The last of the sisters, Jeanne-Marguerite, was known as Tonton. She too played the harp well and had a charming voice; she was pretty and very *chic*. With all its gaiety and constant music-making, the Caron household must indeed have been a very lively one; the girls, playing the harp or 'cello, would be accompanied by their brother on the viola or flute, and – with the gift in that direction which they all possessed – they would improvise their own couplets and set them to music.

Young Pierre's actual schooling, however, was a very brief one. He was sent to the École d'Alfort, but at the early age of thirteen, he left to be apprenticed to his father. Not surprisingly, in such a lively home, the boy's mind was hardly fixed very firmly upon clock-making; for he was now precisely the age of Chérubin, page to Count Almaviva, and it is clear that he himself was just as precocious as the character he was eventually to create. (Already, like Chérubin, as he later recalled, his 'heart pounded at the sight of a woman', and, as Julie tells us, he was already writing verses to his girl friends.) As he grew up, he gave his father more serious concern by his association with companions whom the elder Caron considered to be thoroughly undesirable. By the time that Pierre had reached the age of eighteen the father decided that drastic action must be taken and he made a show of driving his son out of the house – having first arranged with some friends that they should receive Pierre into their home until he showed proper signs of repentance. When these signs were duly observed and the prodigal begged to be allowed to come home, his return was made conditional on his acceptance of a sort of peace treaty drawn up by his father. This truly curious document throws a revealing light on the character of an eighteenth-century parent and on the misdemeanours of his son:

First: you shall not make nor sell, nor cause to be made or sold, directly or indirectly, anything which is not for my account; and you shall yield no more to the temptation of appropriating to yourself anything whatever beyond that which I give you. You shall receive no watch for repair or other work under any pretext whatever, or for any friend, no matter whom, without notifying me; you shall never touch anything without my express permission. You shall not even sell an old watch key without accounting for it to me.

Second: you shall rise in summer at 6 o'clock and in winter at seven, and you shall work till suppertime without reluctance at whatever I give you to do; I do not propose that you shall employ the faculties which God has given you, except to become celebrated in your profession. Remember that it is shameful and dishonouring to lag behind and that if you do not become the first in your profession, you are unworthy of any consideration; the love of so beautiful a calling should penetrate your heart and be the entire preoccupation of your mind.

Third: you shall sup no more in town, and shall not go out in the evenings; suppers and evenings out are too dangerous for you. But I consent to your dining on Sundays and holidays with your friends on condition that I know always to whom you are going and that you will definitely return before nine o'clock. From now onwards, I exhort you not even to ask for permission contrary to this article, and I advise you not to take it yourself.

Fourth: you shall abandon entirely your wretched music, and above all the company of young people. I will not suffer any of these things: the one and the other have been your undoing. Nevertheless, in consideration of your weakness, I allow you the viole and flute; but on the express condition that you never play them except after supper on working days, never during the daytime, and then only without disturbing the rest of my neighbours or myself.

Fifth: I shall avoid as far as possible sending you on errands, but in cases where I shall be obliged to do so for my business, remember above all else that I shall accept no poor excuses for your being late. You know beforehand how repellent this article is to me.

Sixth: I will give you your board and eighteen livres a month, which will serve for your maintenance and little by little enable you to pay your debts. It would be too dangerous for your character and very improper for me to require you to pay me board and to assess with you the price of your work. If you devote yourself, as you should, to the improvement of my business, and if by your talents you procure me more, I will give you a fourth part of the profits of all that comes to me through you. You know my way of thinking; you know from experience that I never allow myself to be surpassed in generosity; deserve then that I do more for you than I promise; but remember that I give nothing for words, that I accept only actions.

If my conditions suit you and if you feel strong enough to carry them out in good faith, accept them and sign your acceptance at the bottom of this letter, which you shall return to me. In that case . . . make yourself ready to return with me to take the place which I was very far from believing you would occupy so soon, if ever at all.

The bottom of the document bears the following declaration in the delinquent's own writing:

Monsieur, very honoured, dear father,

I sign all your conditions in the firm desire to execute them with the help of the Lord. But how painfully all this recalls to me the time when such laws and ceremonies were necessary, to engage me to do my duty! Yet it is right that I should suffer the humiliation that I have justly deserved, and if all this, joined moreover to my good conduct, can procure for me and merit entirely the return of your good graces and of your friendship, I shall be only too happy. In faith of which, I sign all that is contained in this letter.

A. CARON *fils*

So was parental authority upheld in the eighteenth century! The prodigal returned home and was received with joy by his family. Pierre seems indeed to have learnt his lesson, and he kept his side of the bargain by applying himself to his profession to such good purpose that three years later, in 1753, he invented a new escapement for watches. In those days watches, which were worn by the rich in fobs, were poorly regulated, owing to faulty design of the escapement mechanism, which was in the shape of a cylinder. The young watch-maker of twenty-one designed a new form of escapement in which the length of the cylinder was extended by a tail shaped like a comma – hence its name of *virgule* – which, when the escape-wheel tooth slid along it, imparted an extra impulse to the balance. Two *virgules* were used in this form of escapement, which had many theoretical advantages over the ordinary cylinder type (though its extreme fragility and difficulty of making were later to make its popularity short-lived). With a pardonable pride in his achievement, however, Pierre Caron confided details of his invention to the watch-maker Lepaute, a colleague of his father, and one of some importance since he was clock-maker to the King. Lepaute, apparently with Pierre's consent, adapted the invention for use in clocks. Then, evidently considering that he had nothing to fear from the apprentice son of a small watch-maker, he calmly announced the escapement to be his own invention. But he had yet to learn, as a great many more people in France would one day learn, of what stuff Pierre was made; while Pierre was to have his first experience of the bitter fruits which success may bring. But he lost no time in his defence; on 13 November 1753 he sent a petition to the Academy of Sciences, expressed with the clarity and precision which were to be characteristic of his writings. In it, he said:

... Instructed by my father since the age of thirteen in the art of watchmaking, and animated by his example and counsels to occupy myself seriously with the perfecting of this art, it will not be thought surprising that from my nineteenth year I have endeavoured to distinguish myself in it and to merit public esteem. Escapements were the first object of my reflections. To diminish their defects, simplify and perfect them, became the spur which excited my ambition. Finally, in July last, I thought I had reached my goal. M. Lepaute soon heard of it and came to congratulate me on the 22nd or 23rd of the same month. With the fullest confidence in him, I not only let him see my escapement, but I placed my microscope in his hands, so that he could the better study it. . . . But what sorrow for me if M. Lepaute succeeds in taking from me the honour of a discovery which the Academy would have crowned! I do not speak of the calumnies which M. Lepaute has written and circulated against my father and me; they show a desperate cause and cover their author with confusion. It is sufficient for the present that your judgment, Gentlemen, assures to me the honour which my adversary wishes to take from me, but which I hope to receive from your equity and from your insight.

CARON, fils.

At the same time, with this letter, Pierre forwarded to the Secretary of the Academy a sealed box containing the successive stages of his experiments. Not content with this, he also demanded, through the Minister of the Royal Household, to be confronted with Lepaute – who promptly vanished. Then Pierre took up his pen again and wrote to the editor of the journal, *Le Mercure*, in which Lepaute had complacently published the announcement of his 'invention':

I have read, Monsieur, with the greatest astonishment, in your September number, that M. Lepaute, watch-maker to the Luxembourg, there announces as his invention a new escapement for watches and clocks which he says he has the honour of presenting to the King and to the Academy. . . .

It is true that on the 23rd July last, in the joy of my discovery, I had the weakness to confide this escapement to M. Lepaute, allowing him to make use of it in a clock which M. de Julienne had ordered, and whose interior he assured me would be examined by no one, because of the arrangement for winding of his own invention, and because he alone had the key to the clock.

But how could I imagine that M. Lepaute would ever venture to appropriate to himself this escapement which it will be seen I confided to him under the seal of secrecy?

. . . M. Lepaute evidently wishes to avoid all explanation, for he declares that his escapement resembles mine in no way; but from the announcement which he makes, I judge that it is entirely conformable to it in principle.

He ends by saying that he will not pursue the matter any further at the moment, but will await the decision of the Academy. Three months later, on 23 February 1754, the Academy of Sciences gave its considered judgment on the affair, concluding with the statement that

. . . We therefore believe that the Academy should regard M. Caron as the true inventor of the new escapement and that M. Lepaute has only imitated the invention; that the escapement of the clock presented to the Royal Academy on the 4th August by Lepaute is a natural consequence of the escapement for watches of M. Caron; that in its application to clocks, this escapement is inferior to that of Grabain, but that it is in watches the most perfect that has been produced, although it is the most difficult to execute.

Thus was Pierre Caron triumphantly vindicated, in the first of the many battles which he had to fight on his journey through life, and in which his pen was to be his chief weapon of defence. But this first success was to have very far-reaching results; for the battle of the watch-makers had not passed unnoticed by the jaded royal eye at Versailles. Pierre was invited to come to Court and explain his invention. Within a few months, he was able to write joyfully to a cousin in London:

I have at last delivered the watch to the King, by whom I had the happiness to be recognized at once, and who remembered my name. His Majesty ordered me to show the watch to all the noblemen at the *lever*; never was an artist received with so much kindness. His Majesty wished to know about the minutest details of my invention. . . . Mme de Pompadour's watch in a ring is only four lines* in diameter; it was much admired, although it is not yet finished. The King has asked me for a repeater in the same style. All the lords followed the King's example, and each wishes to be served first. I have also made a curious little clock for Mme Victoire, in the style of my watches; the King wished to make her a present of it. It has two dials, and whichever side it is turned, one can see the time.

Now he calls himself *horloger du roi* when he writes again to *Le Mercure*, refuting the suggestion that the use of his escapement prevents watches from being made flat or very small:

I make watches as thin as may be desired, thinner even than have been made before, without in the least diminishing their quality. . . . The first of these simplified watches is in the hands of the King. His Majesty has carried it for a year and is well satisfied. . . . I had the honour to present to Mme de Pompadour a short time ago a watch in a ring, which is only four lines and a half in diameter, and a line less a third in thickness between the plates. . . .

The wave of success had carried the young watch-maker up the first rungs of the ladder.

* A line is a measurement used by watch-makers.

8

Chapter 2

A WATCH-MAKER AT COURT

LOUIS XV, who had been King of France since the age of five, was now a melancholy, secretive man in his forties, who furtively conducted his own foreign policy behind the backs of his ministers and whose only real interests in life were women and hunting. Although by this time Mme de Pompadour had ceased to be actually the King's mistress, she remained the power behind the throne through the close friendship which was to endure between them until her death in 1764. As for the rest of the Court, the life they led was of a quite devastating dullness, particularly in the case of the King's daughters, known as Mesdames de France. His plain Polish Queen Marie Leczinska had done her duty in providing her husband with ten children, before she retreated into the consolations of her religion, in which she became more and more deeply engrossed; as did her son the Dauphin, who made no attempt to conceal his disapproval of his father's way of life. Six daughters had survived to grow up, of whose existence the King was sufficiently conscious to pass daily through their apartments on his way to and from hunting. Mme Campan, their reader and lady-in-waiting, describes these occasions:

Louis XV saw very little of his family; he would go down every morning by a private staircase into the apartment of Mme Adelaide. He would often bring with him, and drink, some coffee he had made himself. Mme Adelaide would ring a bell informing Mme Victoire of the King's arrival; Mme Victoire would ring Mme Sophie, who in her turn rang Mme Louise. The princesses' apartments were extremely large and Mme Louise was lodged in the furthest one. This last daughter of the King was deformed and very small, and in order to get to this daily gathering, the poor princess would run as fast as she could through the great number of rooms; but in spite of her haste, she often would only have time to embrace her father, before he set off for his hunting.

When the King returned, punctually at six o'clock in the evening, Mme Campan was usually reading to the Princesses and would break off so that another gathering could take place. But this one was more ceremonious. The Princesses would put on the enormous panniers which were the fashion, underneath skirts speckled with gold or brocade, and, covering themselves with large mantles of black taffeta to conceal any shortcomings in costume, they were then escorted, in solemn procession with lighted torches, to visit their father. He would perfunctorily peck each daughter on the forehead and the ceremony then ended, often within a quarter of an hour; after which the girls would return to their reading.

After the death of the twins Louise-Elizabeth and Henriette – the two of whom their father was really fond, and whose death genuinely grieved him – the Princesses were reduced in number to four, of whom Mme Adelaide was the leader. She does not seem to have been a lovable character, for like her great-niece the Duchesse d'Angoulême, Louis XVI's daughter, she was haughty and ungracious in manner, with the same masculine energy. Mme Campan declares that Mme Adelaide had at first a very attractive face, but that her charm disappeared very rapidly as she grew older. She had, however, a good brain, and was keenly interested in music, herself playing several instruments including – believe it or not, says Mme Campan – the horn! Mme Victoire, the next sister, was both pretty and graceful, with a charming expression and a smile which reflected her kind heart. The unfortunate Mme Sophie, on the other hand, was extremely plain, and shy to the point of oddity. 'Never did I see anybody who had such a frightened look,' says Mme Campan. 'She walked with great rapidity, and in order to recognize without looking at the people who made way for her, she had acquired a habit of glancing sideways like a hare. This Princess was so exceedingly diffident that one might be with her daily for years without hearing her utter a single word.' Mme Louise, the fourth member of the quartet, was secretly nourishing the desire to become a nun, though for the time being she kept her wish to herself. (But when Mme de Pompadour died, and her place was presently taken by Mme du Barry, the Princess's concern for the soul of her incorrigible parent impelled her to lose no more time in obtaining his permission for her to become a Carmelite, and in September 1770 she took the veil as Sister Thérèse-Augustine.) It was no doubt the King's distinctly peculiar sense of humour which caused him to bestow on his daughters a series of nicknames which were considered to be the lamentable result of his habit of mixing with low company, Mme Victoire being known as Sow* (because, as she explained placidly to

* Coche.

the scandalized Mme Campan, she was the plumpest of the Princesses),
while Mmes Adelaide, Louise, and Sophie were known by names
which may be euphemistically translated as Rag, Tag and Crow.*

A great excitement in the dull lives of these Princesses was evidently
the occasion in 1749 when Mme Victoire had just left school and, the
King being absent on a visit to northern France, they sallied forth
from their gilded cage to give Mme Victoire her first view of Paris.
The whole sisterhood, as Barbier relates, set forth in a brilliant caval-
cade, magnificently attired and blazing with diamonds and other
precious stones. They drove in state, first to hear Mass at Notre-Dame,
and then to the palace of the Tuileries, the way being lined with large
crowds which had gathered to see them pass. A few years later, another
outing is recorded, when, accompanied this time by their brother the
Dauphin, the Princesses drove the entire length of the fashionable
promenade of the rampart boulevards, amid a great concourse of
people and many carriages which were drawn up on both sides under
the trees. But these obviously were only very special occasions, since
they are considered worthy of particular mention by the chronicler.

Now, however, into the dreary existence of Mesdames there came
suddenly a fresh interest. The young watch-maker of the Rue Saint-
Denis, whose new invention had caused such a stir, was found to be an
extremely personable young man: tall, well-built and good-looking,
with a witty tongue and an air of complete assurance, he possessed a
degree of charm which was to attract towards him most women who
met him, and which did not pass unremarked by the more discerning
members of his own sex. 'I have seen few men more favoured by
nature,' says his contemporary, the literary critic La Harpe; 'his face
and voice were equally lively, lit up by eyes full of fire, with as much
expression in accent and look as of delicacy in the smile. Above all, he
had a sort of assurance inspired by the consciousness of his own powers,
and which he knew how to communicate to others.' But best of all
from the point of view of Mesdames, this interesting young man was
found to be a very competent performer on both the flute and the
harp. This latter instrument had become extremely fashionable in
France since the invention of pedals by a Bavarian in 1720, an inno-
vation which had revolutionized harp-playing, not only by freeing the
player's hands but by giving the instrument a number of complete
major and minor scales. The pedal mechanism, however, was still far
from perfect, and before long the young watch-maker was to give

* Loque, Chiffe and Graille.

further proof of his inventive talent by devising an improved system of pedals. Within a short time he was composing songs and figuring as the principal performer at the little concerts held in the royal circle, while the Princesses took lessons from him in harp-playing.

Obviously, such success could no longer be contained within the boundaries of the Rue Saint-Denis, though it was the ancestral trade which was to open the door of escape. For one day there entered into the little shop of *Caron père et fils* a certain Mme Franquet, her ostensible purpose that of bringing a watch to be repaired. She was a good-looking woman of about thirty, married to an elderly and ailing husband who held the office of Clerk Controller in the Royal Household. Her visit to the shop resulted in the formation of a friendship between the young watch-maker and the Franquets, and it was not long before Franquet was persuaded to yield his office to young Pierre Caron in return for a life annuity from Caron *père* – for such was the strange manner in which Court appointments could be bought and sold at this period. At the end of 1755, therefore, Pierre was able to abandon the family profession and became a Court official whose duty it was to escort the royal meat to table, walking in front of it with drawn sword. Two months later, Franquet proved to be even more accommodating: he departed from this world altogether, leaving a well-endowed and attractive widow, with whom Pierre was already on friendly terms. The death of his mother in this year probably made him feel the need of a household of his own, and in November he married Mme Franquet. In addition to financial assets, the bride possessed some property, notably a little domain in the village of Beaumarchais, in Brie, the province from which the elder Caron had originated. The new Clerk Controller of the Royal Household considered that the name of Caron was not sufficiently imposing for a Court official, and he decided to add to it the name of his wife's estate. It is therefore from this time that Pierre Caron, the young watch-maker of the Rue Saint-Denis, emerges from his chrysalis bearing the name under which he was one day to be famous throughout Europe.

Beaumarchais' first marriage, however, lasted only ten months, for at the end of September his wife was carried off by a fever which appears to have been typhoid. But in fact the marriage was not turning out to be a great success, and discord had already begun to arise between the two. For while Beaumarchais, as always throughout his life, was never able to resist the charms of attractive women, Madeleine-Catherine Franquet was not the type to look with an indulgent eye upon the wandering fancy of a husband ten years younger than herself and with whom she was passionately in love. Under the terms of her marriage contract her money was to go to Beaumarchais; but owing to the obstructive tactics of her family, who disapproved of the marriage, the contract had not yet been registered at the time of her death, so that he therefore received nothing from her estate – a fact, which however, would not prevent his enemies from declaring in after years that he had poisoned her.

It was not to be expected, of course, that the meteoric rise of an obscure young watch-maker to the highest favour at Court would fail to raise up against him a host of jealous enemies. Their first attacks took the form of attempts to humiliate him; one day, as Beaumarchais came from the apartments of Mesdames, where he had been giving them their usual music-lesson, he was stopped by a courtier, who, holding out a very beautiful watch, said to him: 'Monsieur, you are an expert in watch-making. Tell me, I beg of you, whether this is a good watch.' Beaumarchais, conscious that the eyes of a group of courtiers were fixed upon him, replied smoothly, 'Monsieur, now that I no longer work at this art, I have become very clumsy.' 'Ah, Monsieur,' persisted the other, 'do not refuse me.' 'So be it,' replied Beaumarchais, 'but I am only warning you that I am clumsy.' Taking the watch in his hand, he opened it, raised it in the air, and pretending to examine it, he let it slip out of his hand and fall from his full height. Whereupon, with the deepest of bows to his tormentor, 'I warned you, Monsieur, of my extreme clumsiness,' said he, and took his departure, leaving the other to pick up the ruins of his watch amid the malicious laughter of the onlookers.

On another occasion, his enemies tried to turn Mesdames against him by saying that he was on bad terms with his father, who they said had finally cast him off. But Beaumarchais was again their match. Hurrying to his father, who had always expressed a wish to see Versailles, he explained that he had a splendid opportunity that very day of showing him all round the *château*. He brought the old man out to Versailles, and made a point of appearing with him in front of Mesdames at all places where he knew they would be passing by during the day. In the evening he went to pay his usual visit to the Princesses, bringing with him his father, whom he left in the ante-room while he went in. He found Mesdames chilly, embarrassed and trying not to look at him. At last one of them, probably Mme Victoire, said to him impatiently: 'With whom have you been all day?' 'Madame,' he replied, 'with my father.' 'His father, Adelaide!' she cried sharply to her sister. 'That cannot be; we know that you have fallen out with one another.' 'I, Madame? I spend my life with him!' was Beaumarchais' reply. 'He is in the next room. I have come to take your orders, and he is waiting for me. If you would deign to see him, he will give you proof of the respect I bear him and of the affection I have never ceased to have for him.' The old man was duly brought in, and the lying tale exposed in all its malice. Certainly the elder Caron's letters to his son a short time later give the lie to any tales of their being on bad terms. At the beginning of 1763 the old clock-maker writes:

What father is happier than yours? I bless heaven with emotion to find in my old age a son of such admirable disposition, and far from being downcast at my present situation, my spirit is raised up and warmed at the touching thought that it is to him alone, after God, that I owe my well-being.

A year later, he writes again to his son, who was then in Spain:

You suggest modestly that I should love you a little. That is not possible, my dear boy; a son like you is not made to be loved only a little by a father who thinks and feels as I do. The tears of emotion which are falling from my eyes on to this paper are the proof of it. The qualities of your excellent heart, the strength and greatness of your mind, fill me with the tenderest love. My son, my dear son, honour of my old age, how can I have deserved of God the favour which He showers upon me in my dear son?

(This was, of course, the age of great 'sensibility'; but times indeed had changed since the days of the watch-maker's unruly apprentice!)

Yet there were more dangerous methods of attack than those of the tongue. A brave but misguided gentleman, the Chevalier de C--, was persuaded by Beaumarchais' enemies of the need to remove the upstart. Since he was a man of honour, he used no underhand methods, but sent Beaumarchais a challenge to a duel in the proper form. The latter could do no less than accept the challenge, and they met in the park of Meudon, where Beaumarchais was sufficiently skilful to run his adversary through the chest. But as he withdrew the blade and saw his opponent fall to the ground bleeding profusely, his naturally kind disposition got the better of him and, horrified at what he had done, he hurried to the fallen man and tried in vain to stop the flow of blood with his handkerchief. 'Save yourself, Monsieur,' gasped the Chevalier, 'you will be lost if you are seen, and they discover that you have taken my life.' 'You need help,' replied Beaumarchais firmly, 'and I am going to get you some.' He leapt on to his horse, galloped into Meudon, found a surgeon and told him where the wounded man was lying. He then set off at full speed to return to Paris, to consider what he should do next; for his position was indeed one of the greatest peril. But the gallant Chevalier de C – –, as he lay dying, refused to name his opponent, saying only that, 'I have got what I deserve; in order to please people for whom I have no esteem, I provoked an honest man who had in no way offended me.' He took the secret of his opponent's identity with him to the grave.

Before the Chevalier's death, however, since there was always the possibility that his family might somehow discover the identity of his killer and take vengeance, Beaumarchais had sought the protection of Mesdames, to whom he gave a full account of the whole affair. They informed their father, and the King, with his masterly capacity for warding off the prospect of any impending trouble for himself, replied briefly: 'My children, see to it that nobody mentions it to me.'

Chapter 3

HIGH FINANCE – AND PAULINE

IN the financial world of this period the four Pâris brothers played a leading part. One of them, Pâris de Montmartel, was Keeper of the Royal Treasury; but it is with the third brother, Pâris-Duverney, that we are concerned. The latter, a protégé of Mme de Pompadour, had been responsible, among other activities, for the provisioning and equipment of the French armies in Germany and the Low Countries during the War of the Austrian Succession. He was now an old man, but still active in the numerous financial enterprises in which he had made not only his own fortune, but that of several other people, including Voltaire. (It was largely owing to Pâris-Duverney that the sage of Ferney had become a wealthy man, able to devote himself whole-heartedly to literature and to his cherished causes, without the distracting necessity of having to earn his daily bread.) Duverney was a man of public spirit, as well as being a rich financier, and he devoted a part of his great fortune to the project of founding a military school which should give the French nobility some much-needed training in military science and in discipline. The fine building which was being constructed on the Champ de Mars would house five hundred young noblemen without means, between the ages of nine and twenty, first preference to be given to the sons of those who had been killed on active service, or who had died of wounds.

Unfortunately, however, Duverney's alliance with Mme de Pompadour was sufficient to set a large proportion of the Court against him. Weighed against such a damning fact, a project to provide efficient officer-training for the French Army paled into insignificance, and ten years after the royal edict authorizing its foundation the École Militaire was languishing, while Duverney tried in vain to raise enough money to finish the building. In his despair, he at last appealed to the young man who had risen to such a favoured position at Court. Beaumarchais, always with a keen eye on his future, was quick to see the advantage which might accrue to him by making himself useful to the great financier. He took pains to arouse the interest of Mesdames by speaking of the fine new School and its purpose. Their curiosity was aroused, and an excursion was made to see the building, where they were received with suitable honours and shown round by Duverney himself. Naturally, their enthusiasm for what they had seen was communicated in due course to their father; with the gratifying result that, on 18 August 1760, the King visited the School in state and officially inaugurated it.

For Beaumarchais personally the result was even more satisfactory. Duverney was grateful, and his friendship was to prove as profitable to the rising young man as it had been to others who had come within the old financier's golden orbit. Beaumarchais' financial position was just then far from easy. Not only had he received nothing from the estate of his late wife, but she had even left debts for which he found himself liable. His father's business had declined, too; to the extent that it was now the son who lent money to his father, to the tune of 50,000 francs. However, in any case it was not seemly that a Court dignitary should have a father who pursued the humble trade of watch-making, and the elder Caron was presently persuaded to give up altogether his never very lucrative calling. But even the favour of Mesdames was proving to be somewhat costly, for they were given to sudden whims whose gratification, essential though it might be, was often expensive, and one could not of course press for a refund of expenses which might be slow in coming.

The alliance of Beaumarchais with Duverney came therefore at a particularly fortunate time. Beaumarchais himself said later that it was Duverney who taught him the business of finance. 'Under his direction I built up my fortune; on his advice I embarked on numerous enterprises. In a few, he supported me with his capital or his credit; in all with his counsels and experience of the world.' The full extent and nature of their dealings together will probably never be known, for in their correspondence with one another they used a secret code which has made it impossible to unravel the threads of their activities. Nor were any proper deeds drawn up, specifying the exact nature of the transactions between them. In view of Duverney's advanced age Beaumarchais was constantly pressing him to do this, but with the obstinate procrastination of old age Duverney kept putting it off. In the not very distant future the old man's failure to legalize their dealings in the proper manner was going to cost Beaumarchais dearly.

However, a more immediate result of Duverney's support was that Beaumarchais was able to climb higher up the ladder by buying himself for 85,000 francs – of which Duverney provided 55,000 – the office of Secretary to the King, which carried with it the status of nobility. He did indeed aim even higher, at the office of Grand Master of Waters and Forests, which would have cost him 500,000 francs. But the other Grand Masters would not tolerate such an intrusion into the rarefied region into which many of them had only recently risen themselves, and Beaumarchais was obliged to content himself with the office of 'Lieutenant-General of Hunting in the Capitainerie of the Varenne du Louvre'.* The Lieutenant-General acted as assistant to the President of the tribunal which sat to try infringements of the hunting laws, and as the President, who was the Duc de la Vallière, was chiefly conspicuous by his absence, it usually fell to the lot of the Lieutenant-General to preside in his place over a tribunal which contained many noblemen of high rank; it was indeed a far more imposing office than that of Grand Master of Waters and Forests to which he had previously aspired. Beaumarchais was to continue to hold this office right up to the time of the Revolution, administering the laws without fear or favour – even when it meant falling foul of so great a personage as the Prince de Condé, who on one occasion had torn down a certain wall, which Beaumarchais, ever the champion of the rights of the individual, had caused to be rebuilt. The Prince was at first very angry, but, with a fairness of mind unusual in a great noble of those days, he expressed himself willing to discuss the matter on a purely legal basis, without taking advantage of his rank and position. Beaumarchais, we are told, explained the legal aspects of the affair with such clarity and tact that in the end the Prince honestly avowed that he was in the wrong.

Beaumarchais' position, both financial and otherwise, now seemed assured. Yet he himself certainly did not think it to be beyond improvement. For he set to work – as his father before him had done – to educate himself, reading solidly in the classics and in French literature; even Richardson, that popular novelist of eighteenth-century England, did not escape his attention. As he read, he would jot down in a notebook any words or phrases that he thought worth remembering. Perhaps it was his association with Mesdames – particularly the intellectually

* The *capitaineries* were areas in which the right of hunting was the exclusive prerogative of the King, and that known as the Varenne du Louvre was a district extending some sixty miles round Paris.

inclined, if grim, Mme Adelaide – which had made him painfully conscious of the gaps in his own education. Or perhaps it was because he had himself already begun to write. In his preface to his first play, *Eugénie*, he declares that he began it about 1759; certainly, between that time and about 1763 he wrote several of the extremely racy little pieces known as *parades* for the benefit of the private theatre of Le Normant d'Étioles, financier husband of Mme de Pompadour. (For, strange to say, Mme de Pompadour had a husband, who was now doing his best to console himself with charmers from the Opera.)

Beaumarchais, however, was now the sole support and mainstay of his family: his widower father (who had given up his own career in order that he should not handicap his son's), and his two unmarried sisters, Julie and Tonton, who like himself he had equipped with new names, Julie being given the name of Beaumarchais and Tonton being whimsically christened 'Mlle de Boisgarnier', after one of his uncles. In 1763 he purchased a large house in the Rue de Condé and brought them all to live under his roof. And what an amusing household it must have been! 'Our house is a dovecote where everyone lives on love and hope,' writes Julie; 'I am the one who laughs more than the others, because I am the least in love.' She was being courted by a Chevalier de Séguiraud, but was obviously not taking him very seriously. 'He is as loving as an angel, passionate as a seraph,' she writes mischievously, 'while I am as gay as a linnet, and malicious as a demon.' Meanwhile, Tonton was being courted by a solemn young man called Janot de Miron, Caron *père* was contemplating a second plunge into matrimony with a widow he had known for years, and the head of the household, now an eligible widower too, was beginning to fancy himself taken with one of Julie's friends, a young girl called Pauline Lebreton. It seems clear that Pauline was much in love with Beaumarchais – it was usually to be that way round – but it is doubtful whether Beaumarchais on his side was so deeply committed; though he was unquestionably attracted by her; for Pauline was of a delicate beauty, with a charming voice and some musical ability. But marriage, as distinct from the passing love-affair, was a serious business arrangement – as it still is in France – not to be embarked upon without careful consideration. Pauline, a creole who had been left an orphan early in life, had been brought up in Paris by an aunt, and though the family estate in Santo Domingo had been valued at two million francs, it was in poor condition and heavily encumbered with debts. In other words, Pauline, for all her charm, might turn out to be a financial liability.

Beaumarchais, always the prudent man of business, therefore decided to send his uncle Pichon out to Santo Domingo to investigate, sending with him 20,000 francs in money and a cargo of merchandise. But it would obviously be some time before he could hope to receive any report from his uncle, so in the meantime he must temporize with Pauline. He writes to her:

... There is only one thing which deters me, my amiable Pauline: with management and a reasonable economy, I consider that the actual condition of my affairs is such as to provide you with an agreeable future, which is the sole wish of my heart; but if, through some frightful misfortune, all the money which I am sending to Santo Domingo should be engulfed in the ruin of an affair of which we have as yet no knowledge except through the testimony of others, this amount deducted from my fortune would no longer permit me to support the condition which I would have given you. And what would be my sorrow then! ... This disquietude is the only reason that has forced me to delay the demand for your hand, for which I have sighed softly for so long.

But Pauline had also a wealthy uncle, and there would be no harm in making a few tentative soundings in that direction:

I do not know what claims you have upon the property of your dear uncle, either with regard to your late aunt's dowry or for the debts of which I have heard indirect mention. It would be unseemly for me to broach this subject, either to you or to him. ... Nevertheless, my dear Pauline, in order to spend a happy future life one must be without uneasiness as to the future, and no sooner should I have you in my arms than I should be trembling lest some misfortune were to make us lose the funds sent to America; for I have put aside no less than 80,000 francs for this purpose. There, my dear Pauline, is the cause of a silence which may appear strange to you after what I have done. There are only two ways out of this difficulty, if you accept my courtship: the first is to have patience until the entire success of my plans and of the money advanced permits me to offer you an assured condition; the second is that you get your aunt – if my views are agreeable to her – to sound your uncle about his dispositions with regard to you. ... Think carefully over what I am writing to you, and give me your opinion in reply. My tenderness for you will come first over everything, even over my prudence. My fate is in your hands; yours is in those of your uncle.

All this may have been the cautious foresight of a prudent man of business, but it was hardly a young girl's dream of an ardent suitor, and Pauline was obviously much hurt – 'Your letter, Monsieur my good friend, has thrown me into extreme distress.' However, she made no mention of the letter to her aunt, but went direct to her uncle, who agreed to discuss matters with Beaumarchais. What exactly took place at this meeting is not clear, but it did not produce any tangible results, and nothing therefore remained but to await news from Santo Domingo.

The affair had reached this stage when circumstances made it necessary for Beaumarchais to visit Spain.

Chapter 4

A VISIT TO SPAIN

TEN years after Beaumarchais' journey to Spain, when he was defending himself with his pen against the attacks of powerful enemies, he published an account of his visit to Madrid and the reasons which he declared had led up to it.

According to this narrative, told with the dramatic power of the future playwright, the story begins one day in February 1764, when Caron *père* received a letter from his eldest daughter Mme Guilbert, who, with her younger sister Lisette, was living in Madrid. The letter unfolded a melancholy tale: a certain José Clavijo, a Spanish literary man, had been courting Lisette, and had gone so far as to make a definite proposal of marriage, to take place as soon as he should obtain a remunerative position. He had in fact become Keeper of the Crown Archives and editor of the journal *El Pensador*, but, far from keeping his word to Lisette, he had twice drawn back on the very brink of marriage. 'The dishonour which this event has cast upon her,' wrote Mme Guilbert, 'has plunged us into the deepest seclusion. I weep day and night, lavishing upon the poor girl such consolation as I am not in a state to accept for myself.' Their fond father, in tears, hurried to Versailles and implored his son to go to Madrid and see what he could do for the two women: 'they are no less your sisters than the others.' Beaumarchais explained the circumstances to Mesdames and applied for leave of absence, which they gave, approving his mission. He then set forth for Spain, accompanied by a merchant friend of his family. Travelling day and night by chaise, they reached the Spanish capital on the morning of 18 May 1764. Beaumarchais at once sought out Clavijo, and without revealing his identity told the Spaniard that he had been charged by a French literary society to make contact with the most eminent men of letters in Spain, and that he was naturally therefore addressing himself to the moving spirit of *El Pensador*. Clavijo fell into the trap and, much flattered, invited Beaumarchais to take chocolate with him on the following morning. Beaumarchais duly presented

himself, accompanied by his friend, who would be a witness for what
was to follow, and when the Spaniard, in the usual formula of polite
society, placed his services at the disposal of his guests during their stay
in Madrid, Beaumarchais unfolded a tale to explain, he says, the purpose of his visit to the Spanish capital.

A certain French merchant, with a family and only moderate means, had nevertheless many business connections in Spain. One of the richest of these, passing
through Paris nine or ten years ago, made him this proposal: 'Let me have two
of your daughters to take back to Madrid. I am an old man, without relatives;
they can take charge of my business and will eventually succeed to the richest
establishment in Spain.' The eldest daughter, already a married woman, and
one of her sisters were put in his charge, the father undertaking to provide the
new·branch in Madrid with all the French merchandise they might want.

Two years later, the old Spaniard died, leaving the Frenchwomen without
any benefit, and in the awkward position of having to carry on a commercial
business all alone. In spite of their straitened circumstances, their sensible
behaviour and wit preserved to them a number of friends, who hastened to
increase their credit and their business. At about this same time, a young man
from the Canary Islands got himself introduced into the house. [Here, says
Beaumarchais, Clavijo's smile froze on his face.] In spite of his lack of means,
the ladies, seeing in him a great enthusiasm for the study of the French language
and of sciences, provided him with the means of making rapid progress in
these. . . . Finally he conceived the idea of giving the city of Madrid the novel
pleasure of reading a periodical journal on the lines of the English *Spectator*, and
then, spurred on by hope of success in making his name, he dared openly to
propose marriage to the younger of the two Frenchwomen. . . . Touched by
the merit of the man who sought her, she refused several advantageous matches,
and preferring to wait until he who had loved her for four years had fulfilled
the hopes of success which all his friends entertained for him, she encouraged
him to publish his first philosophical journal, under the imposing title of *El
Pensador*. [Here, says Beaumarchais, I saw my man ready to faint.]

The work [pursued Beaumarchais icily] had a prodigious success; even the
King gave public marks of goodwill to the author. He was promised the first
honourable employment which should fall vacant. Then he drove'away all
other suitors by paying open court to the girl; the marriage only awaited the
attainment of the promised appointment. At last, after six years of waiting on
one side, and of cares and attentions on the other, the appointment materialized
– and the man fled. [Clavijo was now breathing hard.]

The affair had caused too much stir for such an outcome to be viewed with
indifference. The ladies had taken a house capable of holding two households;
the banns had been published. The outrage incensed all their friends, who set
about avenging the insult. The French Ambassador took the matter up. But

when the man in question discovered that the Frenchwomen were employing more powerful support against him, fearing for an influence which might overthrow him and destroy in one instant his rising fortune, he threw himself at the feet of his exasperated mistress. In his turn he enlisted the aid of all his friends to bring her back, and as the anger of a deceived woman is hardly ever more than disguised love, everything was set right. The preparations for the marriage were resumed, the banns were published again, and the wedding was fixed to take place in three days' time.

He came back, indeed, two days later; but instead of leading his victim to the altar, he sent word to the poor soul that he had changed his mind a second time and would not marry her. Her indignant friends rushed to him at once; the insolent wretch no longer beat about the bush, but defied them to do their worst, saying that if the Frenchwomen sought to worry him, they had better take care that he did not bring about their final ruin, in a country where they had no protection.

At this news, the young French girl fell into a state of convulsions which caused fears to be held for her life. In their despair, the elder one wrote to France of the public affront which had been put upon them; this account so moved the heart of their brother that, instantly demanding leave to come to Spain and elucidate such a complex affair, he leapt at one jump from Paris to Madrid. *I am that brother*, who has left everything – country, duties, family, pleasures – to come to Spain to avenge an innocent and unhappy sister, to unmask a traitor and write his infamy in letters of blood upon his face – and *you are that traitor*!

The wretched Clavijo began to stammer excuses, but 'Do not interrupt me, sir,' thundered Beaumarchais; 'you have nothing to say to me, and much to hear from me.' Beaumarchais then relates how he compelled Clavijo to declare, in front of the witness he had brought with him, that Lisette had done nothing whatever to deserve such treatment, and that the reason for his behaviour towards her was that he had been 'urged on by others'. The French merchant then departed, leaving the two men alone together, and Beaumarchais demanded that Clavijo should sign a declaration acknowledging the wrong done to Lisette and asking her pardon; the alternative being that they should fight a duel. After various attempts at evasion, Clavijo agreed to sign – probably with the idea of gaining time. He then seems to have set to work not only to make his peace with the two women, but to try to gain their brother's friendship as well. (Beaumarchais' response to these overtures was perhaps not uninfluenced by the fact that the French Ambassador, when consulted by him, had already expressed the opinion that Clavijo was definitely a young man with a future and that he would therefore be a good match for any girl – however poor a specimen, presumably, he might be in other ways.) Soon after this, Clavijo wrote to Beaumarchais, expressing once more his desire to marry Lisette, and asking for her brother's help in bringing about a reconciliation. This Beaumarchais was glad to do, having, as he tells us, convinced himself that she still cared for Clavijo. Once more, everything was made ready for the wedding. But when Beaumarchais applied for the usual authorization of the marriage, he was informed that there was an obstacle: a young woman, a chambermaid, was claiming that she had received a promise of marriage from Clavijo some nine years earlier. Beaumarchais exploded in a justifiable fury of resentment, whereupon Clavijo once more disappeared, and from his place of concealment lodged a judicial complaint against Beaumarchais for having compelled him at the pistol's point to sign an undertaking to marry Lisette. The French Ambassador, when appealed to by Beaumarchais, now warned him that he was in a position of considerable peril: Clavijo, he said, would have the backing of the Court, and was using his influence in an attempt to have Beaumarchais arrested; in fact the Ambassador had already had the greatest difficulty in preventing him from being seized, and perhaps put away for life in some dungeon. Beaumarchais would be wise to lose no time in getting out of the country and returning to France. But Beaumarchais, as in all the crises of his life, was never one to admit defeat; after spending the night walking up and down, considering what to do next, as dawn broke he decided to go direct to the chief Minister, Grimaldi, and lay the whole story of the Clavijo affair before him. While waiting in an ante-room to see the Minister, he had the good fortune to meet the very man who had been responsible for Clavijo's appointment, and who listened with sympathy and with growing horror as the extent of his protégé's malefactions was revealed. Beaumarchais was taken into the presence of the King, to whom he read the pamphlet setting forth the facts of the case which he had already read to the Minister. The final outcome was that Clavijo was deprived of his post and disgraced. Retreating into a Capucine monastery, the villain of the piece wrote an abject letter to his triumphant adversary, reiterating his willingness to marry Lisette; a letter which moved Beaumarchais to ask (though his request was not granted) that Clavijo might receive back his appointment – for 'I no longer hate him; in fact I have never hated anybody.'

So much for the history of this curious affair as given by Beaumarchais himself. But we shall see that during the course of his long career Beaumarchais, in relating basic fact, not infrequently allowed his histrionic sense to get the better of him; the temptation to embroider truth with a few colourful additions proved irresistible to the future dramatist. We find, in the first place, that the 'innocent young girl' of Beaumarchais' legend was in fact a mature woman of thirty-three, older than her brother. It seems clear that her longstanding relations with Clavijo had done no good to her reputation, but so far was she in February 1764 from being thrown into a state of convulsions by his behaviour, that she was contemplating marriage with a compatriot, a merchant named Durand, and a letter exists which she wrote to her father at this exact time, announcing her intention. The old watch-maker was prepared to give his blessing, but his son considered that Durand, a person of no particular consequence, was not a suitable match for the sister of the recently enobled Caron de Beaumarchais. Clavijo, for all his dithering, was a much more promising proposition, and might be useful to Beaumarchais in furthering the real purpose of his journey to Spain – which was to do the business of Pâris Duverney, who had armed him with a credit of 200,000 francs. But first, Lisette's slightly tarnished reputation must be re-established by extorting the signed confession from Clavijo. In the end, however, Lisette married no one, and she disappears from the scene almost unobserved; while Clavijo did indeed attain the eminent position in the literary world that had been forecast for him, crowning his career by becoming Vice-Director of the Royal Institute of Natural History.

But after the Clavijo incident had petered out, Lisette's brother remained on in Madrid for nearly a year, attempting to forward Duverney's various schemes, chief among which were projects for the improvement of agriculture, commerce, and industry in Spain, and for the provisioning of the Spanish armies in Spain and North Africa. For the accession in 1759 of the Bourbon King of Naples to the Spanish throne as Charles III had opened a new era of enlightened progress in one of the most backward countries of Europe, and Spain had become the Mecca of many enterprising speculators, of whom Beaumarchais was only one. The monarch who had already done so much to improve the appearance of Naples now set to work upon Madrid, which up to that time had the unenviable reputation of being the dirtiest capital in Europe. The streets, mostly unpaved, had the usual central drain running through the middle, where water, mud and refuse mingled together. The inhabitants still preserved the pleasing medieval habit of hurling their slops out of the windows; so that the railings along the streets were coated with evil-smelling filth, while gold and silver became tarnished. As for the pedestrian, he naturally walked the streets in the direst peril, for the jaunty cry of 'Water coming!' – when in fact it was already well on the way – was no protection; a thick cloak and wide brimmed hat were essential parts of a man's attire. Nor was it only the pedestrian who became a victim; the Count of Fernan-Nuñez tells how his father once received an unsavoury shower-bath while riding in his coach. Although the municipality of Madrid had a considerable sum earmarked for cleansing the city, most of it, says Fernan-Nuñez, stuck to the fingers of those handling it. But Charles III took steps to remedy this state of affairs; to such good purpose that Beaumarchais was able to write at the end of 1764 to the Duc de la Vallière:

Since the obstinacy of the reigning prince in cleansing the town of Madrid has overcome the persistence of the Spaniards in living in the midst of filth, this town is one of the cleanest I have seen, well spaced out, ornamented with numerous squares and public fountains ... the air keen and delicious.

It was indeed to Charles III that Madrid owed not only her paving, cleansing and efficient street-lighting, but also such fine buildings as the Prado Museum.

But not all Beaumarchais' energy and powers of persuasion could overcome the inertia and obstructive conservatism of the Spanish Government when it came to the question of Duverney's various projects, and when Beaumarchais eventually left Spain he had still made no real progress. He was considerably more successful, however, in persuading some of his father's Spanish clients to pay their long-outstanding accounts, and was able to write to him that

I am on the way to receiving payment from all your grandees – their self-esteem is so mixed up with it that I think I shall manage to obtain all they owe you. My letters to them are polite but proud. . . . Let me manage it in my own way.

Old Caron writes back gratefully to his son:

I see what you have done and what you are doing among my debtors, from whom I would never have extracted anything but for you.

Yet to imagine that Beaumarchais spent all his time in Madrid engaged entirely in work of one kind or another would be to form a completely false impression of his stay in the Spanish capital. He writes to his father:

. . . If you receive news of me through some inhabitant of Madrid, you will be told: Your son amuses himself like a king here; he spends all his evenings at the house of the Russian Ambassadress and at milady Rochford's [the British Ambassador's wife]; he dines four times a week with the commanding officers of the Engineers and drives all over Madrid drawn by six mules; then he goes to the royal palace to see M. Grimaldi and other Ministers. He eats every day at the French Ambassador's, so that his travels are delightful and cost him very little. . . . But you must not suppose that I neglect my business. It is in good society, for which I was born, that I find the means I need.

From which it will be clear that the Lieutenant-General of the Varenne du Louvre was moving in most elevated circles – which meant in effect those of the Diplomatic Corps, for the Court played no part in the social life of Madrid. The Queen had died in 1760, and Charles III, who remained a widower for the rest of his reign, was a man of peculiarly regular habits, who liked nothing better than to do the same thing at precisely the same time each day; with the result that the Court was a dull, stiff, ceremonially bound machine, producing none of the gay and brilliant gatherings to be met with at Versailles, Schönbrunn or St Petersburg. Social life therefore centred on the foreign diplomats and their wives, and in this circle there moved a certain Marquise de la Croix. A niece of the Bishop of Orleans, her husband was a lieutenant-general of artillery in the service of the Spanish King. The beauty and musical talent of Mme de la Croix made her one of the most popular figures in the diplomatic set, and when she met her compatriot, who at thirty-two was in the prime of life, handsome and self-assured, the inevitable soon happened, and Beaumarchais was writing home:

I have this afternoon been to the French Ambassador's in the carriage of Mme la Marquise de La Croix, who has the goodness to drive me everywhere with her six mules. She is a charming lady who has great credit here by her rank, but still more by reason of her intelligence and the graces which make her dear to everyone. Her society dissipates the dust, the inaction, the boredom, the impatience which seize everyone who remains long in this place. I should die in this dull city if it were not for this delicious company.

By the end of another two months the situation had progressed to the point where Beaumarchais was able to write to his father:

In the room where I am writing there is a very great and beautiful lady . . . who makes fun of you and me all day long. She tells me, for example, that she thanks you for the kindness you did her thirty-three years ago, when you laid the foundations of the delightful intimacy which I began with her two months ago. I assure her that I will not fail to write to you, and I am doing it now; for what is only a joke on her part has the right to please me as though she really thought it. [Here the Marquise, who was leaning over his chair, adds in her own writing: 'I do think it, I do feel it, I swear to you, Monsieur.'] Do not fail, then, through bashfulness, to thank Her Excellency, in your first letter, for her thanks, and still more for the kindness with which she overwhelms me. I admit that, without the charm of such delightful company, my Spanish business would be full of bitterness.

During this same time, in the 'dovecote' of the Rue de Condé, Beaumarchais' family were equally occupied with thoughts of love-making. He writes with approval of his father's courtship of the widow, Mme Henry:

Monsieur and very dear father,
    I am not surprised at your attachment for Mme Henry; she is cheerfulness itself, and has one of the best hearts that I know. I could wish you might have been so fortunate as to inspire a more lively return of affection. She would make you happy and you would certainly render agreeable this union founded upon reciprocal affection and an esteem which has lasted twenty-five years.

But, unfortunately, Mme Henry seemed to be in no hurry to change her state, and Beaumarchais writes again to his father:

A man ought not to be alone. One must hold on to something in this life, and the society of your sons and daughters can only be sacrificed to another much sweeter, but which you do not seem on the point of acquiring. . . . What pleasure for me, if on reaching home, I could on the same day see assured the happiness of my father and my sister.

For Tonton, otherwise Mlle de Boisgarnier, was still keeping Janot de Miron dangling. There appears to have been a moment, during his stay in Madrid, when Beaumarchais had thoughts of a different match for his sister, and a sharp correspondence passed between Miron and his prospective brother-in-law, in which the aggrieved suitor hit back with thrusts as keen as any that he received. But, after all, Miron, even if pedantic and lacking in elegance, was a barrister and a member of that awesome body the Parlement of Paris; Tonton could well do worse than marry him. It was no doubt these considerations, as well as his recognition of Miron's undoubted good qualities, which decided Beaumarchais to champion the cause of this faithful, if not very dash-ing, suitor. He sends some sober advice to Tonton, in a letter written to his father:

Miron does not lack any of the solid qualities which are needed to make the happiness of a decent woman; and if my Boisgarnier is less touched by that than put off by the want of a few frivolous graces – which, all things considered, are not even entirely absent in him – then I should say that my Boisgarnier is a child who has not yet acquired the experience which causes happiness to be preferred to pleasure. To say truly what I think, I believe he is right to think himself better than me in many respects in which I feel I have neither his virtue nor his steadfastness; which things are of great price when it is a question of a life-long union. There is no man I should like better as a business associate or as my brother-in-law. I well understand what Boisgarnier will say. Yes, it is true that he plays a hurdy-gurdy, that his heels are half an inch too high, that he is scarcely in tune when he sings, that he eats raw apples in the evenings . . . that he is cold and didactic when he chats, and that he is clumsy in everything he does . . . but a wig, a waistcoat and galoshes should not cause anyone to be chased away when the heart is excellent and the mind cultivated.

Beaumarchais' more serious activities in Madrid were not only concerned with Duverney's projects, or with the collection of the debts outstanding to his father. He also acted as an unofficial diplomat (which was not to be the only time in his career that he would be found in this role), unfolding his views in a memoir to the Foreign Minister of France. Thus towards the end of his stay in Madrid he writes to the Duc de Choiseul about the importance of securing the goodwill of the King of Spain towards France. The marriage arranged between the Prince of the Asturias and a princess of Parma who is 'three-quarters French' is a good move, he tells Choiseul; but it is not enough, and Beaumarchais has thought out what now needs to be done. The King is bored; on twenty occasions his eye has roamed over those about him, seeking some 'object' whose charms, wit and affection could draw him out of the melancholy life he leads. Beaumarchais has discovered just the 'object' required. Who is she? Why, none other than the Marquise de la Croix. It is true that she shows some initial hesitation; but she is introduced to the King, who falls madly in love with her at first sight, while Beaumarchais instructs her to show a certain reserve to begin with, in order to lead on the infatuated monarch. Everything goes according to plan: the Marquise is presented at Court, her husband is kept quiet with a cross of diamonds and is made a Commander of the Order of St James; while Beaumarchais, on the eve of leaving Spain, achieves his first diplomatic success by passing on his mistress to the King. If there is something a little distasteful in this transaction, such were the methods of the time – and is not Figaro here performing his first service to Count Almaviva?

But as it gradually became clear to Beaumarchais that none of the industrial projects he had come to negotiate would make any progress against the lethargy and obstruction with which he was met at every turn in Spain, he decided to return to France. However, as his most famous biographer, Louis de Loménie, has said: 'When Beaumarchais left Spain after a stay of one year, he had failed in his industrial speculations, but returned richer than he himself realized; for he was carrying in his head the first outlines of those sharply-cut and original characters Figaro, Rosina, Almaviva, Bartholo and Basilio, which would one day bring glory to his name.'

At the very time when the future author of *The Marriage of Figaro* was observing fashionable life in Madrid at first hand, the six-year-old musical prodigy who was one day to bring Figaro immortal fame on the operatic stage had been on a visit to Paris with his father and sister. The two young children's performances on the clavier and violin had provided society with a sensational novelty, as they had done about twelve months previously at the Court of Vienna, where the children had been presented to the imperial family. The story goes that when little Wolfgang Mozart had slipped and fallen on the polished floor of the palace at Schönbrunn, the seven-year-old archduchess who as Marie-Antoinette was one day to become Queen of France picked him up and comforted him, while her sister walked on, unheeding. 'You are kind,' said Wolfgang; 'when I grow up, I will marry you.' Not surprisingly, the infant genius who in Vienna had been kissed and petted by Maria Theresa and her daughters was deeply offended when, in Paris, Mme de Pompadour declined to do the same! ('Who is this who does not want to kiss me? The Empress did so.') But his ruffled feelings were soothed by the kind-hearted Queen and Mesdames. When Leopold Mozart and his two children left Paris to continue their tour by paying a visit to London, Beaumarchais was still in Madrid, and it was not until March of the following year, 1765, that he finally left Spain. On arriving home, he then set to work, as he wrote to the Duc de Noailles, to 'scratch the earth' and 'cultivate the garden of my advancement'; for when, as he said, he ceased for a moment to do so, 'what I have cleared is instantly covered with brambles, so that I have always to begin again'.

Chapter 5

A DRAMATIST MAKES HIS BOW

IT was certainly true that Beaumarchais' 'garden' was distinctly in need of attention by this time, for during his absence in Spain, several events had happened to throw a blighting influence over that part which he had cultivated with such care and success at Versailles. Mme de Pompadour was dead, the reign of Mme du Barry had not yet begun, and now the Dauphin, who had always been well disposed towards him, was dying. The Court was plunged into more than its usual gloom; for within the space of little over two years the King was to lose not only his son, but his daughter-in-law and finally his long-suffering Queen, for whom, in his own way, he still retained an affection born of long association. There were no more little concerts in the royal family circle; Mme Campan speaks of 'those grand apartments hung with black, those state armchairs raised upon several steps and overhung by a canopy adorned with plumes, those caparisoned horses, that immense procession in deep mourning'. Indeed, it was at about this time that Beaumarchais' visits to Mesdames ceased altogether.

Naturally, his enemies were not slow in putting forward reasons for this, one being that Beaumarchais had become too familiar with Mme Adelaide and had been told to appear no more at Versailles. It is indeed likely enough that after his social success in Madrid he may have returned feeling even more than usually pleased with himself. Modesty was never one of his outstanding characteristics, and while he was still in Spain we find him writing complacently to Julie:

In the evenings we have cards or music, and then supper, of all of which I seem to be the moving spirit. Society has been increased by all the ambassadors, who before my arrival lived rather isolated lives. They say that they now have delightful evenings because I am there.

Or he may perhaps have been guilty of one of those painful lapses from good taste which he was to perpetrate on more than one occasion during his career. It was not long after this, for instance, that he contrived to offend the King by a piece of ill-chosen ingenuity. Louis XV was at all times of a morbid and introspective disposition, which had been intensified by the recent bereavements in his family circle, and by the sudden deaths of several prominent members of the Court who were of about the same age as himself. In addition, although quite unable to break away from the habits of a lifetime, he was becoming increasingly oppressed by thoughts, not only of death itself, but of the possible fate awaiting him in the next world as a result of his behaviour in this. Now it so happened that on Good Friday 1768 the Duc de la Vallière complained to Beaumarchais of his boredom at the prospect of the usual supper in the King's private apartments, which he would have to attend that evening, and declared himself to be at a loss to think of some witty saying that might bring interest to the occasion. Beaumarchais must needs put forward what he described as 'a moral reflection', to be used if the gathering was in merry mood, to draw attention by sharp contrast: 'While we are laughing here, have you never thought, Sire, that by virtue of the august privilege conferred on you by your crown, Your Majesty owes more livres* of twenty sols than the number of minutes which have elapsed since the death of Jesus Christ, the event whose anniversary we keep today?' The Duc de la Vallière, hoping to be the success of the evening, duly brought out this verbal contribution at a particularly hilarious moment in the party. It was not well received, least of all by the King, who muttered gloomily that it reminded him of the human skeleton carried round in ancient times at banquets. Since the Duc de la Vallière was not usually noted for originality of thought, Louis demanded to know whether the idea was in fact his own. The duke, seeing that his brilliant verbal firework had turned out to be a very damp squib indeed, hastened to confess that it was the work of Beaumarchais; upon which the King, without uttering any further word, rose to his feet and left the table. Beaumarchais afterwards declared that this episode, and the ill-feeling it aroused against him at Court, was the root of the enmity from which he was to reap such a bitter harvest a few years later at the hands of the Parlement of Paris.

* The *livre*, a coin so called because originally containing a pound of silver, circulated alongside the franc up to the Revolution; by which time, however, they were practically equal in value and had become worth less than a shilling. The *livre* was divided into 20 *sous* (older form *sol*, cp. Italian *soldo*) and 12 *deniers*. The *sou*, originally a small silver coin, had already degenerated into a copper one by the eighteenth century.

In actual fact, his idea of calculating the sum total of State debt in terms of the minutes elapsed since some great landmark of human history was not an original one; Voltaire had made a similar calculation some six years previously, by assessing the total figure of English national debt – not to mention that of his own country – as being probably greater than the number of minutes elapsed since the Creation! But Beaumarchais's rather tasteless quip provided what was not to be the only occasion when his tendency to see everything in terms of money would arouse irritation against him, and incite the malicious to recall to memory his origin.

During his absence in Spain, his private affairs had also taken a turn for the worse, as unpleasant news began to reach him from Santo Domingo. The estate of Pauline's family turned out to be in a condition quite as bad as rumour had suggested, and was immersed in debt far beyond its actual value. As Beaumarchais had feared, the capital he had sent out with his uncle looked like becoming a total loss, while to add to his misfortunes, his uncle was suddenly taken ill and carried off by some tropical fever. Beaumarchais, spurred on as always to greater effort when confronted by difficulties, decided that he would marry Pauline and go out to Santo Domingo himself in an attempt to retrieve the situation. But a quite incredible and unlooked-for obstacle to this plan arose: Pauline no longer wished to marry him! The truth was that the Chevalier de Séguirand, tired of his treatment at the hands of the mischievous Julie, had turned his attention to Pauline, who was, after all, his compatriot, since he also came from Santo Domingo, of a good but equally impecunious family. It seems too that Pauline's ardour for Beaumarchais had been considerably cooled by his neglect of her while in Spain (even Julie had urged him to write to her) and even more by the discovery that he had been consoling himself only too well during his absence. Yet who more injured and incredulous than Beaumarchais at this turn of affairs, or more bitterly indignant at the behaviour of the man who had stepped in and plucked the flower to which he had given so little attention? He pours forth his reproaches over Pauline:

You have renounced me, and what time have you chosen to do it? The very moment which I had announced to your friends and mine would be that of our union. . . . If I had not had the intention of marrying you, would I have put so little form into the services which I rendered you? Would I have assembled your friends and mine two months before your refusal, to announce to them my resolution? Everything has turned against me. The conduct of a friend, two-faced and perfidious, in giving me a cruel lesson, has taught me that there is no woman so honest and so tender who cannot be seduced and made to change.

Pauline's reply is concise and cool:

I can only repeat, Monsieur, what I said to Mademoiselle your sister, that my decision is taken not to return; therefore I thank you for your offers, and I desire with my whole heart that you may marry the person who will make you happy. . . . My aunt and I feel it our duty to tell you how distressed we are that you should fail in respect to us by treating so badly a man whom we consider as our friend. I know better than anyone else that you have no right to call him perfidious. You have still several of my letters which I ask you to return. I will beg one of our friends to arrange with you about everything which remains to be adjusted. I am, very perfectly, Monsieur, your very humble and obedient servant . . .'

And she who only a short time before had been signing herself as 'for life' his 'faithful Pauline', now signs briefly with her surname.

So ended the episode of Pauline Lebreton, which, apart from the injury to his own dignity, left Beaumarchais financially poorer. For although a settlement was reached over the money he had put into her estate – punctually, on the day following Pauline's marriage with Séguirand, the discarded lover submitted his account! – there is no trace that any payment was ever made to Beaumarchais, either by Pauline or by any member of her family.

But while Beaumarchais' own matrimonial ship had foundered on the rocks, there were others in his family which safely reached port. A month before his final break with Pauline, his father had at last brought Mme Henry to the altar. (Yet their happiness was to be of short duration, for, with the cruel uncertainty of life in those days, the bride died only two years later, and the old watch-maker, then nearing seventy, returned as a widower for the second time to the house in the Rue de Condé.) In 1767, twelve months after his father's marriage, Tonton married her faithful Janot de Miron, who was soon to become, with the aid of his brother-in-law's influence, secretary to the Prince de Conti.

Meanwhile, the owner of the house in the Rue de Condé was left to reflect on how much he had cared for Pauline, now that, largely through his own fault, he had lost her. But there was little room in his mind for such painful thoughts, for he had much to occupy it: he was writing a drama, *Eugénie*. Drama was a novelty, sponsored by La Chaussée and Diderot, which at that time had only appeared recently in France. This was perhaps its source of attraction for Beaumarchais. 'Drama', he writes in his preface to *Eugénie*, 'holds an intermediate position between heroic tragedy and amusing comedy. It should be written in prose, and must confine itself to painting situations drawn from everyday life.' Which, however, was exactly what *Eugénie* did not do; for it was a piece of the purest melodrama, though the characters were sharply drawn and the plot ingeniously contrived. Beaumarchais had had it in his mind for something like eight years, so that its general lines must have been laid down well before his visit to Spain. Like most of his works, it is an attack on social privilege, and its scene was originally laid in eighteenth-century Paris. But this inevitably brought it into conflict with the strict play censorship, and the location of the piece had to be changed to London. Eugénie, the daughter of a nobleman who has now been made to come from Wales, has been tricked into a bogus marriage by Lord Clarendon, who is contemplating a real union with a rich heiress. Clarendon complicates the situation by saving the life of Eugénie's brother, 'Sir Charles', who has got himself into a variety of troubles. But Sir Charles is horrified to discover the identity of the girl who has been seduced by the man to whom he now owes his life. Further incredible complications lead to Sir Charles in turn saving Clarendon's life, and then challenging him to a duel on account of Eugénie. However, Clarendon repents very properly and in the end really marries Eugénie – who, oddly enough, seems perfectly willing to have him, in spite of the way he has behaved.

It is perhaps not surprising that this amalgam of improbabilities was hissed at its first public performance on 29 January 1767, especially as its author was at this time entirely unknown in the literary world. But Beaumarchais had taken the precaution of enlisting beforehand the interest of Mesdames, the Duc d'Orléans and other eminent persons, including the Duc de Nivernais, who was an Academician and himself of some literary distinction. He gave Beaumarchais much valuable advice on both the style and the construction of his play. So undaunted by the first reception of his piece, its author now set to work to revise it, and, bearing in mind the helpful criticism he had received, he re-wrote some parts of it entirely and cut down others. This brought the play a better reception, and it ended by having a fair measure of success, not only in France but also in England, where Garrick had it translated as *The School for Rakes* and acted in it himself.

It was at about this time that a friend of Julie came to see Beaumarchais one day, for the express purpose of trying to bring about a match between him and 'an amiable woman, recently widowed, and already much sought after'. She said that she and the widow would be going for a drive the following day in an unfrequented part of the Champs-Élysées known as 'The Widow's Drive' and suggested that Beaumarchais should take a ride out there on his horse, so that he could meet them there as if by chance. Beaumarchais was not the man to refuse an invitation of this kind, and all went according to plan; having greeted Julie's friend, he was of course introduced to her companion, and presently took a seat with them in their carriage, leaving his servant to return to the city with the horses. The introduction was a success from the first moment. The widow, Geneviève-Madeleine Wattebled, whose husband Antoine Lévêque had been a Court official, seems to have been a very attractive woman. She was practically the same age as Beaumarchais, and obviously was as much taken with him as he with her. She was also a wealthy woman, for her late husband had left her very well provided for. On 11 April 1768, therefore, Beaumarchais married Mme Lévêque as his second wife, and in the following year a son, Augustin, was born to them.

Fortune seemed indeed at this time to be smiling upon the one-time watch-maker, married to a rich and adoring wife and now the proud father of a son. With his wife's wealth behind him and the assistance of Pâris-Duverney, Beaumarchais was able to turn once more to industrial enterprises, and he bought from the State a large portion of the Forest of Chinon, whose wood provided him with many years of activity in the timber business. A letter written to his wife in July 1769 from Rivarennes in Touraine describes some of the work entailed in this undertaking:

You invite me to write, my dear one, and I wish to with all my heart; it is a pleasant relaxation from the hard labour of my stay in this village. Misunderstandings between managers to be put right, complaints and demands of clerks to be listened to, an account of more than 100,000 écus parcelled out in sums of 20 and 30 sols to be put in order, in regard to which it is necessary to discharge the responsible cashier; the different wharves to be visited; 200 labourers felling timber in the forest and their work, to be inspected; 280 acres of cut wood whose sawing up and transport must be arranged for; to have new roads constructed from the forest to the river and the old ones repaired; to have 300 or 400 tons of hay stacked; to provide oats for 30 cart horses; to buy 30 other horses for 6 more carts to transport all our wood for the Navy, before winter sets in; wharves and locks to be constructed on the River Indre to give us water all the year round at the place where we load the wood; 50 boats awaiting their cargo before going to Tours, Saumur, Angers and Nantes; agreements to be signed with 6 or 7 farms together, for the provisioning of a household of 30 persons; to draw up the general inventory of our receipts and expenses for the last two years: there, my dear wife, is in brief the sum total of my labours, of which part is already done and the rest well in hand.

He then goes on to describe his ruggedly simple, but not unpleasant, mode of living, in a small farm, where from the window of his plainly furnished whitewashed room he looks out over the Indre valley, and can see the men and women working there, singing as they go:

This picture is not without charm. Good coarse bread, a more than modest amount of food and execrable wine form my diet. . . . Farewell, my dearest . . . I am going to bed . . . without you, however . . . that often seems to me very hard. And my son, my son, how is he? I laugh when I think that I am working for him.

All this activity might surely have been enough to provide most men with a full day's work; but Beaumarchais still found time for other occupations as well. The eventual success of his first play *Eugénie* had encouraged him to believe himself cut out for the writing of drama; he had yet to prove to himself and to the world at large that his true genius lay in comedy. Within three years of the production of *Eugénie*, he brought out yet another drama, *The Two Friends*. This is an equally improbable tale about two business-men, Aurelly a silk-merchant and Mélac a tax-collector, who tries to save his friend from bankruptcy by using the tax money of which he has charge. The Farmer-General of Taxes arrives on the scene and calls upon Mélac to account for the missing money. The situation is further complicated by the fact that Mélac is in love with his friend's daughter, who is also being courted by the Farmer-General; the young girl's name, incidentally, is Pauline. However, the true reason for Mélac's action is presently uncovered, and all ends happily, the Farmer-General being so moved by such an act of friendship that he advances the money necessary for Aurelly the silk-merchant to re-establish his business. The play had some success in the provinces, particularly in the industrial towns; its author wrote hopefully that he trusted it would please merchants, since it had 'been made for them, and in general to honour people of the Third Estate'. He reported that it had been given at Lyon, Marseilles and Rouen with the greatest success; but in Paris its reception was, to say the least, unkind. Wags described it as 'an exchange where money circulates without producing any interest', and across the poster advertising *The Two*

Friends an unknown hand scrawled: 'By an author who has none'. The play, produced in Paris on 13 January 1770, ran for only ten performances and was then withdrawn.

This year 1770 was in fact to be a period of great misfortune for Beaumarchais. Before the year was out, he was to lose his wife. After the birth of her son in the previous December, Geneviève-Madeleine had developed tuberculosis, and in spite of all that the doctors could do for her – or more probably because of it, considering the medical methods of the time – she died on 21 November, leaving behind her the child who was to survive her by only two years and the husband who, like his father, was now left a widower for the second time after so few years of happiness. For this marriage seems to have been a success, and Beaumarchais, who had promised his wife when he married her that he would never spend a night away from her, remained devotedly at her side to the end. With Geneviève-Madeleine's death went also her fortune, for she had only a life interest in the money. Her death therefore left Beaumarchais with considerably reduced financial resources, and this at a time when only a few months before, in the summer of this most unlucky year, an event had occurred which was to bring down upon him the troubles which so nearly destroyed him. This event was the death, on 17 July at the age of eighty-seven, of the old financier Pâris-Duverney.

Chapter 6

VINDICTIVE COUNT

AND DEMENTED DUKE

THE heir to Pâris-Duverney's fortune of a million and a half livres was a great-nephew, the Comte de la Blache, who had been brought up under the old man's eye and had recently, through his influence, been made a brigadier. For some strange reason – perhaps no more than the whim of an old man – Duverney had passed over a nearer relative, his nephew Pâris de Meyzieu, who had in fact performed great and useful services to his uncle over the foundation of the École Militaire. Beaumarchais, who was himself treated by Duverney with the favour of an indulgent father, had warmly pleaded the cause of Meyzieu, whom he knew and liked, against that of La Blache. For the latter made no secret of his violent hostility towards Beaumarchais, whose dealings with Duverney he had long viewed with suspicious disapproval. Indeed, in an attempt to keep the two apart, he had practically shut up the old man as a prisoner in his home, so that when Duverney wished to see Beaumarchais, he was obliged to arrange meetings 'by chance' in his carriage. Naturally, the latter's championship of the cause of Meyzieu only added fuel to the flames of La Blache's enmity towards Beaumarchais: 'I hate that man as a lover loves his mistress', he announced to a gathering of his friends. Beaumarchais realized only too well the prospect in front of him with La Blache as Duverney's sole heir, and he had begged the old financier – though in vain – not to leave him in such a position, but to make his friend Meyzieu the heir.

It was thus particularly unfortunate, especially in view of Duverney's great age, that he had omitted to legalize in the proper form his business dealings with Beaumarchais, who since the beginning of their relations together had been urging this course upon the old man. But it was only when Duverney was within three months of his death that he could at last be persuaded to take the necessary action. An agreement was then drawn up in duplicate, by which Beaumarchais undertook to restore to Duverney 160,000 livres' worth of promissory notes and agreed to the dissolution of their partnership over the Forest of Chinon; while on his side Duverney declared Beaumarchais to be discharged from all debts towards him, acknowledged his own debt of 15;000 livres to the younger man, and finally undertook to lend him 75,000 livres free of interest over a period of eight years.

But before these two last clauses could be executed Duverney died, and when Beaumarchais duly presented the agreement to the man who was his bitter enemy, La Blache announced that he did not recognize his uncle's signature and that he therefore did not consider the document valid. He did not dare to accuse Beaumarchais openly of forgery – such a course was too dangerous, although he was challenged to do so by the man he was attacking – but his attitude implied as much indirectly, and he had the effrontery to declare that as a result of the invalidity of the agreement Beaumarchais, far from being a creditor to the extent of 15,000 livres from Duverney's estate, was himself its debtor to the amount of 139,000. 'Thus', observed unctuously the suave and ingenious lawyer engaged by La Blache, 'justice will be done, and honest citizens will have the satisfaction of seeing such an adversary taken in his own snares.' But even worse than the prospect of being called upon to produce a sum totalling 139,000 livres was the fact that unless Beaumarchais could prove the authenticity of the agreement made between him and Duverney he would stand implicitly branded before all the world as a forger.

Battle was joined between the litigants in October 1771, when the case was given its first hearing in the courts. It trailed on until the following spring, when on 22 February La Blache's demand for annulment of the agreement was dismissed, and on 22 March a further official pronouncement ordered the execution of the deed. Beaumarchais had thus won the first round; but it was no more than that, for the vindictive La Blache was by no means yet defeated. Nor did Beaumarchais emerge from the arena unscarred; for in the encounter La Blache had been at pains to stir up the maximum amount of mud against the man he hated, providing the gossip-writers with material which they did not fail to use in blackening the character of his adversary. It was from this time, for instance, that Beaumarchais' enemies began to circulate the vile suggestion that he had poisoned his two wives. La Blache also busied himself spreading the tale that Beaumarchais had been chased from the presence of Mesdames through some grave misdemeanour he had committed. On hearing of this, Beaumarchais wrote to the Comtesse de Périgord, lady-in-waiting to Mme Victoire, begging for some statement to clear his name. Mme de Périgord at once replied that she had communicated the contents of his letter to Mme Victoire, 'who assured me that she has never said a word to anyone which could damage your reputation, knowing nothing about you which could give her cause to do so. She has authorized me to pass this on to you.' Publication of this letter as it stood would have adequately met the case, but, most unfortunately, Beaumarchais must needs try to improve the situation by embodying the letter in a memorandum of his own, in which he spoke of La Blache's attempt to deprive him of the 'protection that Mesdames had always accorded' and concluded with the ill-advised statement that he was 'authorized by Mme Victoire to publish the letter'. La Blache did not fail instantly to use the weapon which Beaumarchais had thus laid in his hand; hastening to Versailles, he informed Mesdames that Beaumarchais was making an unauthorized and improper use of their names, and that he was having the audacity to claim that they were supporting him in his lawsuit. The Princesses were not unnaturally much displeased, and La Blache had no difficulty in obtaining from them a statement which he hastened to have printed and published everywhere:

We declare that we take no interest in M. Caron de Beaumarchais, or in his affair, and did not give him permission to insert assurances of our protection in a printed and public memorandum.

MARIE-ADELAIDE   VICTOIRE-LOUISE

SOPHIE-PHILIPPINE

Though this note did not influence the judges at the first hearing of the case, as they had seen Mme de Périgord's letter, it did immense harm to Beaumarchais in the eyes of the general public, who now saw him as a fabricator not only of false documents but also of the Princesses' alleged support. Too late, Beaumarchais realized what a false move he had made; but he did not dare to publish the Comtesse de Périgord's letter, for fear of giving further offence.

However, while La Blache was initiating the next round of the battle by carrying an appeal against the verdict to the Grand Chamber of the Paris Parlement, the highest court of justice in the land, Beaumarchais was trying to console himself for his troubles by starting to write *The Barber of Seville*. This was actually an adaptation of one of the early *parades* he had written for Le Normand d'Étioles, and he was now proposing to enlarge it into a comic opera which he hoped to get produced at the Comédie Italienne. But much was yet to happen before this famous work made its first appearance on a public stage.

It was also at about this time that Beaumarchais made the acquaintance of the man who was to be his most devoted lifelong friend, and indeed his Boswell: Gudin de la Brenellerie. A Protestant and the son of yet another clock-maker, Gudin had come to Paris to pursue a literary career; which he did with an energy and profusion more noteworthy than his talent. Verses, political essays, philosophy and history alike poured forth from his pen, though not all achieved publication; his massive *History of France* still reposes among the manuscripts of the Bibliothèque Nationale. By this time Tonton, who had become Mme de Miron, was presiding over a literary *salon* which Gudin began to frequent. 'She spoke to me of her brother,' he says. 'She found me without prejudice for his dramas, but naturally biased in regard to his character, of which I had heard much adverse criticism.' However, one evening Beaumarchais appeared in person, Gudin was introduced to him, and was soon won over by his charm. Gudin's account of what followed gives a vivid picture of the best side of Beaumarchais' character, by one who knew him at first hand:

... Two days later he invited me to his house, presented me to his father, to the one sister who lived with him, and whom I had never met.

I saw him as simple in his domestic circle as he was brilliant in a *salon*. I was very soon certain that he was a good son, good brother, good master, and good father, because he had still a little son, a young child whose infantile words were often repeated to us, which charmed me all the more because it betrayed his paternal tenderness. ...

We soon learned to esteem each other from a similar foundation of severe principles, hidden in his case under an exterior of lightness and gaiety, by a vivid and constant love of the good, the beautiful, the honest, by an equal disdain for prejudice and for all opinions ill-founded. ... The taste for letters, for the theatre, for the arts, the same indulgence for the weaknesses of the human heart, strengthened our union. ...

He never criticized any work; on the contrary he always brought out the beauties which others had not noticed, extolled talent, repelled scandal; he defended all those whose merit he heard depreciated and never listened to slander. 'I am,' he used to say, 'an advocate of the absent.' I noticed that he never spoke evil of his enemies, even of those whom he knew to be most intent on ruining him. One day when I had learned some most damning facts in regard to the conduct of the man who had brought suit against him, I expressed my astonishment that I had not learned these facts from him, but rather from a relative of the man himself. 'Eh, my friend,' was his reply, 'should I lose the time which I pass with you in recalling the things which would only afflict your spirit and mine? I try to forget the folly of those about me, and to think only of what is good and useful; we have so much to say to each other that such topics should never find a place in our conversation.'

It was indeed as well that Beaumarchais could take so philosophical a view of life, for worse afflictions to his spirit were about to fall upon him than even those connected directly with the Comte de la Blache.

He had recently become friendly with the Duc de Chaulnes, surely one of the most singular characters of his time. The Duc, thirty years of age, was of the ancient house of Luynes, the last member of a younger branch – which was perhaps just as well, for he was notorious for the unbalanced violence of his disposition.

His character [writes Gudin de la Brenellerie] was an unusual combination of good qualities and the most contradictory faults: he had wit but no judgment, pride but no dignity; a vast but disordered memory; a great desire for knowledge, but an even greater taste for dissipation; prodigious bodily strength; a violence of disposition which clouded his always rather confused judgment; frequent accesses of fury in which he resembled a drunken savage, not to say a ferocious beast. Always swayed by the impression of the moment, regardless of consequences, he had more than once brought trouble on himself. Banished from the kingdom for five years on one occasion, he employed his time of exile in making a scientific expedition, visited the Pyramids, foregathered with the Bedouins of the desert, and brought back many objects of natural history, and an unfortunate ape which he beat savagely every day.

He was also passionately interested in chemistry and had even made some original discoveries in it. For some time now he had been much enamoured of a certain Mlle Ménard of the Comédie Italienne. A bouncing young woman of fine physique, though apparently of somewhat mediocre musical ability, she yet possessed both charm and ambition; which was probably the reason why she had become the Duc's mistress, for, as was only to be expected, she found him a brutal and madly jealous lover, whose violence soon extinguished in her every feeling but that of fear. For the sake of peace, she had abandoned her career on the stage, but her *salon* was frequented by many distinguished men who were friends of the Duc de Chaulnes. One day the Duc brought in and introduced his latest friend Beaumarchais, and it was not long before the famous charm produced its usual effect, especially when seen in contrast to the uncertain moods of the Duc. But the latter was not long in perceiving what had happened, and Mlle Ménard begged Beaumarchais in terror to cease his visits. However, the Duc's violence became so insupportable that she was herself obliged to take refuge in a convent. After some weeks in seclusion she emerged again, and, evidently hoping that the storm had blown over, sent word to Beaumarchais to resume his visits. But some while later Gudin paid a call on her and found her in tears, complaining of the Duc's brutality. The latter happened to come into the room while she was speaking of the charges against Beaumarchais and expressing the hope that he would be able to refute them. 'What need is there,' retorted the Duc, 'to justify a rascal like Beaumarchais?' 'He is a perfectly honest man!' she cried, with a fresh burst of weeping. 'You love him!' shouted the Duc, leaping to his feet. 'You humiliate me. I declare to you that I shall go and fight him.' And thrusting aside the efforts of Mlle Ménard and Gudin to restrain him, he rushed out of the house. Gudin at once hurried out by another way to warn Beaumarchais of his peril, and meeting his friend's carriage in the Rue Dauphine he leapt at the horses' heads to stop them. 'The Duc is looking for you to fight you,' he explained breathlessly. 'Come back to my house; I will tell you the rest.' 'I cannot,' replied Beaumarchais calmly, 'I am going to the Capitainerie to hold court. When it is over, I will come to you.' He resumed his journey and Gudin turned back for home. But as he was mounting the steps up on to the Pont Neuf, he felt himself seized by the coat-tail, and fell backwards into the arms of the Duc de Chaulnes, who, much bigger and more powerful than he, picked him up 'like a bird of prey' and hurled him into a *fiacre*.

'By what right, M. le Duc,' protested the indignant Gudin, 'do you, who are always talking about liberty, dare to make an attempt on mine?'

'By the right of the strongest. You will find Beaumarchais for me, or——'

'M. le Duc, I am unarmed; you will surely not assassinate me?'

'No, I shall only kill this Beaumarchais, and when I have plunged my sword into his body and have torn out his heart with my teeth, the Ménard woman can go to hell. . . .'

Gudin said stoutly that he did not know where Beaumarchais was, and if he did, would certainly not say. The Duc then threatened to 'give him a thousand blows', at which Gudin retorted that he would return them in good measure. 'What? You would return them on me, duke and peer?' Gudin, undaunted, replied that when it was a question of violence all men were equal. This put the madman into such a frenzy that he fell upon Gudin, trying to seize him by the hair. But he only succeeded in catching hold of Gudin's wig, which came off in his hand, to the great joy of the passers-by whose attention had been attracted by the Duc's behaviour and who now gathered round to watch the scene. The Duc next seized Gudin by the throat, and the latter, defending himself as best he could, called to the guard for help; which slightly quietened his demented assailant. When at last they arrived at Beaumarchais' door, Gudin slipped quietly out of the carriage, thinking that the servants could be relied upon not to reveal their master's whereabouts. But unfortunately they were intimidated into letting out that he had gone to the Louvre; whereupon the Duc de Chaulnes hurried off there, and burst into the court where Beaumarchais was giving judgment. Striding straight up to the Lieutenant-General of the Varenne du Louvre, he announced that he had something of great importance to say, and asked Beaumarchais to come outside. The latter at first replied that he could not do so, since his duty to the public service compelled him to finish what he had begun; but fearing that the Duc would make a scene in court, he finally consented to go with him into an adjoining room. 'There,' as Beaumarchais related in his own account of the affair, 'he told me in the language of the markets that he was going to kill me, tear out my heart and drink my blood, for which he was thirsting.' To this Beaumarchais coolly replied: 'Is that all, M. le Duc? You must allow business to come before pleasure.' Unmoved by the Duc's threat to tear out his eyes forthwith, he then turned and went back into the court to conclude the rest of his official business. This took about another two hours, after which the Lieutenant-General of the Varenne du Louvre, having disrobed and reappeared, demanded to know what grievance the Duc could have against a man he had not seen for six months. 'No explanations,' snarled the other. 'We fight right away or I shall make a scene here.' They would go and get as a witness the Comte de la Tour du Pin, who would be able to lend Beaumarchais a rapier in place of the small mourning sword he was wearing at that moment. The count, however, on being found, regretted that an important engagement at the Luxembourg would detain him until at least four o'clock in the afternoon. The Duc then demanded that Beaumarchais should come back with him to his house and wait there. But Beaumarchais, wisely, would not risk putting himself completely in the power of a man who was so obviously a maniac, and he ordered the coachman to drive to his own home in the Rue de Condé – despite a roar from the Duc to the effect that he would stab Beaumarchais if he got down out of the carriage.

When they arrived at the house, its owner ordered dinner for two to be served upstairs in his study, in order to avoid a painful scene in front of his old father, and, alone with the madman, tried to talk him into a more reasonable state of mind. But suddenly the Duc seized the small mourning sword which Beaumarchais had just taken off, and, grinding his teeth in fury, rushed at him. The latter seized his attacker's arms and holding them down, pushed him towards the bell; whereat the Duc, seeing his intention, thrust his fingers into his opponent's eyes, whose face he scored with his finger-nails until blood flowed. Nevertheless, Beaumarchais succeeded in reaching the bell and summoning his servants. 'Disarm this madman!' he cried. His cook, a big hulking fellow as strong as the Duc himself, was preparing to knock him out with a great piece of wood; but Beaumarchais called out quickly: 'Disarm him, but do not hurt him, or he will say that I have tried to assassinate him in my house.' The servants dragged the sword from him, but the Duc instantly made a leap at Beaumarchais' hair, tearing out a handful from the front of the head. In his pain, Beaumarchais let go of his adversary, but with the full strength of his arm he dealt him a heavy blow in the face with his fist. 'Wretch!' bellowed the madman, 'you are striking a duke and peer!' The incongruous absurdity of this remark would have made Beaumarchais laugh at any other time, but, as the Duc was much stronger than he and now had him by the throat, there was no time for amusement. Struggling desperately, with the servants trying to separate them, the two men were now practically at the top of the stairs, when the Duc suddenly fell, and, rolling on top of the servants, dragged Beaumarchais down the stairs with him. At this exhilarating moment, there was a ring at the door and Gudin reappeared, in time to hear the Duc declare that he would cut into pieces anyone who tried either to come in or go out of the house. He was now in fact making so much noise that a large crowd was gathering outside Beaumarchais' door, to be presently rewarded for its interest by seeing one of his female servants put her head out of the window, shrieking that her master was being murdered. Indoors, the battle continued, as the Duc drew his own sword and made a fresh onslaught on Beaumarchais, whose face by this time was streaming with blood and his clothes badly torn. The servants now contrived to wrest the Duc's sword from him, whereat he ran into the kitchen in search of fresh weapons. Fortunately, everything suitable had been hidden, and meanwhile Beaumarchais seized the opportunity to arm himself with a pair of large fire-irons. Provided with these, he went downstairs again in search of the Duc – to find him seated at the dining-table, hurling down his throat the food which had been left upon it!

At this stage a Commissioner of Police at last arrived. Beaumarchais' statement of what had happened caused a fresh outbreak of berserk rage from the Duc, whose fury, however, was now turned on to himself. Tearing his own hair for a change, he beat himself in the face for his failure to finish off his enemy; after which, he coolly ordered the lackey whose head he had gashed in the fight to dress his hair. He then departed in his coach, leaving the servants and their master to attend to their wounds and clear up the battlefield.

It is a measure of Beaumarchais' resilience that, after such a day and with the scars of battle fresh on his face, he was still able, as Gudin tells us, to devote the same evening to giving a reading of his new play *The Barber of Seville* to a large assembly at the house of one of his friends, finishing up the entertainment with a witty account of the day's events, and finally singing an assortment of Spanish *seguidillas* to his own accompaniment on the harp. 'It was thus', says Gudin, 'that, in all circumstances of his life, he gave himself entirely to the thing on which he was engaged, without being turned from it either by what had happened or by what must follow; so sure was he of his faculties and of his presence of mind.' Yet even Beaumarchais could hardly have been prepared for the final sequel to his battle with the Duc de Chaulnes.

The Commissioner of Police duly made his report on the affair to M. de Sartines, the Lieutenant-General of Police. But with the discretion befitting one having to deal with such a delicate matter as the peccadilloes of a duke and peer, he took care to stress the fact that he had arrived on the scene only in the concluding stages of the affair. However, the matter was considered sufficiently serious to be brought before the Tribunal of the Marshals of France, who were the judges of disputes between noblemen. In the meantime, the Duc de la Vrillière, Minister of the King's Household, was proposing to banish Beaumarchais to the country while the case was pending; but Beaumarchais protested vigorously that such a procedure, in view of the threats of the Duc de Chaulnes, would compromise his honour: he was therefore allowed to remain under house arrest in his own home. When the case came before the Tribunal of the Marshals, the judges were not slow in deciding against the Duc de Chaulnes, of whose outrageous behaviour there could be no question. The Duc was sent to cool his heels – and his brain – in the fortress of Vincennes; Beaumarchais, summoned before the tribunal, was exonerated and told that he was free.

This was very gratifying, if only just; but to make quite sure that everything was in order, Beaumarchais called on the Duc de la Vrillière to confirm that he was indeed free. Finding the Duc absent, he went to M. de Sartines and asked him the same question. On the latter replying that he could now consider himself as entirely free, Beaumarchais felt that he could once more go about Paris in his usual manner.

But he had counted without the Duc de la Vrillière. The Tribunal of the Marshals had taken upon itself, in the name of the King, to revoke measures taken under the same august authority by the Minister of the King's Household. That was an affront both to the Minister's dignity and to his personal vanity. Possibly too, as Loménie has suggested, it was considered outrageous that a duke and peer of France should be sent to Vincennes while the son of a mere clock-maker – even if recently ennobled – was discharged, to repair as best he could the ravages made on his face by the same duke and peer. Whatever the reasoning in the great brain of the Duc de la Vrillière, there was no doubt about its result. On 24 February, under his orders, still in the name of the King, Beaumarchais was summarily arrested and, at the very moment when he should have been preparing his defence against the new onslaught of La Blache, found himself shut up in For-l'Évêque, a prison used for the confinement of refractory stage-players.

Chapter 7

THE PRICE OF

COUNCILLOR GOEZMAN

THE Parlement of Paris, before which La Blache was now about to bring his appeal, was, up to the time of the Revolution, the High Court of Justice. Originally deriving, like its English namesake, from the medieval King's Court where all kinds of business came under discussion, it had become by this time a mainly judicial body, owing to the great amount of legal business – particularly appeals from lesser courts – which through the centuries had increasingly fallen upon it. Another important function of the Parlement, however, was the registration of royal decrees. These, in the event of the Parlement being refractory, could be forced through by the King in person, in a ceremony known as a *Lit de Justice*. During the reign of Louis XV the Parlements, now no longer cowed by the awesome presence of the Roi Soleil, had in fact become extremely refractory, and those in the provinces took their cue from the attitude of the Parlement of Paris. The latter body, a group of highly privileged magistrates known as Councillors, headed by a President, had set themselves up as champions of constitutional liberty; in which role they conducted a ceaseless campaign of obstructive opposition to any attempts at reform, since their real concern was with the preservation of their own privileges. At the beginning of 1771 matters had at last come to a head, when the able Chancellor Maupeou had carried the war into the enemies' camp by clearing out the entire Paris Parlement with *lettres de cachet* exiling its members to far distant corners of the country, while he set up new courts in Paris under royal nomination. There was, needless to say, a furious outcry from all those whose vested interests lay with the deposed Parlement – the nobility, the Parisian *bourgeoisie*, and, with the notable exception of Voltaire, even some members of the literary world – but there was also a strong feeling in some quarters that with the overthrow of the Parlement

had gone a powerful and very necessary curb on royal absolutism.
It was, then, the new Parlement, known scornfully to its enemies as
the 'Parlement Maupeou', before whose Grand Chamber the appeal of
La Blache would be brought. It was the custom to depute one of the
Councillors to collect and report on the written documents of a case,
including the proceedings of the court of first instance, the Councillor
acting in this capacity being called a *rapporteur*. While he was engaged
on this work, it was also usual for litigants to make contact with him,
in order that they should be personally known to him – and to make
sure that he was in possession of all information relating to the suit.
This was what Beaumarchais should have been doing at the very time
when he found himself shut up in For-l'Évêque, leaving his enemy La
Blache in undisputed possession of the field.

Beaumarchais, with the irritation of a citizen unjustly used, took up
his pen – that ever-ready weapon of his defence – and began to bom-
bard the Duc de la Vrillière with memoranda, pointing out that he had
committed no wrong and even demanding to know why he was being
held in detention. M. de Sartines, who was his friend, tried to give him
the hint that such methods were not those to be employed against the
Minister of the Royal Household; but Beaumarchais had not yet
learned his painful lesson, and merely replied that: 'The only satisfaction of a persecuted man is to render testimony that he is unjustly dealt
with.' Sartines, who realized the particular peril of Beaumarchais'
position in view of the impending law case, tried to put as much pressure as he dared on the Duc de la Vrillière to allow his prisoner to
come out of confinement for a few hours daily, so that he could prepare
his case for the Parlement. But the only reply received from the Duc
was: 'That man is too insolent; let him pursue his affair through his
attorney.' Beaumarchais poured forth his wrathful frustration in a
letter to Sartines:

It is completely proved to me that they desire me to lose my suit . . . but I
admit that I was not prepared for the derisive answer of the Duc de la Vrillière
to have my affair conducted through my attorney – he who knows as well as I,
that it is forbidden to attorneys to do so. Ah, great gods! cannot an innocent
man be lost without laughing in his face! Thus, Monsieur, have I been griev-
ously insulted, justice has been denied to me because my adversary is a man of
quality. I have been put in prison, I am kept there because I have been insulted
by a man of quality. . . . A little more and they would say that it was very
insolent of me to have been outraged in every way by a man of quality; because
what is the meaning of that phrase 'He has put too much boasting into this

affair'? Could I do less than demand justice and prove by the conduct of my adversary that I was in no way wrong? What a pretext for ruining an injured man, that of saying, 'He has talked too much about his affair'. As if it were possible for me to talk of anything else.

At this afflicting moment, however, when the hands of so many seemed to be turned against him, Beaumarchais had the pleasure of finding that he had at least one friend: the six-year-old son of Le Normand d'Étioles by his second wife wrote to the prisoner on 2 March:

Sir, I am sending you my purse, because one is always unhappy in prison. I am very sorry that you are in prison. Every morning and every evening I say an Ave Maria for you. I have the honour of being, Sir, your very humble and very obedient servant,

CONSTANT

Obviously much touched, Beaumarchais replied to the little boy:

My dear little Constant,

I received with much gratitude your letter, and the purse you enclosed with it. I have carefully shared out their contents among my fellow-prisoners, according to their several needs and my own, keeping for your friend Beaumarchais the better part – I mean the prayers and the Ave Maria, of which assuredly I have great need – while distributing among poor people, who are suffering, all the money contained in your purse. Thus, in your desire to oblige a single man, you have won the gratitude of several. That is the usual result of all good actions such as yours.

Good-bye, little friend Constant.

BEAUMARCHAIS

To Constant's parents he wrote:

This letter and purse have made me feel as joyful as a child. Happy parents to have a son capable, at six years of age, of such an action! I also had a son, but I have him no longer. . . .

For Beaumarchais' son, the only one he was to have, had survived his mother by no more than two years.

But the weeks were slipping by, and even Beaumarchais began to realize that only by swallowing his pride and displaying an appropriate humility would he be able to make any impression on the Duc de la Vrillière. So, bitterly as it must have gone against the grain of his self-respect, he at last humbled himself to write:

Monseigneur,

The frightful affair of M. le duc de Chaulnes has become for me a series of misfortunes without end and the greatest of all is that I have incurred your displeasure. But if, in spite of the purity of my intentions, despair has broken me and driven me to measures which have displeased you, I disavow them, Monseigneur, at your feet, and beg of you a generous pardon. Or if it seems to you that I deserve a longer imprisonment, permit me to go out for a few days to instruct my judges in the affair most important for my fortune and my honour, and I will submit after the judgment to whatever penalty you may impose. All my family, weeping, join their prayers to mine. Everyone speaks, Monseigneur, of your indulgence and goodness of heart. Shall I be the only one who implores you in vain? You can with a single word fill with joy a host of honest people whose gratitude will equal the very profound respect with which we are all, and I in particular, Monseigneur,

Yours, etc.

BEAUMARCHAIS

Pompous vanity was appeased and satisfied. On 22 March the Duc de la Vrillière was graciously pleased to accord the prisoner permission to go out during the day, under the escort of a police officer; but he must still return to eat and sleep at For-l'Évêque. There was no time to be lost; March was drawing to an end, and the Parlement would meet on 6 April to consider the report on the suit of La Blache against Beaumarchais.

The Councillor deputed to act as *rapporteur* in this case was a certain Louis Valentin Goezman, a lawyer of some eminence who had held a similar position in Alsace; although since coming to Paris in 1768 his reputation had not been of the best. However, Beaumarchais lost no time in trying to obtain an interview with him, though greatly hampered by the necessity of having to return each evening to For-l'Évêque. Three times during the afternoon of 1 April, and again the following day, he called at Goezman's house begging for an interview, only to be informed by the concierge that Goezman did not wish to see anybody and that it would be quite useless calling again. On one of these occasions Goezman could be plainly seen watching from behind the curtains of his study on the first floor. Since there was only a day or two left before the Councillor was due to make his report to Parlement, it was clear that La Blache had been taking the fullest advantage of his undisturbed possession of the arena. Beaumarchais, scarcely knowing which way to turn in his despair, called on his sister Madeleine-Françoise, wife of the clock-maker Lepine, and a man called Dairolles who lodged in the same house suggested that help might be obtained from the bookseller Le Jay, who had business dealings with

53

Goezman and was on friendly terms with both the Councillor and his wife. It appeared that Mme Goezman – a frivolous young woman whose pursuit of pleasure was as expensive a hobby as her husband's pursuit of women – had declared to Le Jay on one occasion, in the hearing of a number of people, that it was impossible for them to live honestly on what they received, but that they had 'the art of plucking the fowl without making it cry out'. It appeared that Mme Goezman would not be adverse to receiving a 'present' which might cause her husband's door to open – though it might have to be as much as 200 louis.* Since Beaumarchais, in his desperate situation, could not readily lay hands on this amount, a kind friend lent him 100 louis and he made up the other 100 by adding a watch of that value, studded with diamonds. These offerings were accepted with alacrity by Mme Goezman with the assurance that they would be returned if the case went against Beaumarchais; but she made a further request for 15 louis, on behalf, so she said, of her husband's secretary. At last, at an inconveniently late hour in the evening, Beaumarchais, was admitted to the long-sought interview. But Goezman's remarks on the case were so little to the point that Beaumarchais expressed the fear that the Councillor might be insufficiently acquainted with all the details to act as *rapporteur* upon it in only two days' time. Goezman replied, with a peculiar smile which Beaumarchais did not like, that the case was a simple one and that he knew enough of it to give an exact account to the court. Filled with misgiving, Beaumarchais requested another interview; but this was refused, and Mme Goezman, when again approached, remarked soothingly that Beaumarchais had no cause for alarm, and as for the expression he had noticed on her husband's face, it was only his usual one.

On the 6 April the case came up before Parlement, and on the report of Councillor Goezman the verdict of the court of first instance was set aside, and the agreement between Pâris-Duverney and Beaumarchais declared invalid. Beaumarchais, now by implication stamped as a forger, found himself faced with a payment of 56,300 livres together with five years' interest, plus the costs of the proceedings. (He was probably lucky not to have been called upon to pay the whole 139,000 livres demanded by La Blache; but even Parlement, it seems, had to draw the line somewhere.) As if this were not enough to fall on a man at any one time, other claimants were now encouraged by La Blache's success to come forward, like jackals to the feast. Even the relatives

* 1 louis (= 24 livres) was worth a little over a guinea.

Beaumarchais
Aged 23
From the portrait by Nattier (1755)

Mme Adelaide (1756)   Mme Victoire (1748)

Mme Louise (1748)   Mme Sophie (1748)

MESDAMES DE FRANCE

From the portraits by Nattier

William Henry Zuylestein,
Earl of Rochford, British
Ambassador in Madrid,
1763-6; later, Secretary
of State for the Northern
Department

From the portrait by Perronneau

Charles Gravier,
Comte de Vergennes
From the portrait by Callet

David Murray, Viscount
Stormont
British Ambassador in
Paris, 1772-8

The Chevalier d'Eon de
Beaumont as "Mlle Lia
de Beaumont"

*Angelica Kauffman's copy of
the portrait by Latour*

Pierre-Augustin Caron de Beaumarchais
From the pastel by J. B. Perronneau

Le Mariage de Figaro
Act I, Scene IX
From an engraving by Liénard

All that remained of Beaumarchais' house by the early
nineteenth century

From an etching by A. P. Martial

The Bastille and the Porte Saint-Antoine from the site of Beaumarchais' house

After J. Rigaud

of Beaumarchais' first wife thought the moment a timely one to put forward claims, although nothing of her estate had come to Beaumarchais except debts; but it was only after several years of litigation that their attempt was eventually defeated.

The fortunes of Beaumarchais were indeed at their lowest ebb. His house in the Rue de Condé had to be sold up to meet the payments he had to face: his furniture went with it, and his father had to go to lodge with a friend, while Julie retreated for the time being to a convent. But the unhappy Beaumarchais himself was still shut up in For-l'Évêque. On 9 April he wrote a letter to M. de Sartines which seems to show that, for once, even Beaumarchais' indomitable spirit was near breaking-point:

I am at the end of my courage. . . . My credit has gone, my business is in ruins; my family, of which I am the father and support, is in a state of desolation. . . . Is there no limit to the vengeance to be taken on me for this wretched business of Chaulnes? My imprisonment has cost me a good 100,000 francs . . . and while I am kept in this horrible prison I have no chance of retrieving my losses. I have strength to bear my own troubles, but none against the tears of my respected father, 75 years old, who is dying of grief at the state into which I have fallen; nor have I more against the sorrows of my sisters and my nieces, who are already haunted by the fear of want, arising out of the state into which my detention has thrown me and my affairs. . . . My situation is killing me. . . . the infected air of the prison is destroying my health.

At last even the Duc de la Vrillière relented. The insolent upstart had been chastised; ruined and well chastened, he could now be allowed his liberty. No doubt he would take to heart the lesson he had been given. So on 8 May 1773 the gates of For-l'Évêque opened to let out the prisoner, after two and half months of disastrous seclusion.

Now on the evening of the fatal 6 April Mme Goezman had duly sent back the 100 louis and the diamond watch. But the 15 louis had not been returned, and Beaumarchais soon discovered that Goezman's secretary, the alleged beneficiary, had not received a particle of the money. The secretary was in fact an honest man who had only accepted with the greatest reluctance a tip of 10 louis which Beaumarchais had pressed upon him before the court hearing. Beaumarchais, irritated at the outcome of the case, and suspecting that La Blache had financed Goezman more heavily than he, decided to write to Mme Goezman – which he did on 21 April – demanding the return of the 15 louis. This was indeed a perilous course to take, since it would almost certainly embroil Beaumarchais in open conflict with a magistrate. On the other hand, if he could convict Goezman, through his wife, of venality, the very foundations of the verdict which had just been given against him would be shaken. On his release from For-l'Évêque in May, he made it his business to ensure that all the Paris *salons* should know that Councillor Goezman had his price. Such a piece of scandal about a member of the detested Parlement Maupeou was a juicy morsel indeed.

The result of Beaumarchais' letter to Mme Goezman was what might have been expected. She declared loftily that she had been offered presents by Beaumarchais in order to win for him the support of her husband, and that she had of course rejected such nefarious overtures. Her husband, who seems to have been at first unaware of his wife's part in these transactions, thought to stifle the whole affair at one blow by having Beaumarchais put away with a *lettre de cachet*. But Sartines, when appealed to by Goezman in a confidential note (dated 5 June 1773), refused to oblige. Beaumarchais had already spread too much of the affair all over Paris, and the Government simply dared not risk taking such a measure. Goezman had to lay other plans. He began by summoning the bookseller Le Jay to his house, and browbeat him into supporting Mme Goezman's false statement. For Le Jay had already started to blurt out the truth, and he had to be persuaded to copy out and sign a statement dictated by Goezman, retracting what he had previously said. This inconvenient point having been dealt with, Goezman then formally denounced Beaumarchais to the Parlement for having libelled the wife of a judge, after having vainly attempted to bribe her, and through her, of course, her husband.

Beaumarchais had now landed himself in very serious trouble indeed. For the charge against him was a criminal one, which, according to the horrifying legal procedure of the time, would be tried in secret and judged behind closed doors; while the penalty could be of the utmost severity short of death. Moreover, no advocate would dare to take on his defence, in the face of such redoubtable judges. In this desperate situation he turned to that unfailing weapon of defence, his pen. He would be his own advocate; he would let the full light of publicity into the dark recesses of that chamber where his judges sat behind closed doors; in brief, he would enlist the aid of that most powerful of allies, public opinion. It was fortunate indeed that he had the capacity to do this, that he was able to produce what La Harpe described as 'those remarkable writings which were at once a plea, a satire, a drama, a comedy, a gallery of pictures, and finally a kind of arena opened for the first time where it seemed that Beaumarchais amused himself by leading in so many personages like performing animals assembled to amuse the spectators'. It must be remembered that, up to this time, Beaumarchais' literary output had amounted to little more than two distinctly mediocre dramas; the matured talent of his two great comedies had yet to be revealed. But in his pamphlets against Goezman the curtain rises to uncover the true quality of his mind. Yet Beaumarchais was not the unaided author of the famous pamphlets, though he always wrote the final versions himself; he had a devoted band of co-operators in the relatives and friends who rallied round him to help: his old father, with experience of life covering three-quarters of a century; his sister Julie, with a wit as sharp and brilliant as his own; their brother-in-law Janot de Miron, himself a barrister and a man of keen intellect. The legal profession was further represented by a young and distinguished member, Falconnet by name, whose assistance was invaluable in dealing with technical points of law. The faithful Gudin also brought his pen to his friend's assistance, and finally there was a Provençal doctor named Gardane, whose co-operation was to be particularly useful when his two compatriots Marin and Bertrand joined the ranks of the enemy. This was the band which the Goezmans, when they found themselves to be getting the worst of the encounter, referred to as the *clique infâme*. They assembled at the house of Beaumarchais' sister, Mme Lepine, where he was himself lodging, since he no longer possessed any home of his own. There they would discuss the composition of the pamphlets, the drafts of which were always written out by Beaumarchais himself. The most brilliant parts were often redrafted three or four times, for the collaborators did not hesitate to make pungent criticisms of any portions they considered below standard, and at this period in his career Beaumarchais gladly accepted their advice – he was to become less amenable to criticism after full success had come to him on the stage.

On 5 September Beaumarchais published the first of his four pamphlets dealing with the Goezman case. In it, he gave a straightforward account of his attempts to see his *rapporteur*, of the payments made to Mme Goezman, and of the unsatisfactory interview at last obtained with her husband. He then gives the text of his letter to Mme Goezman demanding the return of the 15 louis, records how Le Jay has repented of signing the false statement dictated by Goezman and, supported by the strong-minded Mme Le Jay, has now returned to the true version of the affair; although Goezman has tried in vain to bribe him into going to Holland until the affair has blown over. Finally, Beaumarchais relates how Marin, Director of the *Gazette de France* and a friend of Goezman, suggests that the whole business could be amicably settled without mention of 'those wretched fifteen louis'. Beaumarchais points out firmly that, on the contrary, they are the keystone of the whole edifice, for Mme Goezman, who now denies having received the price of her husband's audience, is left without a leg to stand on if asked to explain how she comes to be still in possession of the 15 louis, if it is true that she has rejected all the rest. If she has not got them, the only alternative possibility is that Le Jay has them; in which case, he would be assumed to be in possession of the whole amount, and an unfortunate man would be ruined, to save the real authors of the transaction. What does it matter, replies Marin airily, if a rascal like Le Jay is sacrificed? It is no great matter, if it gets everyone else out of a mess.

This first pamphlet of Beaumarchais, written in direct and simple language without any personalities or sensationalism, was read avidly all over Paris, in cafés and *salons* alike, and with not least interest at the Court; in fact the supply of copies was exhausted within a week. It drew forth five replies from the enemy camp. The first, a massive bundle of no less than seventy-four pages, purported to be the work of Mme Goezman; but the ponderous construction of the document and its frequent use of sonorous legal terminology and Latin quotations could leave no doubt as to its actual authorship. As Beaumarchais remarked: 'They announce to me an artless woman, and present a German publicist.' But while ridiculous enough in its form, the pamphlet was offensively personal in tone, as was the second of the series, obviously written by Mme Goezman herself and full of the hysterical abuse of an angry and frightened woman. The remaining three were from various persons who had their own reasons for wishing to please Goezman and therefore took his side: the stockjobber Bertrand, the writer Arnaud-Baculard, and lastly Marin, the most venomous and virulent of them all. It was when maddened by the scurrilous personal attacks of these ruthless antagonists that Beaumarchais began to hit back against them in real earnest, with no holds barred, in an intensity of bitter fury which is not found in the first memoir.

In his second pamphlet, which appeared on 18 November, Beaumarchais gives an account of the confrontations between Mme Goezman and himself in the Registrar's court, where each had the right to cross-examine the other. On being first asked formally if they knew each other, Mme Goezman replied that she did not, and had no wish ever to know Beaumarchais; while his reply was that, 'I have not the honour of knowing Madame either: but in seeing her, I am unable to prevent myself from forming a wish quite different from hers'. After this promising beginning, Beaumarchais then plays out a scene with Mme Goezman which might well have found a place in one of his comedies; his ironic flippancy and subtle wit leaving her so flustered and disconcerted that she either contradicts herself or is stricken with complete loss of memory. The scene terminates with his demanding of Mme Goezman to explain why she persists in giving her age as thirty, when her face contradicts her by showing her to be no more than eighteen. Mme Goezman is so captivated by this remark that she proposes to leave the court room on the arm of Beaumarchais – that *homme atroce* of a few moments before – when the scandalized Registrar hastens to point out the unseemliness of such a procedure on the part of two adversaries. The whole situation was one after the heart of all Paris, especially among the enemies of the Parlement Maupeou, who were watching the course of the battle with glee, and the second pamphlet had as great a public success as any theatre comedy. Indeed, Mme du Barry played it as such in front of the King, to his enormous amusement.

But Beaumarchais' enemies, becoming ever more venomous in their attacks, had now reached the stage when no mud was too vile or stinking to be flung at their adversary. He was next obliged, in his pamphlets, to refute their allegations that he had poisoned his two wives; charges levelled at him in spite of the fact that in each case his wife's death had left him financially a poor man. But he was not one to lie down under such onslaughts; he would give as good as he received, and, after citing the evidence of the doctors who had attended his wives, he counter-attacked by producing a deadly missile which he considered himself to be fully justified in hurling at his chief enemy. On 15 December 1773 he laid before the Procureur-Général the fact that a couple named Dubillon had made a well-attested statement to the Archbishop of Paris to the effect that Councillor Goezman, godfather to their daughter Marie-Sophie, had had a child by her for whose maintenance he had completely failed since then to provide, although he had pledged himself to do so. Beaumarchais having gone to the parish of Saint-Jacques de la Boucherie to consult the register, found that the child's father, duly entered as the godfather of Marie-Sophie, had, however, given a false name and address. Here indeed was an interesting piece of information; for while the Councillor's amorous adventures were unlikely to have any influence on the court case, the falsification of a parish register was a different matter: it was a criminal offence, all the more serious when the culprit was no less a person than a magistrate of the High Court of Justice. 'I am uncovering a fact', wrote Beaumarchais soberly, 'which it is important for my judges and the public to know. I denounce him to M. le Procureur-Général . . . who will make of it the use which his prudence and his well-known exactitude may dictate.'

In his fourth and last pamphlet (he had intended to write a fifth, but the case came to court before he could do so), Beaumarchais not only gives his own account of his visit to Spain – about which his enemies were putting about all manner of tales – but he also castigates the most virulent of them, Marin, the play censor, journalist and unscrupulous purveyor of the vilest gossip, in a famous passage which was to set all Europe laughing:

Eloquent writer, skilful censor, veracious newsmonger, hack journalist; when he crawls on the ground, he slithers along like a serpent; when he rises up, he flops down like a toad. In short, dragging himself along and climbing up by leaps and bounds, but always with his belly on the ground, he has done so well by his daily toil that nowadays we find the bandit going to Versailles, drawn by four horses, and bearing, as a coat-of-arms on the panels of his carriage, on a shield in the form of an organ-case: Fame, on a field of gules,* her wings cut, her head down, croaking into a megaphone,† and supported by a disgusted figure representing Europe; the whole enclosed by a short cassock lined with journals, surmounted by a square cap, with this inscription on the top-knot: 'What's that?‡ Marin.'

At Versailles this description of Marin caused such merriment that the milliner of the gay young Dauphine, Marie-Antoinette, invented a new headdress for smart women, the *Quesaco*, consisting of a bunch of three feathers worn at the back of the head. No one was more amused at Beaumarchais' pamphlets than the King; the only person who did not laugh – and with reason – was the unfortunate Chancellor Maupeou. For Beaumarchais' cause, the struggle of one man against the detested Parlement Maupeou, personified in Councillor Goezman, had now become, as it was said, the 'cause of the nation'. During the six

---

* A play upon the words *gueules*=gules (the heraldic colour red) and *gueule*= mouth (of animals) or face in the vulgar sense of 'mug' or 'phiz'; hence *homme fort en gueule*=a foul-mouthed or abusive man.

† *Trompette marine!*

‡ *Qu'es-aco?* (Provençal dialect) Marin's stock expression.

months between the late summer of 1773 and the early spring of 1774, no important events occurred to distract the volatile public attention, so that all Paris followed the course of Beaumarchais' battle with breathless interest and amusement.

Indeed, the pamphlets spread all over Europe. Horace Walpole wrote from England to Mme du Deffand that he had received them all and was just reading the third with much amusement:

This man is extremely clever, reasons well, and has great wit; his jokes are often excellent, but he is too pleased with himself. . . . I forgot to tell you of the horror that seized me at the judicial procedure in France. Is there a country in the world where they would not have severely punished this Mme Goezman? Her deposition is a frightful piece of impudence. Is one then allowed to lie, to contradict oneself, to insult one's adversary, in such an unbridled manner? What has become of this creature and her blackguard of a husband? Tell me, I beg of you.

In Vienna and St Petersburg, Beaumarchais' pamphlets provided the respective Courts of Maria Theresa and Catherine II with greatly enjoyable reading throughout the winter of 1773-4; while in Germany Goethe read them aloud with enormous success at social gatherings in Frankfort, finally extracting from the fourth pamphlet the material for his drama *Clavijo*. The pamphlets even reached America, where the political and judicial aspects of the case were carefully studied by serious thinkers.

But nowhere were they received with greater interest and amusement than at Ferney. Voltaire's sympathies at first inclined towards the Chancellor Maupeou, and hence towards his Parlement. Moreover, he had business relations with Marin, by whom the banned works of Voltaire were smuggled into France and peddled round the houses of the great – which, however, did not prevent Marin from denouncing and bringing to the galleys any competitors in the same line of business. All this, as well as the certain amount of popular prejudice against Beaumarchais as a man of doubtful character with a charge of fraud just pronounced against him, made Voltaire's first reaction to the pamphlets one of cautious, if amused, interest. But on 30 December he was writing to the Comte d'Argental:

I have read all Beaumarchais' pamphlets and have never been so much amused. I fear that this brilliant madcap may, at bottom, be in the right against everyone. But heavens! what roguery! what horrors! what degradation in the nation! How unpleasant for the Parlement. . . . Once again, we live in strange times. . . .

And a few days later he wrote to the Marquis de Florian:

The pamphlets of Beaumarchais are the most curious, the most powerful, the most comic, the most interesting, and the most humiliating for his adversaries, of any that I have ever seen. . . . I have read the fourth pamphlet; I am still much affected by it; nothing has ever made more impression upon me. There is not a comedy more amusing, a tragedy more moving or a story better told, and above all, no intricate affair better clarified.

Beaumarchais had in fact sent Voltaire all his pamphlets, but the cautious old sage had not thought it prudent to write and thank him, fearing that Marin might hear that he had been in communication with the enemy; for he was still dependent upon Marin for the distribution of his works in Paris. But he was now forming his own opinion about the case, and about Marin's part in it, and we find him writing again on 25 February to the Comte d'Argental:

I flatter myself that you no longer believe the tales they tell you about Beaumarchais, and that, like me, you are undeceived. A man who is lively, passionate, and impetuous can give a slap to his wife, and even two slaps to his two wives – but he does not poison them.

Yet such tales were like pebbles thrown into a pond, whose ripples spread far. On a certain occasion during a performance of *Eugénie*, when Beaumarchais had slipped in among the audience unobserved, to discover at first hand their reactions to his piece, he overheard one of them arguing against Voltaire's opinion. 'The members of Parlement are certain,' declared this busybody 'that he [Beaumarchais] has poisoned his three wives—' Here, Beaumarchais interrupted him: 'It is so true that this wretch has poisoned his three wives, although he has only been married twice, that they also know in the Parlement Maupeou that he has eaten his father in a game stew, after having smothered his mother-in-law between two thick slices of bread and butter. And I am the more certain of it, since I am this Beaumarchais in question, who will strangle you if you do not clear off forthwith.' Exit the know-all, amid a burst of laughter from the bystanders.

But the time for the Parlement to give its judgment was now at hand. On 26 February Mme du Deffand was writing to her adored Horace Walpole:

We await today a great event: the judgment on Beaumarchais. . . . M. de Monaco has invited him this evening to give us a reading of a comedy of his which is entitled *The Barber of Seville*. . . . The public dotes upon the author;

he is being judged while I write to you. They expect the sentence to be severe, and it may be that instead of supping with us, he will be condemned to banishment, or even to the pillory. That is what I will tell you tomorrow.

Mme du Deffand did not hear *The Barber of Seville* that night; for its unfortunate author had been before his judges since six o'clock that morning, and as evening approached without their having arrived at a decision he wrote a short note to the Prince of Monaco, explaining the circumstances and begging that the reading might be postponed. Then, utterly exhausted, he went back to his sister's house, retired to bed and fell into a deep sleep. 'He slept,' says Gudin, 'and his judges sat up . . . divided among themselves', torn between their desire to punish the author of the pamphlets, yet painfully aware that their own enemies stood solidly behind him. At last they reached a decision which they hoped would give some satisfaction to the public as well as to themselves. The chief characters in the drama, the Goezmans and Beaumarchais, were alike condemned to *blâme*, a condition of infamy which carried with it the loss of all civil rights – including, of course, the capacity to hold any public office. The pamphlets which had wrought such havoc in the battle were to be suppressed. The sentence meant the end of Goezman's professional career and the ruin of the couple; but it also meant ruin for Beaumarchais, especially in view of the fact that he had already lost the La Blache case. Yet as it presently appeared that he had only escaped the pillory, branding and the dreaded galleys by a majority of no more than six votes, he was still to be accounted lucky.

Gudin tells us that Beaumarchais was awakened from his sleep at the house of Mme Lepine to be informed of the result of the judges' deliberations. He arose calmly and went out of his sister's house with Gudin, who in this hour of calamity remained loyally at his side. They feared that unless Beaumarchais disappeared from all his known haunts he would be arrested for the full carrying out of the sentence, which required that he should receive it on his knees before the assembled court, whose President would then pronounce the words: 'The Court blames you and declares you infamous.' But the verdict had already been so badly received by those assembled outside the court, and the judges spat upon as they came out – though some made their escape from the building by secret corridors unknown to the public – that it was hastily decided to proceed no further in fulfilling the letter of the law.

But on 5 March Beaumarchais' pamphlets against Goezman were solemnly torn up and burnt in the courtyard of the Palais de Justice.

They had provided all the principal capitals of Europe with entertaining reading and had carried their author's name even as far afield as America; yet, at the same time, they were double-edged weapons, not without a certain danger to their author, as well as to the enemies from whom he had received such provocation. In the opinion of La Harpe, they left on the public an indelible impression of a dangerous man whose resentment and enmity knew no limits; 'one cannot make oneself feared up to this point without being hated'. Yet, as Loménie has rightly pointed out, Beaumarchais was obliged to 'give to an affair of little interest in itself all the interest of a drama, a comedy and a novel'; for if he had confined himself to a sober statement of the facts he would never have caught the attention or interest of the volatile public, and without their attention and support he would certainly have been lost.

Chapter 8

M. DE RONAC, SECRET AGENT

THOUGH the outcome of the Goezman case had completed the financial ruin of Beaumarchais, it brought him at the same time great social success – and acquaintance with the woman who was eventually to be his third wife. For the man who had fought the Parlement Maupeou single-handed and sent it reeling towards its fall, the man who, according to that rather acid commentator Baron Grimm, had been a year previously the most hated in Paris, had now become, to supporters of the old Parlement, the hero of the hour. Immediately after the announcement of the verdict the Prince de Conti (head of the house of Bourbon-Condé, a younger branch of the royal family) and the Duc de Chartres hurried to call upon Beaumarchais and invited him to a brilliant gathering on the following day, where some forty prominent people were present. 'We are of a sufficiently great house', said the Prince, 'to give an example of the way in which one ought to treat a man who has deserved so well of France.' Following these illustrious examples, many other people, of course, called to attest their support.

Among those who gathered round Beaumarchais at this time was a new admirer, a young woman of Swiss origin, Marie-Thérèse Amélie Willermaula, whose father had held a post in the service of the King's Grand Master of Ceremonies, the Marquis de Dreux-Brézé. She was now at twenty-three years of age an orphan, for both her parents had died quite young. Those who knew her have described her as being distinctly good-looking, with sparkling blue eyes in which there was a glint of slight mockery, auburn hair, a good figure, and, above all, great dignity and poise. 'Nature', she once said of herself, 'has endowed me with a courage, strength, gaiety of character, and a kind of instinctive everyday philosophy which suffices for all my needs, and finds me prepared for all those events which come to spoil the present and the future.' Her disposition, in fact, was in many ways like that of Beaumarchais himself. She was also a musician of some competence, and a brilliant conversationalist. She possessed a fiery temper, but no one was more humiliated than she when, as occasionally happened, she lost control of it. She was well read, and her letters show her as a woman of character, intelligence and wit. Having read all Beaumarchais' pamphlets, she was burning to make his acquaintance, and she therefore sent a mutual friend to beg him to lend her his harp. Such a request, in such circumstances, was a sufficient indication of her intention. Beaumarchais understood, and replied that he did not lend his harp, but that if she cared to call, in company with their mutual friend, they would be able to hear one another play. She came, and Gudin becomes quite lyrical in his discussion of them both:

I was a witness of their first interview. I have already said that it was difficult to see Beaumarchais without liking him. What impression was he not bound to make, when he was acclaimed by all Paris, when he was regarded as the defender of oppressed liberty, the avenger of the public! It was even more difficult to resist the looks, the voice, the bearing, the conversation of this young woman, and the attraction which both inspired at first sight was increased from hour to hour by the variety of their charms and the number of excellent qualities that one discovered, in proportion as one knew them better. Their hearts were united from this moment, in a tie which no circumstances could break, and which love, esteem, confidence, time and the law rendered indissoluble.

The law, it may be mentioned, did not take its share in the affair until their union had lasted twelve years, for the last nine of which they had a daughter. It is true, however, that at the time of their first meeting Beaumarchais was a man deprived of civil rights – which included that of marriage. But they seem to have been two congenial spirits who had found each other at last, and Marie-Thérèse Willermaula was described by Gudin as 'a woman endowed with a tender heart and a firm character, well fitted to sustain him in the cruel trials which were yet to fall to his lot'. Through all these vicissitudes she certainly remained his steadfast and loyal companion, while he on his side seems to have been genuinely fond of her: though being himself (*toujours le même*, in the words of his own popular and much-quoted song) he was of course quite unable to keep his attention from wandering in other directions. But no doubt Marie-Thérèse's 'everyday philosophy' enabled her to accept him as he was and not to expect the impossible from her 'Pierrot'.

Yet in spite of all the acclamation in certain quarters, there could be no disguising the unpleasant aspect of the situation in which Beaumarchais now found himself placed. Financially and civically a ruined man, his reputation was in even worst state. The outcome of the first case concerning La Blache had left him under the stigma of forgery, while however useful he had been as a political brickbat to the enemies of the Parlement Maupeou his efforts to defend himself in this second and even more serious case had earned him the King's displeasure – a poor look-out for 'the garden of his advancement'. For though Louis XV had laughed as much as anyone at the brilliant wit of Beaumarchais' pamphlets, he realized only too well that the case had dealt a mortal blow to his Parlement – that, as the wags put it, the Parlement of *Louis Quinze* had been overthrown by *quinze louis*. No doubt, too, in his relief after his ordeal, Beaumarchais was now going about Paris doing a good deal of talking about it. Sartines, his friend, wrote to him, sounding a note of warning:

I advise you not to show yourself any more publicly. What has happened is irritating to many people. It is not enough to be blamed, one must be modest as well. If an order came from the King, I should be obliged to execute it in spite of myself. Above all, do not write anything, because the King wishes you to publish nothing more upon this affair.

The fact that the unhappy man, by the use of his only weapon of defence, his pen, had fought to save himself from being judged in secret and condemned unheard to a fate often worse than death, could of course scarcely count less, in an age living under a ferocious penal code which permitted, and employed, even more savage penalties. (Though it appears that Beaumarchais had made up his mind to kill himself if condemned to the pillory and the galleys.) But in the agitated purlieus of Versailles he was already being called 'the French Wilkes', after the notorious demagogue who on the other side of the Channel was making himself a thorn in the flesh of George III, to whose horror 'that devil Wilkes' would succeed in this very year in getting himself elected as Lord Mayor of London. After his expulsion from Parliament in 1764, Wilkes had paid two visits to Paris, where he frequented the *salon* of Baron d'Holbach, who had been a fellow student at Leyden University and whose house was the meeting-place of a band of brilliant philosophers and wits such as Helvetius, Diderot and d'Alembert. These, with their agnosticism and their declared war on all forms of absolutism and privilege, were the heroes of the hour; though Horace Walpole writes of them in 1765:

I sometimes go to Baron d'Holbach's; but I have left off his dinners, as there was no bearing the authors and philosophers and savants, of which he has a pigeon-house full. They soon turned my head with a new system of ante-diluvian deluges, which they have invented to prove the eternity of matter.

There were in truth certain points of resemblance in the characters of Beaumarchais and Wilkes: their interest in politics, with the same instinctive rebellion against arbitrary encroachment on individual liberty; the same genuine interest in literature and classical studies, and a similar zest for convivial living – though Beaumarchais never carried his to the outrageous level of debauchery reached by Wilkes.

Beaumarchais, recognizing that the Goezman case had sounded the death-knell of the Parlement Maupeou, decided not to appeal immediately for a second judgment – which with the same set of judges might only confirm, or even worsen, the first – but to bide his time and secure from the King, if he could, a reprieve which would allow him to postpone his appeal. So he wrote to his friend La Borde, a Farmer-General of Taxes who happened at the same time to be the King's First Valet de Chambre, a letter which while addressed to La Borde was really meant for the King's ear. In it Beaumarchais lamented his unfortunate position, especially with regard to Louis XV:

The thing which has most cut me to the heart in this melancholy affair is the unfortunate impression that has been given of me to the King. He has been told that I was aiming at a seditious notoriety, but he has not been informed that all I have done was to defend myself. . . . Ought I to have let myself be crushed without justifying myself? If I did it with too much ardour, is that a reason to dishonour my family and myself, to cut off from society a decent man whose talents might perhaps have been usefully employed in the service of King and State? . . .

The letter achieved its purpose, especially in view of the masterly point raised in the last sentence. For Louis XV had a piece of urgent and very confidential business which required careful handling by a man of just such talents, and here was a chance for Beaumarchais to work his way back into royal favour.

There was living in London at this time a certain Théveneau de Morande who had been compelled to exile himself from France in some haste as a consequence of the disorderly life he had led there. Finding himself in England without means of subsistence, he devised a lucrative source of income as a purveyor of scandal and defamatory libels – the more lurid the better – which he would then cause to be smuggled into France. No one, great or small, was immune from his attacks; he had even tried to blackmail Voltaire, but the old sage was too experienced a war-horse to be stampeded by such a gadfly, however vicious. But there were many others who had skeletons in their cupboards which would not bear the light of day, and among these unfortunates Morande's demands for money inspired considerable terror. At the beginning of 1774 he had had a really brilliant inspiration in fixing his attention on one whose cupboard was not only crammed with a varied assortment of skeletons, but who was in the position of being least able to afford having them displayed to public view. He therefore wrote to this latest victim, no less a person than Mme du Barry, informing her that he was about to publish the story of her life in four volumes under the pleasing title of *Mémoires secrets d'une femme publique*. The unhappy woman appealed to her royal lover, whose first move was to put forward a demand, through his ambassador in London, for Morande's extradition. This request could not be granted officially, but the Secretary of State for Foreign Affairs, Lord Rochford, informed the Ambassador unofficially that the affair could be carried through *sub rosa* if the French used a discreet secrecy, so as not to arouse the tender susceptibilities of the London populace. Preparations were duly made by the French police, but Morande got word of them, and, posing as a political refugee seeking asylum on English soil, he appealed to the Londoners for protection. A body of sympathizers shadowed the police agents from the moment of their arrival, with the result that when they confronted Morande they found him guarded by a hostile mob, who seized them and very nearly threw them into the Thames. Encouraged by this success, Morande now posed as a defender of public morals and pressed on with the publication of his work – 3,000 copies of which, he declared, were already in print, for distribution in Holland and Germany – spurning the further attempts made by various emissaries of Louis XV to treat with him.

This was the state of affairs in March 1774, and it was now intimated to Beaumarchais, through the medium of La Borde, that here was a chance for a man of talents to prove his worth in the King's service. Beaumarchais was only too glad to seize the opportunity offered; the mission not only provided him with a chance to rehabilitate himself in the King's favour, but the circumstances appealed to his dramatic instincts. He therefore set about creating a suitable atmosphere to explain his sudden departure from Paris, pretending that threats were being made against him and that he was liable to arrest at any minute. His champion, the Prince de Conti, seems to have been completely taken in by this tale, and arranged for the Prince de Ligne to facilitate

Beaumarchais' 'escape'. The former in his memoirs relates how he was deputed to meet Beaumarchais at the corner of the Rue Colbert under an extinguished street lamp, and take him in a *fiacre* as far as Le Bourget. Here the 'fugitive' was to be put into one of the Prince's own carriages and sent to an agent in Ghent who would see to it that he reached England. 'This extraordinary man,' says the Prince de Ligne, 'pretended that without our help he would be arrested; yet eight days later, he was already back in the study of Louis XV, who had sent him on a secret mission, which he covered up with this play-acting in order to mystify us!'

On arrival in London, Beaumarchais called himself the Chevalier de Ronac (which was simply an anagram of Caron) and sought out Morande. Under the influence of Beaumarchais' persuasive charm the blackmailer agreed to discuss terms; he finally demanded a payment of 20,000 livres down, and a pension of 4,000 livres a year thereafter as the price of his future silence. It was the bringing of these terms back to the King that caused Beaumarchais to reappear at Versailles only eight days later. Louis sent him to the Foreign Minister, the Duc d'Aiguillon, who was much more concerned with tracking down Morande's accomplices in France than he was with the troubles of the King and his mistress. But Beaumarchais firmly refused to act the part of a police informer in a policy of terrorism, especially as Morande's word was not to be relied on and he might well accuse innocent people; he begged the King that he might be excused from this role. But the Duc d'Aiguillon nursed a grudge against him for his refusal, and sent his own agents to follow Beaumarchais on his second journey to England; he appears also to have been the author of anonymous letters which reached Morande warning him against Beaumarchais, and which caused the latter to make a quick journey back to Paris to obtain evidence of the King's confidence in him. Louis finally resigned himself to the offer of a settlement for a single payment of 32,000 livres, on the express condition that all copies of the work were destroyed. Beaumarchais then returned to England bearing these terms; he not only persuaded Morande to accept them and to agree to the burning of his work on Mme du Barry, but he ended by enlisting the miscreant into the secret service of France. On 27 April the life-history of Mme du Barry was duly incinerated in a brick-kiln in the parish of St Pancras, and Beaumarchais wrote triumphantly to the King, recording the fulfilment of his mission in the flamboyant language that was typical of him:

At last, after having travelled day and night, after having covered nearly 700 leagues in six weeks, after having worked unceasingly and spent more than 500 louis of my own money, I have managed ... to have consumed by the flames the 3,000 volumes which existed of one of these libels and to destroy the engravings and manuscripts of several others, and I have so tied up the author with the fear of punishment, and the hope of benefits that he has submitted himself, in the most authentic legal covenant, to all the rigours of the laws of England at the first word he writes from henceforth *against France*, and, repentance succeeding crime, with the aid of a modest pension and of some other subsistence promised to him, from the execrable fellow that he was, I have made of him a vigilant spy *for France*.

Beaumarchais does not mention the large amount of fatherly advice which he bestowed on Morande, urging him to mend his ways. (But one begins to suspect that this was a role which Beaumarchais rather enjoyed.) After the burning of the du Barry libels, he wrote to Morande:

You have done your best, monsieur, to prove to me that you have returned in good faith to the feelings and conduct of an honest Frenchman, from which your own heart reproached you, long before I, with having turned away. It is in persuading myself that you intend to persist in these praiseworthy resolutions that I take pleasure in corresponding with you.

Perhaps, after all, Beaumarchais' good advice bore fruit, for Morande, after his extremely shady youth, did eventually settle down to an astonishingly respectable old age, and during the Revolution was even to be found bravely writing in support of the monarchy.

Beaumarchais remained a little while longer in London, during which time he succeeded in obtaining, on behalf of Louis XV, an agreement through Lord Rochford – whom he had known well in Madrid – whereby England and France mutually agreed on the application of more rigorous measures against blackmailers. He then set off to return to France, happy in the knowledge that he had not only fulfilled successfully the main part of his mission, but had laid the foundations of other work of future benefit to France. It now only remained for him to hasten to Versailles, see the King and reap the reward of his labours. He landed at Boulogne on 7 May – to be met with horrifying news which dashed all his hopes to the ground.

Chapter 9

M. DE RONAC BEGINS ALL OVER

AGAIN

ON the morning of 27 April, the very day on which a certain bonfire was taking place in a St Pancras brick-kiln, Louis XV, who was at the Trianon, arose feeling slightly unwell and dizzy. He went out for his usual day's hunting, but in the evening returned exhausted and spent a bad night. By the following afternoon he was no better, and as he was apparently developing what might prove to be a serious illness the doctor in attendance insisted on his being brought back to Versailles. Enveloped in a dressing-gown, he was bundled into his coach and brought back to his apartments in the main palace, where he was soon surrounded by a full complement of medical advisers – six doctors, five surgeons and three apothecaries! – who lost no time in bleeding the patient with their usual vigour. But they were not long to be kept in doubt about the nature of his illness; the rash which soon began to appear on the King with fearful profusion told its own terrible tale – smallpox, that scourge of the eighteenth century, in its most virulent form. The young Dauphin and his brothers, who had as yet refused to follow the example of the Empress Catherine of Russia in undergoing the newly discovered process of vaccination, were hastily removed from that part of the palace, together with their wives. Only Mesdames Adelaide, Victoire and Sophie, the last three members of the band of princesses (Mme Louise was now a Carmelite), remained courageously at their father's bedside, in spite of the fact that none of them had had smallpox. Nor did Mme du Barry forsake him, though she might scarcely have been blamed if her courage had failed her. For some fifty persons about the palace are said to have died from the infection – including one poor man who did no more than put his head round the door of the King's apartment to enquire how he was – and the three Princesses were later to pay for their devotion with sharp attacks of the disease.

Round the stricken monarch there now began to rage a most unseemly war of intrigue between the two rival Court factions: the
supporters of Mme du Barry, which meant the party of the Duc
d'Aiguillon, *versus* that of the Duc de Choiseul and the old Parlement,
with whose overthrow Mme du Barry was thought to have been
concerned, since Choiseul was her bitter enemy. (Actually, Jeanne du
Barry took no part in politics, but it was always assumed as a matter
of course that every royal mistress did so.) The Choiseul faction were
doing all they could to hurry on the King's confession and reception of
the sacraments; not that they had the smallest concern for his soul – far
from it, for they were philosophic sceptics – but merely because they
knew that before Louis could receive absolution Mme du Barry would
have to be sent away. For precisely the same reason the rival party, led
by Aiguillon's kinsman the Marshal Duc de Richelieu, were equally
determined to postpone the King's confession as long as they dared,
under the plea that for him to make his confession would cause him to
realize his condition and agitate him beyond hope of recovery. According to Mme Campan, when the Archbishop of Paris presented himself
on 1 May he was intercepted at the door of the King's antechamber by
the Duc de Richelieu, who was – very fittingly in view of his character,
it has been said – First Gentleman of the Bedchamber, and who advised
the Archbishop 'not to bring about the King's death with a theological
proposition' such as had, he declared, killed off so many invalids. The
old reprobate further added that, 'If you are anxious to hear some nice
neat sins, sit down there, M. l'archevêque, and I will confess. You will
hear some the like of which you have never heard since you have been
Archbishop of Paris.' Then, more seriously, he pointed out that to
send away Mme du Barry would mean the triumph of the Archbishop's enemy Choiseul, whose overthrow, declared Richelieu, she
had done so much to bring about. The Archbishop, himself a very
sick man, became unnerved, and departed muttering about the sacrament being a question for the Grand Almoner. The Curé of Versailles,
however, was made of sterner stuff; when, on his own initiative, he
exhorted the dying King to make his confession, and Richelieu's
worthless son the Duc de Fronsac threatened to throw him out of the
window, the undaunted priest retorted: 'If I am not killed, I shall come
back.'

But by the 4 May the nature of his illness could no longer be concealed, as it had been up to now, from the sick man. He asked for a
mirror, and having studied his face intently in the dim light of the

room he was heard to mutter: 'I have smallpox; at my age, one does not recover from this disease; I must put my affairs in order.' That evening he bade farewell to Mme du Barry and sent her away; only Mesdames still remained at their father's side. The horrible disease now relentlessly pursued its course, and its victim would not last much longer. On the very day that Beaumarchais was landing at Boulogne so full of hope for his future . . . Louis XV was receiving the sacrament, and on the following day he was given extreme unction. The end came on the afternoon of 10 May, when the candle which had been burning in a window overlooking the main courtyard of the palace was extinguished. Almost immediately afterwards a noise like thunder was heard inside the building, as the courtiers rushed from one end of it to the other, in order to salute the new monarch, a boy of twenty. On this same day Beaumarchais wrote:

I am amazed at the strangeness of the fate which follows me. If the King had lived in health for eight days longer, I would have been reinstated in my former condition, which iniquity has taken from me. I had his royal word for it.

Yet if the death of Louis XV was a great misfortune for Beaumarchais in some ways, there was one feature of the changed situation which was greatly to his advantage, though not to that of the country as a whole: the fall of Maupeou and consequently of his Parlement. Maupeou's place was taken by the veteran ex-Minister Maurepas, who had served the late King for many years until he had made the mistake of attacking Mme de Pompadour. Now, at the age of seventy-three he was recalled from his retirement to guide the uncertain footsteps of the new occupant of the throne. The fall of the Parlement Maupeou meant, of course, the recall of its predecessor; but as the Ministers, Gudin informs us, were divided in opinion as to the best means of doing this, 'they consulted Beaumarchais and demanded of him a short elementary memorandum where his principles should be exposed in a way suitable to instruct every clear mind'. Beaumarchais duly produced a pamphlet entitled *Elementary Ideas on the Recall of Parlement*, but, needless to say, his advice was not followed. 'Everyone', says Gudin, 'was too flattered by the return of the old time magistracy to think of the future' – or, presumably, to reflect that, as the former magistracy came in again, any hope went out of achieving the reforms which had made a promising beginning under Maupeou and his Parlement. However, in the midst of all this reshuffling, Beaumarchais did

not intend to let his own case be forgotten, and he sent a reminder to
Sartines, who had now become Minister of the Marine:

I hope that you do not wish me to remain *blâme* by that vile Parlement which
you have just buried under the debris of its dishonour. All Europe has cleared
me from its odious and absurd judgment, but that is not enough. There must
be a decree to destroy the one pronounced by it. I shall not cease to work for
this end, but with the moderation of a man who fears neither intrigue nor
injustice. I expect your good offices for this important object.

Your devoted
BEAUMARCHAIS

It was unfortunate for Beaumarchais that the new sovereigns were at
first distinctly prejudiced against him, for they had strongly disapproved of his activities in the Goezman case. Moreover, Louis XVI
was not likely to set the same value on Beaumarchais' services to Mme
du Barry as his grandfather had done. Yet it was not very long before
he too began to have need of such services. For the infamous band of
professional libellers who operated from London were now looking
about for fresh victims, and their choice next fell upon the inoffensive
young couple who had just mounted the throne of France, and who
after four years of marriage were as yet without children – as were also
the King's two brothers. Only six weeks after the beginning of the new
reign Morande, the reformed criminal now turned informer, reported
the preparation in London of a pamphlet entitled *Notice to the Spanish
Branch [of the Bourbons] on their Rights to the Crown of France, in Default of
Heirs.* . . . The publication purported to be a political thesis, but it was
in reality a scurrilous attack upon Marie-Antoinette, her entourage,
and even upon her mother, the Empress Maria Theresa. The authorship of the piece of garbage was unknown, but its distributor was alleged to be a Venetian Jew called Angelucci, who in London went
under the name of Atkinson. He was, it appeared, proposing to publish
the libel in Amsterdam as well as in London.

Beaumarchais had already offered his services, through Sartines, to
the young King, for anything he might wish, 'promptly, quickly, and
secretly: here I am. At his service I have a head, a heart, and arms, but
no tongue.' Since Beaumarchais was still in a state of *blâme*, his services
could not be used officially, but he could act once more as a secret
agent. So in June he again set out for England, which, according to his
own account, he reached only after a somewhat hazardous journey,
the small boat in which he first attempted to cross the Channel having
run aground in heavy seas, which gave him a sufficiently unpleasant

crossing on the following day. Before commencing his journey he had been very anxious to secure a written authorization from Louis XVI in person; but this the King refused to give, evidently distrusting the use which Beaumarchais might make of it. He therefore had to leave without anything of this nature; but with characteristic tenacity he did not fail to refer to it, on every variety of grounds, in each letter he wrote to Sartines. He assured the Minister that he could do nothing without it. Lord Rochford, whom he had known so well as British Ambassador in Madrid, could be most useful to him as Secretary of State for Foreign Affairs; but he would do nothing to help Beaumarchais unless he could be sure that it was really a question of a personal service to Louis XVI. Without the necessary proof of this he could only look on Beaumarchais' mission as an affair of police espionage and would have nothing to do with it; in fact, at the mere mention of the affair, said Beaumarchais, the English Minister's manner changed from friendliness to icy coolness. As for Sartines himself, his own position might be imperilled if Beaumarchais failed in his mission from the lack of a personal authorization from the King. For if the libel is published, he pursued, the Queen's anger will turn on to the Minister who could and should have done what was necessary. If the Du Barry libel could be stopped, she will argue, why not this one? She need only drop a word in the King's ear to the effect that Sartines is a clumsy Minister of little resource and not fit for the handling of great affairs. These sinister suggestions had the desired effect: Sartines made out for the young King's signature a brief statement which was simply a copy of the draft provided by the resourceful Beaumarchais himself:

M. de Beaumarchais, charged with my secret orders, will leave for his destination as soon as possible; the discretion and zeal which he will put into their execution will be the most satisfactory proof that he can give me of his devotion to my service.

Marly, 10 July, 1774   Louis

Beaumarchais immediately had this precious document placed in a flat gold box which, as he informed the King, he then hung round his neck on a gold chain as his most precious possession.

For the history of the negotiations with the blackmailer and Beaumarchais' subsequent adventures we have only his own account, in his letters and his report to the King. According to this, Angelucci was bought off for £1,400, while the manuscript and 4,000 copies of the English edition were burnt. Beaumarchais says that he then went over with Angelucci to Amsterdam, where the Dutch edition of the work was duly rounded up and likewise destroyed. But after Angelucci had departed, Beaumarchais says that he discovered that the Jew had another copy with which he was now on his way to Nuremberg, to have it published there. He writes in his most flamboyant style to Sartines:

I am like a lion. I have no more money, but I have diamonds and jewels; I shall sell everything, and with rage in my heart I shall take to the road again. . . . I do not know German, the roads I am going to take are unknown to me, but I have just got hold of a good map, and I see already that I must go to Nymegen, Cleves, Düsseldorf, Cologne, Frankfort, Mainz and finally Nuremberg. I shall travel day and night, if I do not drop with fatigue on the way. Curses on the abominable creature who forces me to do another three or four hundred leagues more, when I was hoping for a rest! If I find him on the road, I shall despoil him of his papers and kill him, as the price of the vexations and trouble he causes me.

After having delivered himself of this outburst, Beaumarchais then, as he relates, sets off in pursuit of Angelucci, *alias* Atkinson, across Germany. Here his narrative begins more and more to resemble a cloak-and-dagger romance. Angelucci, we are told, is overtaken on the outskirts of the forest of Neustadt, near Nuremberg, ambling along on a pony. At the sound of the approaching post-chaise, he turns round, recognizes Beaumarchais, and decamps hastily into the forest. The latter leaps from the chaise, pistol in hand, and gives chase. The fugitive's horse is presently brought to a standstill by the density of the trees, enabling Beaumarchais to overtake him. He seizes Angelucci by the boot, jerks him out of the saddle, and forces him to turn out his pockets and his valise, at the bottom of which is found the remaining copy of the libel. His heart softened by this success, Beaumarchais not only allows the miscreant to go, but even leaves him some of the money he has previously paid him. He then turns back across the forest to regain his carriage, when suddenly two bandits appear, one of whom, armed with a long knife, tries to hold him up. Beaumarchais fires at the man with the knife, but his pistol jams and he is knocked down from behind by the other. The man brandishing the knife then lunges at his chest; but fortunately the blade's point encounters the gold medallion he is wearing round his neck, and, slipping off, glances upwards and inflicts only a superficial wound on the chest, though it pierces his chin. Beaumarchais struggles to his feet and snatches the knife from the bandit, cutting his own hand badly while doing so. He throws the man to the ground and is preparing to tie him up when the second miscreant, who had disappeared, now returns with some accomplices, and the situation is looking very ugly when the providential arrival of Beaumarchais' manservant, together with a blast from the postilion's horn, combine to put the band to flight. Beaumarchais then continues on his way to Nuremberg, and on arrival there makes a statement about the incident to the Burgomaster and the chief postal officer. But this statement already shows curious deviations from his previous account. There is no mention of his pursuit of Angelucci into the wood; it is one of the two bandits, the man with the knife, who has now become mounted on horseback, who looks like a Jew and who is called 'Angelucci' by his companion; while the latter, on being thrown to the ground by Beaumarchais, is addressed as 'Atkinson' by the so-called Angelucci. Having made this statement, Beaumarchais presses on to Vienna, finishing his journey to the capital by Danube boat, the reason given by him being that he now found travel by road too painful for his wounds – or could it be to place himself out of reach of officials asking awkward questions?

But what Beaumarchais did not know was that the postilion from whom he had parted at Emskirchen, an honest fellow named Dratz, had himself put in a report at Neustadt about his curious fare, an 'Englishman' knowing no German, whom he had driven to Emskirchen, and whose behaviour had been so odd that he could not be sure whether the gentleman was in his right mind or not. For it appeared that when nearing Neustadt this very strange character had stood up in the chaise and taken out of his trunk some toilet equipment, a mirror and a razor. Dratz could not help feeling that it was a little unusual, to say the least, for a passenger to consider shaving while the chaise was in motion; but as they approached the Leichtenholtz wood the gentleman ordered him to stop. He then got down and walked into the wood, carrying only a cane in his hand, having told his servant – who spoke German and who remained in the chaise – to order Dratz to drive on slowly. By the time they had reached the limit of the wood there was no sign of the traveller reappearing, and they waited for him about half an hour. While they were waiting, three carpenter's men passed them, coming home from work, with their axes on their shoulders. Presently the missing traveller reappeared out of the wood, but with his hand wrapped in a white handkerchief. He announced that he had seen some bandits, a remark which his servant repeated in German to Dratz; the latter, however, suggested that he might have mistaken the carpenter's men for robbers. Presently, Dratz noticed that the traveller had blood on his hand and also a little on the side of his neck and on his cravat; in reply to the postilion's enquiry he said that he had been fired on. Dratz concluded his report by giving it as his own opinion that the stranger's wounds were self-inflicted with the razor, and in any case did not seem serious – but that he would not allow anybody to examine them. Dratz himself had seen no one in the locality except the carpenter's men, and had heard no shot. The stranger, he said, had refused to lay any complaint in the villages adjoining the scene of the incident; he reserved his narration for the Burgomaster and postal officer of Nuremberg, and Dratz was afraid that if the traveller made trouble there, it would give the whole district a bad name.

It will be only too clear from all this that Beaumarchais was allowing his dramatic instincts full play in this affair – as in the earlier episode of Clavijo in Spain – and that the drama was being well built up towards a fitting climax in Vienna. For he had determined to present himself in person to the mother of Marie-Antoinette, and two circumstances have been cited as evidence that he intended to do this from the beginning. Of these two, the most suspicious is that before leaving London he took care to engage a servant who could speak German; the other is his persistence in demanding a personal letter from Louis XVI. This would certainly be essential for his appearance at the Austrian Court; yet while it would hardly be necessary for his direct dealings with obscure writers of libels, it might also have carried useful weight with Lord Rochford, who, as a Secretary of State in His Britannic Majesty's Government, might well have been forgiven for looking with a dubious eye upon the activities of his late boon companion in Madrid.

On his arrival in Vienna, Beaumarchais wrote to the Empress announcing, with his usual flourish of trumpets, that he had 'hurried night and day from the confines of Western Europe' on a matter affecting her own happiness, and of such importance that, in spite of the 'terrible sufferings' resulting from his having been 'cruelly assaulted and desperately wounded by brigands near Nuremberg', he had lost no time in making for Vienna. The only reason he had travelled by the slower method of Danube boat was, he said, because the agony of wounds made it impossible for him to endure the jolting of the journey by road. He now begged the Empress to send to him a person of confidence through whom a private and secret audience with her could be arranged; for what he had to say was for her ear alone. Maria Theresa

deputed Count von Seilern, the Governor of Lower Austria, to interview Beaumarchais, who, when summoned, appeared after slight
delay, caused, he explained, by his spitting blood as the result of his
recent wounds (it was necessary to make this point, as the wounds
had healed with rather tiresome rapidity). Count von Seilern was now
regaled with a dramatic account of Beaumarchais' adventures up to the
point of his encounter with the brigands; there, the narrator paused
and insisted that the rest of the tale was for the Empress's ears alone,
since it concerned her daughter. The Count then escorted him to
Schönbrunn, where Beaumarchais was received by the Empress, and
having shown her the authorization of Louis XVI, whose writing she
recognized, he once again plunged with his usual vivacity into the
recital of his adventures. According to the account of this interview
which he gave in a report subsequently written to Louis XVI, 'at each
circumstance [of the story], clasping her hands together in surprise, the
Empress reiterated: "But, monsieur, where have you acquired such a
burning zeal for the interests of my son-in-law and, above all, of my
daughter?"' After finishing the narration of his adventures, Beaumarchais, at the request of the Empress, read to her the libel, which
she then asked him to allow her to keep until the following day,
promising to return it through Count von Seilern. The audience ended
and Beaumarchais returned to his lodging; but, on thinking the matter
over, he evidently realized that the copy of the libel he had left in the
hands of the Empress was the only one he now possessed and he would
have nothing to show to Sartines if she did not return it. He therefore
wrote her a long letter, suggesting the wisdom of making a revised
version of the work for Louis XVI from which some of the grosser
attacks on Marie-Antoinette could be expurgated. Maria Theresa,
however, would not countenance such a procedure; but neither did
she return the document.

Now even more unfortunately for Beaumarchais, the Austrian
Chancellor, Prince von Kaunitz, happened to have been in Paris at
the time of the Goezman trial, so that he was well aware of the accusations which had been levelled at Beaumarchais in France. He now compared the latter's own version of his adventures with the depositions
made by the Burgomaster of Nuremberg and by the postilion Dratz,
together with the fact that the most stringent police investigations had
completely failed to discover any trace of either the bandits or the so-
called Angelucci. We need not ask what was the conclusion reached by
Kaunitz after careful consideration of all this evidence. At nine o'clock

one evening a platoon of grenadiers with fixed bayonets under the command of two officers with drawn swords appeared at Beaumarchais' lodging in the wake of Count von Seilern's secretary, who bore an order from the Count inviting the former to consider himself under house arrest. His belongings, including all his papers, were put under seal, and he remained a prisoner under these conditions for thirty-one days – or, as the erstwhile clock-maker calculated with professional precision, 44,640 minutes. During this time he busied himself once more with his pen, writing to the Empress and to Sartines, protesting at his treatment. In point of fact, Kaunitz himself wrote to Sartines, enquiring what the French Minister would like to have done with the prisoner; for, as there was no denying the authenticity of Louis XVI's note, the situation was distinctly delicate. It was equally so for Sartines, who could do no less than acknowledge Beaumarchais as his agent, try to explain what had happened as best he could, and ask that the prisoner should be released and allowed to come home. Kaunitz, while yielding to Sartines' request and restoring freedom to Beaumarchais, could not forbear making some pungent comments to Mercy-Argenteau, the Austrian Ambassador in Paris, on the subject both of Sartines and of his agent. The French Minister, of whose character Kaunitz had no very high opinion, had no doubt his own reasons, declared the Austrian Chancellor, for employing such a man and for defending his actions. As for Beaumarchais, Kaunitz strongly suspected him to be himself the author of the libel. However, he recommended the Empress to speed the parting guest with a present of 1,000 ducats, which was indignantly refused by Beaumarchais, who declared that he did not accept benefits except from the King his master, and least of all from a foreign Power which had just treated him so odiously. On being told that he was taking a great liberty with the Empress in refusing her gift, he declared loftily that 'the King my master will decide whether or not I am wrong in taking this line; but until he gives his decision, I cannot and do not wish to take any other'. It appears, however, that Beaumarchais did not refuse the gift of a large diamond ring of equivalent value. On the evening of that same day he set off to return to Paris, which he reached after a journey of nine days. Here, he said, he hoped to find some enlightenment about his imprisonment in Vienna. 'The only thing that M. de Sartines has said to me on the subject,' he complained to Louis XVI, 'is that the Empress took me for an adventurer.' Which is exactly what she had done; writing to her Ambassador in Paris on 28 August that

. . . I am vexed that this man was arrested. I had thought that he should have been treated as a miserable impostor, and have been sent away from here in two hours, even out of my dominions, it being made clear to him that we are not his dupe and that we are acting thus out of kindness, not wishing to destroy him as he deserves.

In point of fact, the unhappy Sartines, finding himself entangled in the complicated web of fact and fiction with which Beaumarchais' vivid imagination had clothed his adventures, scarcely knew what to make of the affair, and he was presently to confide in his turn to Mercy-Argenteau that he was becoming more and more tormented by the suspicion that Beaumarchais was himself the author of the libel which he had then come forward to denounce. Yet if Sartines' suspicions had finally crystallized into even a near certainty, such a man would scarcely have been employed again, as Beaumarchais was, on even more important confidential missions of French secret service. Surely, too, for a man already under the grave sentence of *blâme*, from which his whole efforts were directed to earning remission, it would have been altogether too risky a procedure to have produced such a work? He had too many bitter enemies for whom the discovery of his authorship would have been the perfect weapon for his final destruction, the most important among them being the Duc d'Aiguillon, ally of Maupeou (and therefore champion of Goezman), who was particularly concerned with French secret service operations in England. Beaumarchais himself attributed the authorship of the pamphlet to disgruntled courtiers and place-seekers who had fallen out of favour under the new régime. This is a likely enough possibility, and indeed the Empress Maria Theresa strongly suspected the originators of the libel to have been the enemies of the pro-Austrian Duc de Choiseul, whose fall from power at the end of 1770 had been brought about only a few months after the marriage he had arranged between her daughter and the future Louis XVI. Gudin de la Brenellerie, in his biography of Beaumarchais, says that the terms agreed upon between the latter and Angelucci included, in the first place, reimbursement of the cost of printing the pamphlet, with a further payment to Angelucci 'to reward him for his fidelity in the execution of his promises'. Now, strange as it may seem in the light of what had already happened, Angelucci really did exist; for on 12 August 1774 Beaumarchais wrote to a woman whose identity is concealed under the name of 'Fabia' that a bill of exchange he had drawn up in favour of Angelucci for 100 louis had not so far been paid; that, though he had made out the bill, he did not really feel that he ought to be liable for the money, 'my rogue having been false to all the conditions which dragged it from me'. However, if it were presented, his father was to accept it, for it was legitimately due, and Beaumarchais would pay the amount on his return.

All this seems to point to what was often the case with his adventures: that round a nucleus of fact his histrionic talent had woven a romance embroidered almost out of recognition. The key to the whole situation is probably the fact that here was a man who desperately needed, by some outstanding service, to gain the favour of the new monarch in whose hands lay his whole future career, with his rehabilitation as a necessary preliminary. It may well be, as has been suggested, that the courage of the real originators of the libel failed them at the last moment, and that, as the whole business was on the point of petering out, Beaumarchais kept it alive by staging his own version of the affair, complete with brigands and a man-hunt across Europe, with himself in the role of hero. And what could be better calculated to win him the favour of the young sovereigns of France than the approval of the Queen's mother, the Empress Maria Theresa? It was an audacious plan; but its ingenious author omitted to take sufficient care to see that all his various statements tallied; nor did he reckon with the sharp eyes and intelligence of the postilion Dratz.

Chapter 10

THE BARBER OF SEVILLE

IN spite of all the troubles which beset Beaumarchais during the years 1773 and 1774, he had not given up trying to get his *Barber of Seville* produced on the stage. This comedy, telling how the Spanish grandee Count Almaviva, with the aid of his resourceful servant Figaro, wins the young heiress Rosine from under the very nose of her elderly guardian Dr Bartholo, who secretly plans to marry her himself, was the first of a trilogy of plays which Beaumarchais was eventually to write round the lives of his three chief characters. He had originally written *The Barber* in 1772 as a comic opera – which at that period meant little more than light comedy interspersed with songs – basing his music on some of the Spanish airs he had collected in Madrid. He had intended it for the Comédie-Italienne (which a decade earlier had merged with the Opéra-Comique), but they firmly refused it; the reason suggested by the devoted Gudin being that their principal actor had himself started life as a barber! This was true enough; but Loménie, who found amongst Beaumarchais' papers some manuscript fragments of this first edition of the play, concludes that its author was no writer of real verse, in spite of his gift for rhymed couplets, while his musical talent was hardly more than that of a good amateur; so that the Comédie-Italienne no doubt knew what they were about in declining the offer. However, nothing daunted, Beaumarchais next set to work to transform the piece into a comedy for the Théâtre Français (also known as the Comédie-Française), and they accepted it with alacrity. For while only a year before, as Baron Grimm noted, its author had been looked on askance by all Paris, which on the authority of the gossip-writers believed him to be capable of any iniquity, now, since the publication of the Goezman pamphlets, he had become a popular hero, and one moreover who had given proof of the most sparkling wit. The comedians of the revered national theatre had a remarkably keen eye for their own financial profit – of which a minimum amount was usually allocated out of their obscure and quite unaudited accounts to the unfortunate authors; so that even the great Corneille had died in miserable poverty – and they evidently considered that they were now 'on to a good thing'. The piece was duly passed by the censor, to whom all stage plays had to be submitted – and who, at this time, was none other than Beaumarchais' future enemy, Marin – and it was licensed for production on 13 February 1773.

But unfortunately at that very moment Beaumarchais became em-broiled in his ludicrous brawl with the Duc de Chaulnes, the Goezman case came on immediately afterwards, and his play had remained for another twelve months in a state of suspension. It was again billed for production in February 1774, and, as Grimm relates, all seats were sold out for the first five performances, when certain busy-bodies began to circulate statements that the play was full of allusions to the Goezman case. In actual fact, the piece had of course been originally written before the case in question came to court; though Beaumarchais had certainly intended to give Bazile the name of Guzman, for Loménie says that in the manuscript of the play the name occurs frequently and has been corrected. However, we shall see it recurring in *The Marriage of Figaro*, by which time Beaumarchais could afford to be less circum-spect and did not hesitate to christen the judge in the play, Don Guz-man Brid'oison. Meanwhile, these assertions were sufficient to hold up the performance of *The Barber* once more, this time until after its author's return from Vienna. Then he again began to press for permis-sion to present it, and, as if to make some amends to him for his late 'sufferings' in the King's service, permission was at last given to him to have the play performed. But in the interval between the time of receiving this permission and the actual production of the piece Beau-marchais, in a burst of the bitterness pent up inside him, proceeded to insert into the play precisely those allusions to his troubles and his enemies which he had been unjustly accused of putting in before. It was at this stage, for instance, that he inserted the famous speech on the art of calumny which he puts into the mouth of Don Bazile in the second act. The latter is advising Dr Bartholo that slander will be much the most effective way of driving Count Almaviva out of Seville. Bartholo expresses doubts about the success of such a method, and Bazile replies:

Slander, my dear sir: you scarcely know what it is that you despise. I have seen the most upright people nearly crushed by it. Believe me, there is no dull piece of spite, no horror, no absurd story, that one cannot get the idlers of a great city to believe, if one goes the right way about it – and we have here people who are so good at it!... First of all, a light rumour, skimming the ground like a swallow before the storm, *pianissimo*, murmurs and swerves, and sows the poisoned seed in flight. Such-an-one receives it, and *piano, piano*, skilfully slips it into your ear. The evil is done; it sprouts, it creeps, it walks, and *rinforzando* from mouth to mouth, it spreads like the devil; then all at once, you know not how, you see calumny rear up, hissing, swelling, growing before your eyes. It darts forward, extends its flight, whirls, envelops, rends, carries away, flashes forth and thunders, and becomes, thank heaven, a general outcry, a public *crescendo*, a universal *chorus* of hate and denunciation. Who the devil could resist it?

As for Figaro, he is the image of his creator: 'welcomed in one town, imprisoned in another, everywhere rising above circumstances; praised by these people, blamed by those ... mocking the foolish, braving the wicked....'

But Beaumarchais also expanded the length of the play from four acts to five, and added a number of very dubious jokes which must indeed have been of a sufficiently scalding nature to have offended the taste even of that very tolerant age. For La Harpe's withering comment on the first performance of the play was that 'the piece appeared slightly farcical, the length was boring, the tasteless jokes disgusting and the morals revolting'. The rest of the audience must have been of a similar opinion, for the play was hissed; while Voltaire wrote from Ferney that if *The Barber of Seville* was not a success, Beaumarchais had better stage his pamphlets! However, he was quite undismayed, and merely set to work to reshape his play, compressing the five acts back into the original length of four, transposing some of the scenes, and striking out some of the most objectionable passages: all this within forty-eight hours. Mme du Deffand attended the performance of the revised version, as she had done of the original production two days before, and wrote the following day: 'At the first [performance] it was hissed; yesterday it had an extravagant success....'

After this second presentation, on 25 February 1775, there was indeed no doubt of the play's success, and it continued its triumphal career until the end of the season on 20 March (the theatres closed for three weeks at the end of Lent). Even that stern critic La Harpe was appeased, and was later to describe *The Barber* as being, in its final form, 'the best constructed and the best written of all the dramatic works of Beaumarchais.' Ten years later, as the shadows of the gathering storm began to descend upon Versailles, *The Barber of Seville* was to have the unique distinction of being the subject of the last performance of the private theatricals held in the Petit Trianon. Four days after the arrest of Cardinal de Rohan in the painful scandal of the diamond necklace, Marie-Antoinette appeared as Rosine, while the Comte d'Artois (the future 'King of the *émigrés*', Charles X) played the part of Figaro, in the presence of Beaumarchais, and spoke such lines as 'I believe myself only too happy to be forgotten, persuaded that a great lord has done us enough good when he has done us no harm', or – even more startlingly apposite – 'Faith, monsieur, who knows whether the world will last three weeks longer?'

But the players of the Théâtre Français were about to have a very unpleasant shock. Although since 1697 they had been obliged by law to allow an author a twelfth part of the profits of a piece consisting of three acts, or the ninth part of one of more than three acts, they had also a rule which laid down that if the receipts fell twice running below 1,200 livres in winter or 800 in summer, the piece automatically became the property of the players and the wretched author had no further claim to any profit, even if the work were subsequently revived any number of times and played to packed houses. With such a rule in force, it was only too simple a matter for the players to put on a piece at some season when they knew that attendance would be poor, lose the author his right to a share of the profits, and then revive the play to their own advantage as often thereafter as they saw fit. Now when Beaumarchais' first two plays had been put on at the Théâtre Français, they had had, as we have seen, only a very modest success, and since their author was at that time in prosperous circumstances he had been content to make the theatre a present of his two pieces. But now the situation was quite different. During the course of 1775 Beaumarchais' comedy proved to be a gold-mine both for the theatre and for its author who was busy trying to repair his shattered fortune. He had therefore no intention of allowing himself to submit meekly to the sort of treatment the players were in the habit of meting out to dramatic authors, no matter how distinguished, and when at the end of the year he found that they were proposing to give *The Barber* on the same day as a special function at Versailles he began to suspect that they were up to their time-honoured tricks. He protested, and in the following May, by which time *The Barber* had been given thirty-two times, the players were appalled to receive a request for a statement of the profits due to the author. After the lapse of a period of stunned silence, a member of the company recovered sufficiently to ask on how many occasions Beaumarchais wished them to play it for his profit – for example, six, eight or even ten times? This ingenuous proposal, said Beaumarchais, writing of it afterwards, 'seemed so amusing that I replied in the same gay tone, "Since you permit me, I ask you to play it a thousand and one times."

' "Monsieur, you are very modest."

' "Modest, messieurs, as you are just. From what mania do you suffer, wishing to inherit from people who are not dead? My piece not belonging to you until it falls to a very low receipt, you ought to desire that it might never belong to you. . . . I see, messieurs, that you love your interests better than you understand them." '

As disputes between the Théâtre Français and outraged authors were only too common, the old Duc de Richelieu, who was one of the two supervisors of theatrical affairs, supported Beaumarchais, whom he thought admirably suited to deal with the whole thorny question. He therefore provided him with a letter, armed with which authority Beaumarchais called upon the company and asked to be allowed to see their books. Needless to say, this request was refused, but they then tried to buy him off by sending him 4,506 livres, his alleged share of the proceeds of thirty-two performances of *The Barber*. But as no account was attached, Beaumarchais returned the money, with a fresh request for a statement of account. They then sent him an unsigned memorandum; this also he returned, with yet another request for a proper statement. The players now made out that it was impossible for them to arrive at the full amount, except for money taken at the door; 'the other elements can only be guessed at'.

Beaumarchais now writes back, remarking soothingly that while he is sure they are very honest people, anxious to give an author his proper share, he feels that they are like 'all men who are more versed in the agreeable arts than in the exact sciences, and who make phantoms of the embarrassing methods of calculation which the simplest arithmetician would solve without difficulty'. He then proceeds to give them some instruction in the elementary principles of book-keeping! The flustered players say they will take legal advice; but nothing happens, and four months go by 'in a profound sleep' – from which Beaumarchais is sharply awakened by the discovery that repeated requests to play *The Barber* are being met with continued refusals.

The Duc de Richelieu had by this time become wearied of the whole business, but his colleague the Duc de Duras took it up and begged Beaumarchais to get together with other dramatic authors to work out a plan for the equitable sharing of profits. Beaumarchais maintained

that all those who had written for the Théâtre Français ought to have a
say in the matter, and the Duc de Duras being in agreement, the
Bureau de Législation Dramatique (later to develop into the Société
des Auteurs et Compositeurs Dramatiques) came into being on 27
June 1777, when Beaumarchais invited all his colleagues to a dinner.
This procedure, however, came up against certain difficulties: La
Harpe, for instance, would not come because Beaumarchais had already
invited two men with whom he was not on speaking terms; Collé said
that even if he had been in Paris he would not have come, for he was
'old and disgusted to the point of nausea with that *troupe royale*. . . .
From excess of contempt I have become peaceable.' Nevertheless, he
sent his good wishes for the project. Nor would Diderot come, feeling
himself too old for such a battle; but he too sent his best wishes. Yet
there were many who did come, and after the dinner they elected a
committee of four, with Beaumarchais as President, to defend the
interests of their new society and to work out the new regulations suggested by the Duc de Duras. But the task was not an easy one, and it
was not made any more so by the fierce dissensions which broke out
among the authors, whose quarrels, and their President's attempts to
calm them, were to involve the unfortunate Beaumarchais in a mass of
interminable correspondence. Their opponents at least showed a
united front.

But the struggle was in fact to continue until the Revolution came to
put an end to the privileges of the Théâtre Français. On 13 January
1791 the National Assembly, following upon a petition by the Society
of Dramatic Authors, reinforced by a number of pamphlets from
Beaumarchais, decreed that the works of living authors should not be
produced anywhere in France without the consent of those authors;
at the same time, they suppressed all the privileges of the Comédie-
Française. 'The Society of Dramatic Authors,' Sainte-Beuve says truly,
'ought never to meet without saluting the bust of Beaumarchais';
for to the end of his life he constituted himself the special guardian of
their interests.

Chapter 11

THE CHEVALIER D'ÉON:

MAN OR WOMAN?

IN spite of the rather farcical climax to the affair of the Angelucci libel, the man who still remained under the grave sentence of *blâme* was yet held to be sufficiently useful to the Government for further employment as a secret agent, and the spring of 1775 found Beaumarchais once more in London. Of the work that brought him to England there will be much more to say presently, but it was soon after his arrival that he received a visit which was to involve him in the affairs of that extraordinary character the Chevalier d'Éon (or Déon, according to another version of the name).

Charles Geneviève d'Éon de Beaumont was at this time forty-seven years of age. He had been at the start of his career one of the most trusted agents of Louis XV's tortuous secret diplomacy, and that in the most remarkable circumstances. Since the Russian Empress Elisabeth had ascended the throne of her father, Peter the Great, in 1741, she had broken off relations with France to the extent that no male diplomat of that country was allowed to enter Russia. Now it so happened that the Chevalier d'Éon was small and slight in build, with delicate, well-cut features and a high-pitched voice – in marked contrast, it may be added, to the violently militant and eccentric disposition which the passing years were to reveal in him. Louis XV appears to have conceived the extraordinary plan of having d'Éon disguised as a woman, 'Mlle Lia de Beaumont', and sent to the Russian Court to gain access to the Empress and thus renew French contacts with Russia. Now although this story has been dismissed as a myth by some historians, there are facts in existence to support it. In the first place, it was confirmed by the Princess Dashkoff, former favourite of the Empress, when she came to England in 1769. Secondly, the fashionable portrait painter La Tour, who painted Louis XV, Mme de Pompadour and many other members of the French Court, made a portrait of the

Chevalier at about the time of his first visit to St Petersburg, depicting him in female attire (in which, incidentally, he appears as a distinctly attractive young woman). It is highly improbable, to say the least, that d'Éon, a young man of very small private means, could have afforded to employ a painter of such distinction for private purposes, or that he would have chosen to be painted in the dress of a woman. Lastly, and most significant of all, is the existence of a letter, dated 4 October 1763, from Louis XV addressed to the Chevalier in London and written entirely in the King's own hand, in which occurs the sentence: 'You have served me as usefully in the guise of a female as in the dress you now wear.' The whole incident is of considerable importance in d'Éon's career, in view of what was to happen later.

Meanwhile, the Chevalier fulfilled his first assignment so well that in 1756 he was sent again to Russia with a French diplomatic mission whose real purpose was to support the candidature of the Prince de Conti for the throne of Poland, or, failing that, to arrange a marriage between Conti and the Empress Elisabeth. D'Éon was equipped with a copy of Montesquieu's *Esprit des Lois*, concealed inside the binding of which were letters to the Empress and ciphers for use in her correspond-ence with Louis XV behind the backs of their respective Ministers. Two sets of reports were also to be prepared by the emissaries, one for the Foreign Ministry in Paris, the other for Louis XV and the Prince de Conti. Such were the strange workings of the *Secret du Roi*, whose titular head was the Comte de Broglie. Although the various plans for the Prince de Conti came to nothing, the mission did good work in drawing Russia towards the Franco-Austrian alliance, and d'Éon's share in this achievement was duly recognized. When French diplo-matic representation was restored in St Petersburg, he was appointed first secretary – this time under his own name, as the 'brother' of 'Mlle Lia de Beaumont'!

On his return from Russia the Chevalier served with some distinc-tion as an officer of dragoons in the French Army during the last phase of the Seven Years War, and it was at the battle of Villinghausen that he had his first meeting with the Comte de Guerchy, with whom he was to quarrel so disastrously in London a few years later. According to the Chevalier's own account of this occasion, he was sent to find Guerchy with an urgent message from Marshal de Broglie ordering the immediate distribution of 400,000 cartridges to the infantry, the ammunition being in a place which d'Éon would indicate. Guerchy, however, handed back the Marshal's order and galloped off, shouting to d'Éon as he did so that, 'If you have a supply of ammunition, you have only to remove it to a park of artillery you will find at half a league's distance.' D'Éon was left to do this himself, but asserts that Guerchy's failure to carry out the Marshal's order was the cause of heavy losses to the infantry.

At the end of the war the Chevalier d'Éon accompanied the Duc de Nivernais to London as secretary to assist with the discussion over peace terms, and when these were drawn up the Duke returned to France, leaving d'Éon as Minister Plenipotentiary in charge, pending the appointment of a new Ambassador. For his work in connection with the peace treaty the King decorated him with the Order of St Louis, and since he obviously had a high opinion of the Chevalier's intelligence Louis XV gave him a fresh assignment in his secret service. For France, smarting under the humiliating losses of the Seven Years War, was making plans with a view to the invasion of England if war broke out again. The royal instructions sent to d'Éon on 3 June 1763 laid down that

The Sieur d'Éon will receive through the Count de Broglie or M. Tercier my orders on the surveys to be made in England, whether on the coasts or in the interior of that country, and he will comply with the instructions he will receive to that end, as if he received them direct from me. It is my desire that he shall observe the greatest secrecy in this affair, and that he will not make any communications thereon to any person living, not even to any Ministers wheresoever they may be.

He will receive a special cipher for corresponding on this subject, under cover of addresses to be indicated to him . . . and he will communicate to them, by means of this cipher, all the information he is able to obtain on the designs of England, as regards Russia and Poland, the North, and the whole of Germany, so far as will, in his opinion, conduce to the interests of my service, of his zeal and attachment to which I am sensible.

The Chevalier, always with a taste for extravagant living, and now conscious of his importance, proceeded to have the time of his life in London, displaying as much pomp and ostentation as if he were in fact the Ambassador of France – which it seems that by this time he was indeed expecting to become. But he did not receive the appointment; nor did he receive any of the financial assistance for which he presently applied to the Foreign Minister, the Duc de Choiseul, when he began to find himself up to his ears in debt. To make matters worse, the new Ambassador, on whose arrival d'Éon was obliged to take second place, was that same Comte de Guerchy whom he had already met on active service in the late war, and whose only qualification for the post of Ambassador in London seems in fact to have been his rank and the favour of Mme de Pompadour. The Duc de Praslin, Choiseul's cousin and colleague, had grave doubts himself about the appointment, which he confided to the Ambassador's predecessor, the Duc de Nivernais:

I am still very much concerned about Guerchy. I am not sure, however, that we are doing him good service by appointing him Ambassador in London. . . . I dread his despatches like fire, and you know how defective despatches damage a man and his office. . . . I believe our dear friend will do well. I do not think I have anybody better fitted. But he cannot write at all; we must not deceive ourselves on this point.

As can well be imagined, the Chevalier did not welcome the arrival of this man who was to supplant him, nor was his hostility lessened by the fact that the Comte de Guerchy's first action was to hand him an official letter of recall, signed by the Duc de Praslin, ordering him to return to Paris at once, but not to appear at Court. The truth was that an awkward incident had occurred at Versailles: Louis XV, after supping alone with Mme de Pompadour, had dozed off in her presence, during which time she had seized the opportunity to abstract the key of his desk, and as he had afterwards found his papers disarranged he was in terror that his correspondence with d'Éon had been discovered. On the very same day (4 October 1763) as that on which Praslin had written the official letter of recall to the Chevalier, the frightened monarch had written him a letter in his own hand in which, after making the significant remark already quoted about d'Éon's having served him usefully by wearing women's clothes, he continued:

Reassume it [woman's clothing] at once and withdraw into the City.
I warn you that the King has today signed – but only with the stamp, not with his own hand – the order to compel you to return to France; but I command you to remain in England with all your papers, until such time as you receive further instructions from me. You are not in safety in your residence, and here you would find powerful enemies.

LOUIS

On the strength of this letter (no doubt spurred on also by his determination not to yield an inch of his place to the Comte de Guerchy) the Chevalier refused to accept the official letter of recall, on the grounds that it had not been signed by the King in person. The situation now became fantastic. Praslin transmitted to Guerchy an official demand on behalf of the King for the extradition of the Chevalier d'Éon, with special instructions to the Ambassador that he should retain the papers in d'Éon's possession without communicating their contents to anyone. The Ambassador's secretary, Monin, was believed to know where they were. When found, they should remain sealed and in Guerchy's keeping until his next journey to France, when he would bring them over with him and deliver them in person. Again this move was checkmated by the hidden hand at Versailles, Louis XV writing personally to the Chevalier on the very same day:

I warn you that a demand for your extradition, having reference to your person and signed with my stamp, has this day been addressed to Guerchy, to be transmitted by him to the Ministers of His Britannic Majesty, the said demand being accompanied by police officers to give weight to its execution. If you cannot make your escape, at least save your papers, and do not trust M. Monin, Guerchy's secretary and your friend. He is betraying you.

LOUIS

But the British Government would not be a party to such a procedure against a diplomat, even though he was causing considerable scandal with his violent attacks on the new Ambassador and his wild allegations of plots to poison or kidnap him. He was making the maximum amount of publicity out of the situation, and when Guerchy attempted to carry out by force the instructions he had received, the Chevalier barricaded himself into his house, garrisoned it with ex-cavalrymen and defied his enemy to do his worst. Meanwhile, the Count de Broglie, head of the King's secret service, was writing in some agitation to his Royal master, pointing out the hideous consequences which might ensue if d'Éon were driven to desperation:

If, in revenge for the bad treatment he is experiencing, and impelled by the necessity of obtaining a living, he should publish your Majesty's instructions, which he holds, were he even to communicate them to English Ministers, what might not be the unfortunate results? Should we not have to apprehend that the sacred person of your Majesty would be compromised, and that a declaration of war on the part of England would be inevitable?

The warning was sounded none too soon, for before very long the terrible Chevalier published a volume of his papers. His attacks on Guerchy having brought him a prosecution for libel, he retaliated by bringing a charge against the Ambassador of having tried to poison him. When the case came up at the Old Bailey in 1765, the Grand Jury returned a true bill against Guerchy, but the British Government, thinking that the affair had gone far enough and was arousing dangerous national feeling, smothered it by transferring it to the Court of King's Bench, where no further action was taken. But the wretched Guerchy's position in England was hopelessly compromised by the scandal, and he eventually returned to France a broken man.

But Louis XV, realizing that the Chevalier had far too much dangerous material in his possession to be trifled with or driven to desperation, decided to make the best of the situation. He therefore granted d'Éon a life pension of 12,000 livres, in return for the surrender of his most important papers, and retained his services as a secret agent. This arrangement worked satisfactorily for the few remaining years of Louis XV's life; the little firebrand remained quiescent, even if potentially dangerous, and indeed supplied the King with much information on English affairs. At the time of the threatened publication of the du Barry libel, the Chevalier was himself in contact with Morande, and was, so he declared, on the point of buying off the blackmailer for £800 when the latter called upon him 'to inform him that two French noblemen had been to see him that morning, with their pockets full of gold, to invite him to suppress his work against the Comtesse du Barry; but not wishing to conclude any arrangement without first consulting M. d'Éon, who was the first to commence negotiations in this business, the two noblemen had remained in their coach at the corner of the street, and desired to confer with him'. A few days later, as d'Éon wrote to Louis XVI's Minister Vergennes, he had discovered that 'the two unknown nobles were: the unknown noble Caron de Beaumarchais, and the most illustrious and well-known noble Louis François Brancas, Comte de Lauraguais, and that they had concluded an agreement with Théveneau de Morande, in the name of Louis XV, for the suppression of his libel. . . .' From the waspish tone of this account it will be apparent that the Chevalier resented the arrival of Beaumarchais and his bringing the affair to a successful outcome with the support of the Comte de Lauraguais. 'The Sieur Caron de Beaumarchais arrived in London *incognito*, escorted by the Comte de Lauraguais *in publico*', he sneers to Vergennes.

It was somewhere between 1769 and 1771 that curious rumours began to circulate in London as to the real sex of the Chevalier d'Éon. Where these originated is not clear, though they may not have been unconnected with the arrival in London in 1769 of the Princess Dashkoff, who had known the Chevalier in St Petersburg; but what does clearly emerge is that, when it began to be put about that he was in reality a woman, he made no attempt to rebut such statements; indeed he seemed almost to encourage them by the ambiguous manner of his replies, and by 1771 large sums of money were being staked in London sporting circles on possible answers to the riddle. It was, of course, a means of publicity, which was as essential to the Chevalier as life itself; moreover, by this time his financial position was becoming desperate. The pension of 12,000 livres was quite inadequate either to clear off his existing debts or to keep pace with his scale of living. Yet his return to France would present grave difficulties, not least of which was the fact that d'Éon with his viper's tongue had raised up there against himself a host of bitter enemies. Choiseul, even though he had refused to authorize payment of the Chevalier's debts, could scarcely relish being described as having a brain made of 'whipped cream, enclosed within a head of Rouen porcelain, relating pleasantly a quantity of tittle-tattle', and although Guerchy had died, his young son was waiting to avenge his father's memory. It is therefore not impossible that the Chevalier's fertile but decidedly abnormal brain may have seen in the fantastic expedient of becoming a woman a way out of his difficulties – if not in England, then certainly in France, where, as Beaumarchais was presently to remark, all things would be forgiven to a woman.

After the death of Louis XV the Chevalier, hoping to have better success with the new Government of France, had submitted to Vergennes an estimate of his claims: 6,000 livres in respect of a diamond offered to him when he was in Russia by the King of Poland, which, he declared modestly, he had been too honest to accept; 24,000 livres, a sum usually bestowed by the King of England upon Ministers Plenipotentiary at his Court, but which in this case had been lost to him through the machinations of the Comte de Guerchy; 15,000 livres for the loss of revenue over his vineyards in Burgundy, he having been unable to tend them during the ten years 1763-73; 100,000 livres for the 'immense expenses' incurred over the maintenance of 'a simple and decent' household for himself and his cousin during the same ten years in London; together with one or two other items which brought the total up to the modest little sum of approximately 300,000 livres. Small wonder that even the good-natured young King declared that he had never seen 'a more impertinent and preposterous document'. Two emissaries had been sent to negotiate with the Chevalier for the return of his papers on less impossible conditions; but without success. Then the French Government tried to bring him to submission by cutting off his pension and other payments due to him from France. By this time Government opposition circles in England had become alive to the importance of the documents in d'Éon's hands, and were offering him considerable sums for them. It is to the Chevalier's credit that, financially pressed though he was, he did not fall as low as this, but refused the offers made. But, in return for a loan of £5,000 from his friend Lord Ferrers, he did hand over some of his papers as security to the British peer; but the most important, the *grand projet* of Louis XV (which had included plans for a Stuart restoration as well as for the invasion of England), were not among them.

However, in May 1775 d'Éon discovered that Beaumarchais was again in London, made overtures to him through Morande, and finally came to seek his aid. Being evidently well aware of Beaumarchais' reputation with regard to women, the Chevalier opened their interview by confiding, with tears (which came always with wonderful facility when required), that he was really a woman. Now many responsible and serious persons at the time came to accept this as a fact; nor is it altogether surprising that so ingenuous a being as Gudin, who had accompanied his friend to England, should also have done so. But it seems quite unbelievable that a man so astute and so experienced as Beaumarchais should have been really taken in, as some of his biographers, including even Loménie, have invited us to believe. (But Loménie, it appears, was not aware of the existence of the letter written in London by Beaumarchais to d'Éon on 31 December 1775, which begins: 'My dear Chevalier, or whatever it may please you to be with me. . . .') Beaumarchais and d'Éon were men of equally keen wits, not overburdened with scruples, and whether they came to some secret understanding to play out the comedy for what it was worth we shall probably never know. But it is perhaps not without significance that Beaumarchais, when reporting his first interview with d'Éon to Louis XVI, uses curiously ambiguous language which avoids the use of any personal pronouns of definite gender:

I venture to assure you, Sire, that this astonishing creature, if treated with kindness and consideration, will, though soured by twelve years of misfortune, be easily amenable to discipline, and will, upon reasonable terms, give up the papers relative to the late King.

But whatever may have actually passed between Beaumarchais and d'Éon, the former returned to Paris to seek permission to undertake the difficult task of coming to a settlement of the Chevalier's affairs, and after a long conversation with Vergennes, the Minister wrote to Beaumarchais that

His Majesty authorizes you to agree to all reasonable guarantees that M. d'Éon may demand for the regular payment of his pension of 12,000 livres, it being clearly understood that he will not lay claim to an annuity of that amount when out of France; the capital to be employed for the realization of this sum is not at my disposal and I shall have the greatest difficulty in obtaining it. But it is easy to convert the pension in question into a life annuity, of which the title-deed would be given up. The liquidation of debts will be a difficult matter, M. d'Éon's claims in this respect being very great, and he must reduce them considerably to enable us to come to terms. M. d'Éon is of a violent disposition, but I believe him to be an honest fellow, and I will do him the justice to say that I am quite persuaded he is incapable of treachery.

It is impossible that M. d'Éon should take leave of the King of England; the revelation of his sex no longer permits it; it would bring ridicule on both Courts.

You are an enlighted and prudent man, and I have no misgivings that you will make a good bargain with d'Éon, if it is at all possible. If you fail, then we must take it for granted that we cannot expect to meet with success, and make up our minds for the worst.

D'Éon, it will be observed, is now officially considered as a female, but there is no question, as yet, of his wearing feminine clothes. The sole condition for his return to France is the handing over of his papers.

Beaumarchais now returned to London to negotiate with him, and having firmly turned down d'Éon's preposterous demand for 318,477 livres, after a good deal more argument finally made a covenant, dated 5 October 1775, in which d'Éon announced himself to be a woman and undertook to return all the papers of Louis XV in his possession, in return for the 12,000 livres pension, as well as unspecified larger sums for the payment of his debts in England. Thus each side made certain reservations in the transaction, for if d'Éon did not consider that he was getting enough money he could hold back some of the papers, while Beaumarchais on his side had no intention of paying every debt which the Chevalier might choose to produce, but would pay a proportion according to the extent to which d'Éon carried out his side of the bargain. Two other extraordinary stipulations were attached to the convention, which Beaumarchais drew up in the name of the King: that d'Éon should make a public declaration of being a woman, and that if 'she' returned to France it could only be in female dress. Whether or not Louis XVI and Vergennes actually believed d'Éon to be a woman (it seems probable that the young King, at least, did so), the Minister had not concealed from Beaumarchais his anxiety as to what might happen if the Chevalier set foot on French soil, and to compel the truculent little ex-dragoon to assume permanently the role of a woman was one way of putting an end for good and all to his terrifying capacity for making trouble.

D'Éon now revealed that Lord Ferrers held his iron chest – containing, he said, all the papers – as a surety for a loan of £5,000, and he handed the key over to Beaumarchais. But the latter felt that he had no authority to examine the papers, so he made another journey back to Paris to obtain proper authorization. Then, having returned to London, Beaumarchais had the chest opened – to find that it contained papers which appeared to be only of the most trifling nature; though d'Éon assured him that they included such important documents as the instructions given to the Duc de Nivernais before coming to London, his despatches containing details of the peace negotiations, and the secret Bourbon family pact, besides four boxes of other secret despatches. But later he admitted that he was still in possession of the most important of all the papers: his secret correspondence with Louis XV, which he had concealed under the flooring of his room. He (or 'she', as Beaumarchais now wrote in his letters to Vergennes) led the way up to his bedroom, where, having taken up a floor-board, he produced five well-sealed packages labelled 'Secret papers, to be returned to the King only'.

Beaumarchais felt that this piece of attempted trickery dispensed him from the necessity of carrying out in full his side of the bargain regarding the payment of d'Éon's debts, for which the Chevalier had first put in a claim for £13,933, and had then added a further £8,223. Beaumarchais therefore settled only the debt of £5,000 owing to Lord Ferrers, and then set off for Versailles with the papers. He was cordially received by Vergennes, who wrote to him that the King had been very satisfied with the zeal that he had shown on this occasion, as well as with the intelligence and skill with which he had accomplished the mission which His Majesty had confided to him. The King, concluded Vergennes, had commanded him to send Beaumarchais this attestation, in order that it could be of service to him at all times and places where it might be needed.

The Chevalier's attachment to Beaumarchais, whom he called his 'guardian angel', had been so effusively demonstrated in London that wags declared that 'she' was in love with him. ('Who the devil could have thought', the object of these attentions wrote to Vergennes, 'that in order to serve the King faithfully I should have to become the gallant knight to a captain of dragoons?') But from the moment that d'Éon found that his 'guardian angel' had no intention of making any further contribution to the payment of his debts, all was changed. It was now the turn of Beaumarchais to be lashed by the tongue which had already flayed Choiseul, Praslin and other distinguished persons as well as the unfortunate Guerchy. The 'guardian angel' swiftly became 'a fool' and 'a scoundrel', endowed with 'the insolence of a clock-maker's boy who has by chance found the secret of perpetual motion'. The object of these endearing remarks bore them with unruffled calm. 'She is a woman,' he wrote to Vergennes, 'and in so frightful a situation that I forgive her with all my heart.' But he could not afford to dismiss so lightly the rumours which his enemies were circulating to the effect that he had pocketed some of the funds destined for d'Éon. He protested to Vergennes, and the Minister, writing to assure Beaumarchais of his unshaken confidence in him, concluded that, 'Far from your disinterestedness being suspect, I do not forget, monsieur, that you have put in no claim for personal expenses.'

But since d'Éon's debts had not been fully paid, he now refused to discard his soldier's uniform for a woman's dress, and continued to keep himself in the public eye as much as possible by encouraging the bets still being made in London about his sex. Beaumarchais shrewdly advised Vergennes that if he wished to get the Chevalier back to France the best plan was to appear to forget his existence. Sure enough, this method produced results. 'Menaced with oblivion', as Loménie puts it, the Chevalier appeared at Versailles of his own accord, one fine morning of August 1777. But he had ignored the essential condition of his return to France: that he must wear woman's dress. He was at once reminded of it, and had no choice but either to obey or depart. The British Ambassador reported to London that

d'Éon has just seen M. de Maurepas and M. de Vergennes, whom he waited upon in his Uniform and was much pleased with his Reception. He is now gone . . . upon a visit to his Mother, and at his return will be introduced to the King and Queen in Woman's Clothes, which are actually making at Mlle Bertin's.

It will be noted that the Ambassador refers to d'Éon throughout as 'he'. Upon his return to Paris the Chevalier duly assumed female dress, and remained in the capital for some while, affording the *salons* material for ribald mirth over 'La Chevalière d'Éon' and 'her' relations with Beaumarchais, such as they had not had for many a long year – to the latter's real vexation. For oddly enough, the author of *The Barber of Seville* and the Goezman pamphlets was far from being amused when he himself became the butt of society's wit. Whether or not he had been playing a comedy with d'Éon in London, it was altogether a different matter to be made the laughing-stock of Paris, and in such circumstances. However, although the Chevalier did not finally return to London until 1785, he now fades out of Beaumarchais' life and their paths crossed no more.

But before that human fire-cracker, the Chevalier d'Éon, disappears from the scene, it may be noted that after his death (in London in 1810) a post-mortem examination established beyond any doubt that he was in fact a man. To external appearance, therefore, he ended his life as a member of the same sex as that in which he entered it; for the usher of the school he had attended as a child, who had had charge of the boys when they bathed, testified that the young d'Éon was certainly a male. But from a psychological point of view the Chevalier can scarcely be considered to have been a normal person. The evidence seems to indicate, however, that he was caught in a trap of his own making; for after having encouraged the idea that he was of the female sex as a way out of a desperate situation, and having passed himself off to Beaumarchais – with or without success – as a woman, he was finally taken at his word and compelled to dress the part. Whether a Minister so sagacious as Vergennes really believed d'Éon to be a woman is open to doubt; but it was certainly an effective method of discounting possible trouble in the future from one who knew too much of the late King's secret diplomacy. For the Chevalier, having once committed himself to a declaration of femininity as the price of a settlement with the French Government, then found himself in a situation from which it was impossible to draw back without incurring universal ridicule, not to mention the probability of his imprisonment for debt – no light matter in the eighteenth century. In 1779, when France was at war with England and the French Government was making final preparations for an invasion of this country, d'Éon begged to be allowed to resume his uniform as a dragoon and serve in the invading forces. But Vergennes was adamant. So for the remaining years of his life, which were spent in England, the Chevalier continued to dress as a woman.

So ended this extraordinary and most unedifying episode which, if it did nothing to enhance the personal reputation of Beaumarchais, at least earned him the grateful favour of the new King and his Government. But it is perhaps scarcely surprising that Voltaire, octogenarian survivor of the splendid century of the Roi Soleil, should write from Ferney: 'This whole affair dumbfounds me. I am unable to understand d'Éon, nor the Ministry of his time; neither the proceedings of Louis XV and his Ministers, nor those of the present day. This is a world of which I know nothing.'

Chapter 12

BEAUMARCHAIS AND THE

AMERICAN COLONIES

ALTHOUGH Louis XV's secret plans for the invasion of England had remained only on paper, the Government of his successor had not given up the idea of avenging the humiliations of the Seven Years War which had stripped France of her colonial empire, and they were keenly observing the mounting tension between England and her colonies in America. But the Comte de Guines, French Ambassador in London, was not providing very satisfactory reports for his Government, and the real purpose of Beaumarchais' visit to London in the spring of 1775 was the gathering of fuller and more accurate information on the English political and financial scene; particularly the latter, for it was Vergennes' view, as he wrote to the French Ambassador in Madrid, that, 'It is at least as important to beat the English in the economic field as on the battlefield.' Beaumarchais' mission was an assignment after his own heart, for, as he had told the Duc de Noailles years earlier, one of the

follies from which I have been forced to tear myself is the study of politics, a subject thorny and repellent to most men, but quite as attractive as useless to me. I have loved it to madness: reading, work, travels, observation, I have done everything to develop it; the respective rights of powers, the pretentions of princes, by which the mass of mankind is for ever being disturbed, the action and reaction of Governments upon one another; all these are interests made for my soul. . . . Sometimes I have gone so far as to murmur in my unjust humour that fate did not place me more advantageously with regard to those things for which I believed myself suited.

Nearly ten years had passed since Beaumarchais had written those lines, but now he had his chance and he threw himself into it with zest. He was particularly well equipped for the gathering of useful information in London, both from Government and Whig opposition circles.

For on the Government side his old friend of Madrid days, Lord Rochford, was now Secretary of State for the Southern Department and on friendly terms with George III; 'if the idea that we have of Lord Rochford is correct,' wrote Vergennes, 'it should not be difficult to make him talk more than he intends.' At the same time Beaumarchais also had close contacts with opposition circles through his friendship with John Wilkes, the political firebrand who was then Lord Mayor of London. Wilkes had for a long time been in close relations with the moving spirits of revolt in America, notably the organization known as the Boston Sons of Liberty; the Americans had watched his political career with great interest and sympathy, since he appeared to them to be fighting a similar battle for freedom in England, against the same Parliament which had been imposing so much unwelcome taxation upon themselves. It was at the dinners given by Wilkes that Beaumarchais met Arthur Lee, the barrister from Virginia, who was presently to play such an unfortunate role as one of the three American commissioners sent to France by the insurgents.

It is evident too that during his stay in England at this time Beaumarchais took the opportunity of visiting other parts of the country as well as London; for Gudin, who accompanied him, describes how they visited the manufactures of Birmingham, inspected coal-mines and other places of interest, and were particularly struck with the appearance of the countryside covered with cattle peacefully grazing 'without keepers or dogs, as in the golden age'. Gudin, with the astonishment of an inhabitant of eighteenth-century France, enquires of the country-folk: 'I knew well that you had no wolves to devour your flocks, but have you then neither monks to cheat you out of them, nor Farmers-General [of taxes] to hold them up to ransom, nor lesser officials to pillage them, nor Intendants to requisition them?'

When hostilities at last broke out in America with the attack on British troops at Lexington in April, the first official attitude of the French Government was one of cautious disapproval on the part of one monarch towards the rebellious subjects of another. 'What is happening to you in America', said Vergennes to the British Ambassador, Lord Stormont, 'is not to the advantage of anyone'; while Maurepas assured Stormont that 'We do not and will not, directly or indirectly, give them any sort of assistance.' But when it began to be realized that the colonists were not going to be crushed overnight, that the traditional enemy was becoming entangled in a struggle for which she was, as usual, ill prepared, and which could not fail to do material damage to her prosperity, hope began to stir in France that here might be the long-awaited opportunity of paying off old scores. No one was more convinced of this than Beaumarchais, and in the midst of his dealings with the Chevalier d'Éon, he was busily at work on secret projects for American aid. His work was facilitated by the fact that there were many people in England, particularly among the Whigs, who disapproved of the American war; among them was d'Éon's friend Lord Ferrers. Beaumarchais' activities had of necessity to be conducted with great secrecy, not only for their success but also to avoid compromising the French Government, whose official attitude at this time was still one of strict neutrality. Thus, there is practically no written evidence of the details of his operations at this particular period; but a significant passage occurs in a letter he wrote to Vergennes on the 14 July 1775, telling the Minister that he had the key of d'Éon's chest. The letter continues:

I would return at once to give the details of what I have accomplished, if I were only charged with one object. But I am charged with four, and find myself obliged to leave for Flanders with Milord Ferrers and in his vessel.

Now Benjamin Franklin, before he returned to America, had been treating with merchants and armourers not only in London but also in Holland and France for war supplies to America; it seems certain that Beaumarchais was concerned in these projects and that the centre of these operations was sited in Flanders.

As the year 1775 drew towards its close, Beaumarchais became ever more convinced of the necessity for French intervention in support of the American colonists, and we find a situation which assuredly would have astounded Voltaire even more than the d'Éon affair: the man convicted on a charge of forgery in one case, and condemned to loss of civil rights in another, now writes a series of memoranda to the young King and his Foreign Minister, dictating the foreign policy of France. The first long memorandum, which Beaumarchais addressed to the King through Sartines, shows that he was being greatly influenced by Wilkes and his circle, and by the inflated tales of warlike preparations in America brought over by 'an inhabitant of Philadelphia'. He was quite certain that civil war would break out at any moment in the streets of London, and that the English Government would be faced by far worse troubles at home than in America. 'This unfortunate English people,' he writes, 'with their frenzied liberty, can inspire true compassion in a thinking man. Never have they tasted the sweetness of living peacefully under a good and virtuous king. They despise us and treat us as slaves because we obey of our free will; but if the reign of either a weak or a wicked prince has sometimes done France a momentary injury, never has this licentious fury which the English call liberty left an instant of happiness or real repose to this ungovernable people.' Strange words indeed from the creator of Figaro, even though intended for the ears of a young reigning monarch! It was never easy, however, at any time in his reign, to bring Louis XVI to a decision, and least of all in a question where such thorny issues were involved. On 7 December, Beaumarchais returned to the attack with another long memorandum in which he proceeded with forceful if somewhat casuistic arguments to demolish Louis' hesitations and scruples of conscience. England, he declares, is France's natural enemy, the jealous rival whose policy has always been to weaken France. The sovereign law of a state is policy, and the crown of good policy is to found one's tranquillity on the divisions of one's enemies. If England triumphs over the Americans, it will be at enormous expenditure of men and money, the only compensation for which will be to seize the French West Indian sugar islands, making herself the exclusive purveyor of their precious harvest, and the absolute owner for ever of the trade with these islands. If the Americans win, the English, on seeing their possessions diminished by three-quarters, will only be the more eager to seek compensation by the easy capture of France's American possessions. If the opposition comes to power in England and makes a treaty of reunion with the colonies, the Americans will be enraged against France, whose refusal of aid they will consider as having forced their submission, and they will probably join forces with England to carry off the French islands; while a Ministry made up of Lords Chatham, Shelburne and Rockingham would make the most obstinate and cruel war on France.

You will only preserve the peace you desire, Sire, by preventing at all costs the conclusion of peace between England and America, and in preventing the one from triumphing over the other. The sole means of achieving this end is to give to the Americans sufficient help to put their forces on an equal footing with those of England – but no more. And be sure, Sire, that to spare a few millions today can, before long, cost France much blood and treasure.

If it is answered that we cannot help the Americans without offending England and drawing upon us the very storm I wish to dispel, I reply in my turn that we shall not run this danger if we follow the plan that I have so many times proposed, of helping the Americans secretly, imposing on them as a first condition that they shall never send any prize into our ports, and will do nothing to divulge the help which will instantly be lost to them at the first indiscretion on the part of Congress.

He suggests that since success depends on secrecy and speed, the first essential to both is, if at all possible, to get Lord Stormont, the British Ambassador in Paris, recalled; since, by his sources of information in France, the representative of England keeps himself far too well informed of all that goes on in the King's Council. Nor, in point of fact was Lord Stormont in the least impressed with the repeated protestations of the French Ministers regarding their attitude over America. As he wrote to his chief, Lord Weymouth, who had just succeeded Lord Rochford as Secretary of State for the Southern Department:

Though I repeat, as is my duty, the assurances I receive from the Court, tho' I give them credit to a degree for their pacific Wishes and Intentions; yet I hope your Lordship will not think that I am of such easy credulity as to believe that they do not connive at Succours being sent from this Country to America. They could not with the utmost Vigilance prevent it entirely, but I am persuaded that that Vigilance neither does, or ever will exist, and that, on the contrary, they purposely shut their Eyes. This however, my Lord, I never pretend to see, but always seem to rest entirely satisfied with the assurances they give me, and only say that, as it is scarce possible that some illicit attempts should not escape their notice, whenever I hear of anything of that sort, I shall always let them know it.

Obviously the British Ambassador was not easily to be deceived. He was not recalled; he continued to remain in Paris, an uncomfortably watchful observer of the activities not only of the French Government but of Beaumarchais himself, on whose movements some distinctly interesting light is thrown by a report from Stormont to Weymouth in May 1776:

I have good grounds to believe that for some months past, there have been French agents in England, endeavouring to procure sums of money for the Rebels in America, from their Friends in England, in order to convey them in French ships to the French Islands, and from thence to the Congress. M. de Beaumarchais is, I understand, concerned in this business, but he is not alone. Within these eighteen months, he has made eight voyages to London, and in the space of three weeks he went twice.

Although Vergennes had been quietly abetting Benjamin Franklin's efforts to raise supplies for America and had even allowed him to transfer these across the Atlantic through agents operating in Nantes, he was not yet, however, prepared to fall in with Beaumarchais' appeal to transmit direct to American agents the sum of three million livres, either as money or munitions. But presently the prudent Minister thought to find a way by which support might be given to America without compromising his Government. The operation, he informed Beaumarchais, must appear in the eyes both of the British Government and of the Americans as a purely speculative one of individual enterprise, which indeed it must be to some extent in reality. The French Government would secretly give Beaumarchais a million livres, and would try to obtain an equal amount from the Bourbon Court of Spain. With these two millions and the co-operation of private individuals Beaumarchais would found a great commercial house which would undertake at its own risk to supply the Americans with arms, munitions, equipment and any other items necessary for carrying on the war. The arms and munitions could be provided from the royal arsenals of France (the moment was particularly opportune, since the French Army was about to be completely re-equipped with more up-to-date material), but Beaumarchais's new establishment would have to replace them or pay for them. He was not to ask the Americans for any payment in money, since they had none; but they could repay him with the products of their soil (such as tobacco, rice and cotton), whose distribution throughout France would be facilitated by the French Government. Thus, the operation secretly financed by that Government in the beginning must as soon as possible become self-supporting.

This was a proposal which obviously entailed enormous risks, and many a man would have blenched at it; but not so Beaumarchais, to whom difficulties and hazards were like a trumpet-call to a war-horse. (He had, after all, undergone his apprenticeship in large-scale financial operations under the experienced tutelage of Pâris-Duverney.) On 10 June 1776 he signed a receipt testifying that, in conformity with the orders of the Comte de Vergennes, he had received the sum of one million livres, for which he would be accountable to the Foreign Minister. With the signature of this brief document, which would remain filed away in the most secret Government archives until after the fall of the monarchy, our intrepid financier launched himself on to a fresh sea of troubles, which this time would not only last him for the rest of his life, but survive him by thirty-six years to plague his descendants. However, two months after receiving a million from Vergennes, another million was advanced by Spain, so that, with the added funds of various private persons who came forward to support the project, the total soon reached the three millions which had been

Beaumarchais' original aim. The firm of Roderigue Hortalez et Cie now came into being (a name invented by its head and sole director). Beaumarchais rented a large house in the Faubourg du Temple, and filled it with a multitude of clerks and other employees. He presided over it himself, working from early morning till late at night, and superintending with his tireless energy the gigantic and hazardous task he had undertaken. But once again his activities were being duly observed by Lord Stormont, who reported to London on 25 September 1776 that

... a secret agent from the Congress is certainly in constant intercourse with Beaumarchais who was lately not worth a shilling but has now Millions at his command. He keeps a table and entertains Deane and other Americans and friends to their cause. He is likewise, as I am well assured, in regular correspondence with Mr Wilkes. Their letters are not trusted to the post, but sent by private hands. ... He received lately 1,200,000 livres from M. de Sartines. The Reason or Pretence for this Remittance is this. He is appointed Agent to remit to the French West India Islands the money that the French usually coin, out of the Silver Bullion that they purchase at Cadix. ... The giving of it to Beaumarchais affords ... a fair colour for any sums of money the French Ministers choose to put into his hands.

Two months later the ambassadorial sleuth was further reporting that Beaumarchais was also carrying on a constant correspondence with Morande (but by ordinary post, unlike that with Wilkes, which should therefore make it a fairly easy matter to look into it undetected) and that he was even proposing another visit to England for the object of purchasing a 'large forest' near Colchester to provide wood for the French Navy; a scheme which must obviously be nipped in the bud without delay. Within a fortnight of this, however, this tireless industrialist was detected, by the same intelligence service, in an even more astounding plan to arrange with a company of traders at Cork to supply the French and Spanish fleets with salt beef, pork and butter!

But in the midst of all this whirl of activity Beaumarchais had not forgotten a matter of prime personal importance: the clearing of his name from the iniquitous judgment of *blâme*. His collective enemy, the Parlement Maupeou, was now no more, and as soon as he had returned from his mission in London he applied to the Grand Council of Parlement for 'letters of relief' which would enable him to appeal against the verdict, since the statutory period of six months allowed by law had passed while he had been in London. It was just at this particular moment that Beaumarchais found himself obliged to pay a visit to the west coast of France in connection with the chartering of vessels for his supply service to America. 'Go all the same,' said the Prime Minister Maurepas reassuringly; 'the Council can give judgment perfectly well without you.' So, taking Maurepas's word for it, he set off to the west with Gudin, who relates how one evening, on returning to their lodging after a strenuous day's work, they found several letters which had come from Paris for Beaumarchais. These he read while Gudin, tired out, was undressing, and the latter, as he threw himself on his bed, asked Beaumarchais if he was satisfied with the news he had received. 'Perfectly well,' was the answer, given with complete calm. Reassured, Gudin then fell asleep. But in the early morning he stirred to find himself being gently shaken, and woke up to find Beaumarchais standing by his bedside; leaping up, Gudin demanded anxiously to know whether his friend was ill.

' "No," he replied to me, "but in half an hour we leave for Paris."

' "Eh, why? What has happened?"

' "The Council has rejected my demand."

' "Ah, *ciel!* And you said nothing of it to me last night!"

' "No, my friend; I did not want to disturb your night's rest. It was quite enough that I did not sleep; I have been thinking all night what I must do. My stand is taken, my plan is formed and I am leaving to put it into operation. They shall see, those who have said on coming out of the Council, 'Good, we shall see no more of him', they shall see, I say, whether it is I of whom no more is heard." '

Sixty hours later, they were back in Paris, and Beaumarchais had some pungent remarks to make to the smooth-spoken Maurepas: 'So, while I run to the farthest ends of France on the King's affairs, you lose mine at Versailles!' There was no denying the truth of this, nor of Beaumarchais' usefulness to the royal business at that moment. There had been a mistake, he was told, and the Council would have to think again. They did; with the result that the necessary letters of relief were granted, and the case came up for review before the restored Parlement, composed, as Gudin tells us, of 'magistrates recognized and respected by the whole nation'. The result was a foregone conclusion: on 6 September 1776 Beaumarchais' name was completely cleared of the charges arising out of the Goezman affair, and all civil rights restored to him, including his ability to hold the office of Lieutenant-General of the Varenne du Louvre. Outside the court he was carried shoulder-high to his carriage amid frenzied applause from the crowd – though it may be doubted whether their acclamation was not rather for the final rout of the Parlement Maupeou than because of any great concern for that Parlement's victim, who had still to be freed from the stigma of its verdict in the La Blache case. However, Beaumarchais wrote to Vergennes the same day, expressing his joy at the immediate outcome:

Monsieur le comte,

I have just been judged, *déblâmé*, amidst a universal concourse of applause. Never did so unfortunate a citizen receive greater honour. I hasten to announce to you the news, begging you to lay my gratitude at the feet of the King. I am so trembling with joy that I can scarcely write. . . .

Do me the kindness, M. le comte, to announce this very happy news to M. de Maurepas and to M. de Sartines.

Meanwhile, the Secret Committee of the American Congress had appointed one Silas Deane, a delegate from Connecticut, to go to France, 'there to transact such business, commercial and political, as we have committed to his care.' On arriving in France, he was to be 'for some time engaged in the business of providing goods for the Indian trade. This will give you good countenance to your appearing in the character of a merchant, which we wish you to retain among the French in general, it being probable that the Court of France may not like it known publicly that any agent of the colonies is in that country. When you come to Paris, by delivering Dr Franklin's letters to M. Le Ray at the Louvre, and M. Dubourg, you will be introduced to a set of acquaintances, all friends to America. By conversing with them, you will have a good opportunity of acquiring Parisian French, and you will find in M. Dubourg a man prudent, faithful, secret, intelligent in affairs, and capable of giving you very safe advice.' The unfortunate Silas Deane arrived in Paris in July 1776, a quiet and reserved man, and so far from possessing any command of French, Parisian or otherwise, that Beaumarchais was soon writing of him: 'M. Deane does not open his mouth before the English-speaking people he meets; he must be the most silent man in France, for I defy him to say six consecutive words in French.' As for Dr Dubourg, whom Congress had recommended so warmly to Deane, he proved to be something of a menace, officious, indiscreet and far too talkative; so that Beaumarchais wrote to Vergennes that, 'If while we close the door on one side, the window is open on the other, surely the secret will escape. Silence must be imposed on these babblers, who can do nothing themselves, and who hinder those who can.' Dr Dubourg had been on friendly terms with Franklin, having translated some of his writings into French, and as he had been concerned with the supplies provided previously for Franklin, he now

flattered himself that his services would be again in request on behalf of
Deane. He was therefore more than a little injured to find himself sup-
planted by Beaumarchais, and wrote to Vergennes making various
allegations against the former's character and suitability for the undertaking:

Everybody knows his wit, and nobody appreciates more than I do his probity,
discretion and zeal for all that is great and good. I believe him to be one of the
most suitable men in the world for political negotiations, but perhaps at the
same time one of the least fitted for commercial business. He loves display:
they say that he keeps women; he has the reputation of being a spendthrift,
and there is no merchant or manufacturer in France who has not this idea of
him, and who would not hesitate to do the least amount of business with him.
He astonished me very much when he informed me that you had charged him
not only to help us with his wits, but to concentrate in himself alone the whole
undertaking and the details of all commercial operations. . . . I agreed with him
that it might result in making all these operations more secret, but I represented
to him that in taking possession of all this immense traffic and entirely excluding
those who had incurred such great expense, so much fatigue and danger during
the previous year in the service of Congress was most unfair. . . .

The doctor's letter evidently amused even the serious-minded Vergennes, to the extent that he sent it to Beaumarchais, who replied in
his own inimitable style:

I understand well enough that you wished to give yourself time to write to the
Minister on my account, but in order to receive facts was it necessary to offer
him false ones? What does it concern our business whether I am an ostentatious
gadabout who keeps women? The women I have kept for the last twenty years,
monsieur, are your very humble servants; they were five, four sisters and
niece. Three years ago, two of these kept women died, to my great grief. I
now keep only three, two sisters and my niece, which is still rather ostentatious
for a man in my position. But what would you then have thought if, knowing
me better, you had known that I pushed scandal so far as to keep men, two very
young and nice-looking nephews, and even the unfortunate father who put
into the world such a notorious keeper? As for my ostentation, that is worse
still. For the last three years, finding lace and embroidered clothes too poor to
suit my vanity, have I not taken pride in having my wrist-bands trimmed with
the most beautiful plain muslin? The most superb black broadcloth is not grand
enough for me; sometimes I have even been seen to push rascality to the point
of wearing silk, when it is very hot. But I beg of you, monsieur, not to write
these things to M. le Comte de Vergennes; you will end by ruining me entirely
in his estimation. . . .

Let us cease to joke. I am not angered, because M. de Vergennes is not a small man, and I abide by his decision. Let those of whom I ask business advances mistrust me; I can bear it. But let those who are animated by a true zeal for the cause of our common friends which is at stake, think twice before turning away from an honourable man who offers to render every service and make all useful advances to those same friends. Now do you understand me, sir?

Congress had instructed Deane that what they wanted at the moment was clothing and arms for 25,000 men, together with ammunition and a hundred field-guns. He was, however, to proceed cautiously with Vergennes, and, if he found the climate cool, must not try to rush things. The royal arsenals proved to be a splendid source of supply, for with the change in type of weapons for the French Army they were piled with firearms in practically new condition, as well as other military stores which were no longer required. There was one grave difficulty, however, over the brass cannon: they were stamped with the arms of France. This would never do; the incriminating evidence must be obliterated, even if it meant recasting the cannon. But, in spite of all this, Beaumarchais – otherwise Roderigue Hortalez et Cie – was able to collect 200 cannon, 25,000 guns, 30 brass mortars and 200,000 lb of powder, together with enough clothing and tents for the 25,000 men. These supplies he caused to be assembled at Le Havre and Nantes, where Silas Deane had undertaken to provide ships. None, however, appeared, and as the supplies were urgently needed for the forthcoming campaign of 1777, in which the insurgents hoped to retrieve their critical situation, it was finally Beaumarchais who provided the transport.

Naturally all these activities did not escape the penetrating eye of the British Ambassador. Although Beaumarchais had gone to Le Havre in December 1776 under the assumed name of Durand, he could not resist employing his spare time in supervising rehearsals for the representation of his *Barber of Seville*, since the local actors' standard of performance did not meet with his approval; after which, it naturally mattered little what name he chose to assume! On 23 December Lord Stormont reported to London that

Beaumarchais is returned from Havre and has given great offence to the French Ministers by his indiscretion there and the very open and public manner in which he conducted the business entrusted to him. He has likewise had a quarrel with M. Montion, the person to whom the *Amphitrite* belongs and with whom Beaumarchais had agreed for the cannon, arms and ammunition to be sent to the Rebels. It is said that M. Montion has fulfilled this agreement very ill, and that the cannon and firearms are of a bad quality, and many of them absolutely unfit for service. He is strongly accused by Beaumarchais and recriminates in his turn.

Clearly, transport was not the only difficulty that harassed Beaumarchais in his operations. As for the unhappy Deane, he had already reported from Paris to the Secret Committee of Congress that

my arrival here, my name, my lodgings, and many other particulars have been reported to the British Administration, on which they sent orders to the British Ambassador to remonstrate in high terms. . . . The city swarms with Englishmen, and as money purchases everything in this country, I have had, and still have, a most difficult task to avoid their machinations. Not a coffee-house or theatre or other place of public diversion but swarms with their emissaries.

Lord Stormont now launched strong protests at the impending departure of Beaumarchais' ships. As the fortunes of the insurgents were just then at their lowest ebb, neither the King nor Vergennes wished to risk having a rupture with England, and orders were therefore issued forbidding the sailing of the vessels.

The largest of them, the *Amphitrite*, had already put to sea, loaded not only with munitions but with a party of artillery and engineer officers whom the Government had been persuaded to allow to serve in America; but because De Coudry, the officer leading the party – and a source of much future trouble to everyone – did not like his quarters in the ship, the *Amphitrite* put in again at Lorient. Fresh protests to Vergennes followed from Lord Stormont, who found the French Minister much irritated at the publicity which had been thrown on the affair through the indiscretions of Beaumarchais and his associates. 'I answered with a smile,' wrote Stormont, 'that we who wished to be informed were obliged to them for the facilities they gave us' – a remark scarcely calculated to put Vergennes in a calmer frame of mind. However, the ships set sail none the less in the end, by dint of being released at intervals one by one, and having evaded the English cruisers they safely reached America at the beginning of 1777. Putting in at the harbour of Portsmouth, New Hampshire, on 30 April, they were welcomed with great joy and excitement by the inhabitants, who turned out to meet them clapping their hands.

Beaumarchais now naturally awaited some of the return cargoes from America, which were to be the payment for his efforts, and whose arrival within six months had been formally pledged by Silas Deane. But there was not even any acknowledgement of Beaumarchais' letters from the other side of the Atlantic, although he had subsequently despatched two more ships loaded with supplies. Silas Deane, an honest man, was embarrassed by the strange silence, of which he could give no explanation. But the key to the situation was Arthur Lee. A man of overwhelming ambition, he was madly jealous of Deane, who had been given the assignment in France which Lee considered he should have had himself. 'By character and by ambition,' said Beaumarchais, 'Mr Arthur Lee was first jealous of Mr Deane; he finished by becoming his enemy, which always happens to small minds, more occupied in supplanting their rivals than in surpassing them in merit.' Lee's animosity was, however, equally stirred up against Beaumarchais, because since Deane's arrival in Paris the director of the house of Roderigue Hortalez had no longer kept up his former close relations with Lee, but was dealing directly with Deane.

After the Declaration of Independence on 4 July 1776 Congress had decided to appoint three commissioners to go to France to negotiate a treaty of 'amity and commerce' with that country. These were originally intended to be Franklin, Deane (who was already in France) and Jefferson; but unfortunately the latter declined, and the third commissioner appointed was Arthur Lee. Both he and Franklin arrived in Paris in December 1776, and the latter set up his headquarters at Passy, in the Hôtel de Valentinois, which he was to occupy for nine years. (Lee, who characteristically could not tolerate living under the same roof as his colleagues, sought accommodation elsewhere.) Passy was then a country village outside the city limits, and residence in its rustic seclusion had several advantages: it did not obtrude the presence of the American delegates on the public attention, and communication with the French Ministers could take place with less chance of being observed by the ever watchful British Ambassador. Franklin's arrival did not promise well from Beaumarchais' point of view, however, for the old man's mind had been poisoned by Dr Dubourg, with the result that he viewed the firm of Roderigue Hortalez with some suspicion, and informed Deane that he would have nothing to do with any of the dealings arranged before his arrival. Meanwhile, Arthur Lee was busily writing to Congress that 'M. de Vergennes the Minister, and his secretary, have repeatedly assured us that no return was expected for the cargo sent by Beaumarchais. This gentleman is not a merchant; he is known to be a political agent employed by the Court of France.' Lee's spite led him further to the assertion that Deane and Beaumarchais were in league together to swindle both the French and American Governments by making a business operation out of what was intended to be a gift. Congress expressed open bewilderment; they had in any case no surplus cash to spare at this time of acute crisis, and the Secret Committee wrote to Vergennes:

We do not know who the persons are who constitute the house of Roderigue & Co.; but Congress has ever understood, and so have the people in America in general, that they were under obligations to His Majesty's good will for the great part of the merchandise and warlike stores heretofore furnished under the firm name of Roderigue Hortalez & Co. We cannot discover that any written contract was ever made between Congress or any agent of theirs and the house of Roderigue & Co., nor do we know of any living witness or any other evidence, whose testimony can ascertain for us who the persons are who constitute the house of Roderigue & Co., or what were the terms upon which the merchandise and munitions of war were supplied, neither as to the price, nor the time, nor the conditions of payment.

We apprehend that the United States hold themselves under obligation to His Majesty for all those supplies . . . we are ready to settle and liquidate the accounts according to our instructions, at any time and in any manner, which His Majesty and your Excellency shall point out to us.

But that was precisely what His Excellency could not do, if France was to remain at peace with England. He could only write lamely to the representative of the American states that 'the King has not furnished anything, he has simply allowed M. de Beaumarchais to provide himself with what he wanted in the arsenals, on condition of replacing what he took'; no wonder Arthur Lee described the French Government's policy as 'a kind of trembling hesitation'. It must further be admitted that if Congress had genuine misgivings over the firm of Roderigue Hortalez, their doubts were not likely to be set at rest by the letters they were receiving from its head, written in his most exuberantly flamboyant style. It is not hard to picture the reaction of the sober, hard-headed New England merchants who sat in Congress when they received such effusions as the following extract:

Your deputies, gentlemen, can find in me a sure friend, and asylum in my house, money in my coffers, and any means of facilitating their operations. I promise you that my indefatigable zeal shall never be wanting to clear up difficulties, soften prohibitions, and facilitate the operations of a commerce which your advantage, more than my own, has made me undertake.

Silas Deane was doing the best he could for Beaumarchais, writing to Congress in terms of warmest commendation:

I should never have completed what I have done, but for the indefatigable and spirited exertions of M. Beaumarchais, to whom the United States are on every account greatly indebted; more so than to any other person on this side of the water; . . . therefore I am confident that you will make him the earliest and most ample remittance.

But alongside Deane's report, there travelled across the Atlantic a further instalment of venom from Arthur Lee:

The Ministry has often given us to understand that we have nothing to pay for the cargoes furnished by Beaumarchais; however, the latter, with the perseverance usual to adventurers of his type, persists in his demands.

What, indeed, was Congress to make of all this? The actual result was that it split into two warring camps: the supporters of Lee against those of Deane; in the midst of which the unfortunate director of Roderigue Hortalez et Cie was left to whistle for his money. By September 1777 he had in fact shipped to America five million livres' worth of cargoes, and had not had so much as an acknowledgment, although these supplies were to be a vital factor in the campaign of that year, which, with the American success at Saratoga, was to be the turning-point of the war. Beaumarchais was visiting Franklin at his headquarters in Passy one day at the beginning of December when a messenger from Boston, one Jonathan Austin, who had recently landed at Nantes, drove into the courtyard of the Hôtel de Valentinois in the three-horse chaise in which he had made the journey from the coast to Paris at top speed. 'Sir,' said Franklin, 'is Philadelphia taken?' 'It is,' replied Austin. 'But, sir, I have greater news than that: General Burgoyne and his whole army are prisoners.' Beaumarchais leapt into his own carriage, anxious to be the first to carry the news to Paris, and travelled at such speed that the vehicle overturned on the way. 'My right arm is cut,' he wrote to Vergennes, 'the bones of my neck were nearly crushed . . . but the charming news from America is a balm to my wounds.'

But news from America, however charming, was not going to take the place of solid cash, and during the summer of 1777 Vergennes had been obliged to come to the rescue of Roderigue Hortalez et Cie on three occasions, advancing loans to Beaumarchais which totalled over one million livres. In December Beaumarchais was writing to Congress that his money and credit were alike exhausted; that, counting too much on the return cargoes which had been so frequently promised, he had gone far beyond the resources of himself, his friends, and even of 'other powerful sources of aid', which he had obtained on the promise of a swift return. He now sent to America an agent to press his interests, in the person of Théveneau de Francy, a younger brother of Théveneau de Morande, whom fortunately however he did not resemble in character; Francy was in fact a young man of considerable ability who served Beaumarchais loyally. The latter also bought from the Ministry of Marine an old warship, the *Hippopotame*, which he rechristened the *Fier Roderigue*, refitted and armed with sixty-six bronze cannon as well as smaller pieces, and, having loaded her with cargo, had her ready to sail for America. But Lord Stormont's information service was continuing to function with its usual efficiency, and on 11 February 1778 he was reporting to London that 'by intelligence that comes to me from a Person just arrived from Nantes, it appears that the *Hippopotame*, now called *le fier Roderigue*, richly laden, mounting between 50 and 60 guns, is certainly destined for N. America and preparing to sail from Rochefort'. The usual broadside was delivered from Lord Stormont's diplomatic guns, and Maurepas, becoming nervous, forbade delivery of the ship's cargo. Beaumarchais blandly assured the Minister that the vessel was bound for the French colony of Santo Domingo with a detachment of militia for that island. Then the fertile brain of the creator of Figaro set to work thinking of a way by which, while keeping his word to Maurepas that his ship should sail for Santo Domingo, he might yet contrive to get her cargo to the Americans without touching the continent. He wrote to young Francy:

After much thinking, it seems to me that you might arrange secretly with the committee of Congress to send two or three American corsairs immediately to Santo Domingo. . . . They will arrange together that when my vessel sets out, the American corsair will capture it under any pretext he chooses, and carry it off. My captain will protest violently, and threaten to complain to Congress. The vessel will be taken to where you are. The Congress will disavow the brutal act, liberate my vessel, with obliging excuses for the French flag; during the time this takes, you will have unloaded the cargo quickly, and filled the ship with tobacco, and you will send her back to me with just what you have been able to gather together. . . . By this means, M. de Maurepas will be disengaged from his promise made to others, I from mine to him; because no one can oppose himself to violence, and my operation will have been successful in spite of all the obstacles which cross my path.

A plan whose subtle ingenuity was indeed worthy of Figaro; but the *Fier Roderigue* was held up until after the commencement of hostilities between France and England, and the loss to Beaumarchais thereby entailed was, Gudin assures us, something like a million livres.

Since the capitulation of Burgoyne had convinced Europe that England was fighting a losing battle in America, Beaumarchais had become more than ever persuaded of the necessity for active intervention by France, and once more a rain of memoranda from his pen assailed both Maurepas and Vergennes. Once again we have the curious spectacle of the author of *The Barber of Seville* advising the King's Ministers on the foreign policy of France, and what is even more remarkable is that when, in March 1778, the Government of France officially notified the British Government of their recognition of American independence, the substance of their declaration was precisely what Beaumarchais had drawn up, at their own request, after discussions with Maurepas and Vergennes six months before!

The French recognition of American independence was tantamount to a declaration of war upon England, and the *Fier Roderigue* was now therefore free to sail for the West Indies, which she did as escort to a convoy of ten of Beaumarchais' merchant ships. But off the island of Grenada they fell in with the French Fleet under Admiral d'Estaing, who was on the point of engaging a British squadron under Admiral Byron. When d'Estaing's eye fell upon the fine escort vessel flying the French flag, he did not hesitate to conscript the *Fier Roderigue* into his own fleet. Beaumarchais' trading vessels were left to fend for themselves, while the *Fier Roderigue* played an heroic part in the ensuing action – but at disastrous cost to her owner, for her captain was killed and the ship riddled with shot; while the unfortunate merchant vessels which she had been obliged to abandon were either captured or sunk. However, a graceful letter of thanks and appreciation from Admiral d'Estaing for the gallant behaviour of the *Fier Roderigue* in the action was some consolation to Beaumarchais' pride; while the Government paid him an indemnity of two million livres in instalments spread over the following six years, which enabled him to keep afloat financially in face of the continued absence of any returns from America.

In the spring of 1778 Silas Deane was recalled home, ostensibly to report on his work before Congress, but in reality to defend himself (and Beaumarchais) against the poisonous allegations of Arthur Lee, and the attacks of Lee's two brothers, who exercised considerable influence in Congress. Deane was fortunately provided with warm recommendations from the French Government, the King had presented him with his portrait, and it so happened that the newly appointed French Minister Plenipotentiary to the United States, who had just arrived in Philadelphia, had been working under Vergennes in the

Foreign Ministry while Deane had been in Paris. He stoutly championed the cause of Deane, and his opinion of Lee – 'this dangerous and wicked man' – was so damaging to that ruthless mischief-maker that he too was recalled from Paris some months later. It was now beginning to dawn upon Congress that the merchandise which Beaumarchais could send them would be of great value to the young republic, and that if they did not make some attempt to placate him and recognize their liability they would, as Francy did not hesitate to inform them, get nothing more from him; nor would they unless, in addition to acknowledging their past liabilities, they drew up a proper contract regularizing their future dealings. This they were prepared to do, but only in return for a definite statement from the French Government as to whether Beaumarchais was really their creditor for the five million livres worth of cargoes already sent, or whether these were, as Lee continually asserted, a gift from the French Government. A note was presented to Vergennes in September 1778, but in his reply the Minister again took refuge behind his previous statement that the King had provided nothing, but had merely permitted Beaumarchais to draw on the arsenals on condition of a later replacement of the material; as for the ratification of a contract with the house of Roderigue Hortalez, that was a matter, said Vergennes, which did not lie with him. Since this answer implied that Beaumarchais was the creditor of Congress, that estimable body wrote him a high-sounding missive on 1 January 1779.

Sir,

The Congress of the United States of America, sensible of your exertions in their favour, present you with their thanks and assure you of their regard.

They lament the inconvenience you have suffered by the great advances made in support of these states. Circumstances have prevented the compliance with their wishes, but they will take the most effectual measures in their power to discharge the debt due to you.

The liberal sentiments and broad views which alone could dictate a conduct like yours are conspicuous in both your actions and your character. While with great talents you serve your Prince, you have gained the esteem of the infant Republic, and will receive the united applause of the New World.

By order of Congress

This lofty expression of noble sentiments was rather in Beaumarchais' own style, yet it was singularly unsatisfying to a creditor on the brink of financial ruin. Silence fell for nearly a year; then, in October Congress sent letters of credit for 2,544,000 livres, but they were not to be payable until three years had passed, which, as Beaumarchais pointed out with just irritation, would in fact render them worthless in Europe. Two more years went by. Then in 1781 Silas Deane returned to France to wind up his affairs, and he fixed the sum owing to Beaumarchais as 3,600,000 livres. Beaumarchais duly submitted a claim for this amount to Congress; no reply came, and two more years passed. In 1783 Barclay, a new agent of the United States, arrived in Paris and made a fresh – and reduced – estimate of the sum owing to Beaumarchais. But at the same period, the United States wishing to obtain a new loan of 6 millions from the French Government, it was decided to make a thorough review of the financial situation between France and America. Among the various items listed were three millions given by France before the treaty of alliance in February 1778, as well as six millions given in 1781; these nine millions were to be regarded as a gift from the King of France to the United States. The contract was signed by Franklin on 25 February 1783; but, perhaps because he was now an old and tired man, it was only three years later, after his return to America, that he realized that in fact he had only received two millions from the French Government before 1778, although in 1777 he had received a million from the Farmers-General, which had been paid for by 153,229 lb of tobacco. On making enquiries of Vergennes, the Minister replied that the King had nothing to do with the Farmers-General, but that the sum in question was a million delivered by the Royal Treasury on 10 June 1776 – it was in fact the million secretly given to Beaumarchais. The banker who was dealing with the enquiry on behalf of the United States not unnaturally asked for the name of the recipient. He was met with a refusal, being informed that the receipt he was demanding to see had no relation to the affair he was investigating. In face of this attitude on the part of the King's Ministers, Congress considered itself entitled to refuse to make any payment to Beaumarchais at all, on the assumption that the missing million was in his hands. Beaumarchais knew nothing of these secret interchanges between the banker and the Government, and continued in vain to press for payment. The only result of his persistence was that Congress ordered a fresh examination of his account, and delegated the job to – of all people – Arthur Lee, who needless to say found that, far from the United States being Beaumarchais' debtor, it was he who owed them 1,800,000 francs! Four years of protest from Beaumarchais resulted in yet another examination of the position, this time by Alexander Hamilton in 1793, who found that Congress was Beaumarchais'

debtor to the amount of 2,280,000 francs. At the same time, however, he recommended that no payment should be made until a
proper explanation could be obtained from the French Government
regarding the missing million; since if the receipt proved to have been
signed by Beaumarchais, Hamilton considered that the amount should
be deducted from the debt. Buchot, the Foreign Minister of the newly
born French republic, was only too glad to produce the receipt bearing
Beaumarchais' signature from the archives of the lately deceased
monarchy; thereby engulfing the unfortunate signatory in fresh
difficulties. For both Maurepas and Vergennes were now dead –
fortunately for them, before the Revolution which had just swept
away Louis XVI – and Sartines had long since returned to Spain,
whence he had originally come. There was thus no one left who could
vouch for, or even had any knowledge of, the true history of the
missing million and Beaumarchais' part in it.

It would be wearisome to continue to follow in detail the further
history of this sorry affair, but suffice it to say that while Beaumarchais
had been able, with the loyal co-operation of young Francy, to do a
certain amount of profitable business with the individual colonies of
Virginia and South Carolina, he continued to struggle unsuccessfully
through the remainder of his life for payment of the money due to
him from Congress, and particularly when, with the coming of the
Revolution, he saw in that money a possible hope of future subsistence
for his wife and daughter. But it was not until thirty-six years after his
death, when his daughter and grandson themselves made the long
journey to Washington, that they were able to succeed in extracting
the payment of even 800,000 francs, which was to be the only return
that his family would ever receive out of the several millions originally
expended by Beaumarchais in the American cause. The story of his
dealings with Congress is not one which reflects any credit on the
young Republic of the United States; though to their honour it must
be recorded that both Thomas Jefferson and John Jay recognized from
the beginning the obligation of Congress towards Beaumarchais, and
strongly urged payment. But the American historian James Breck
Perkins (who was himself, during the first decade of the present century, a member of Congress and Chairman of the Committee on
Foreign Affairs) wrote* that, 'It is sad to reflect that almost everyone
who attempted business relations with our country at the time of the
Revolution, ended in bankruptcy.' For Beaumarchais was not the only

* *France in the American Revolution*, p. 138

Frenchman so treated. Le Ray de Chaumont, owner of the Hôtel de Valentinois, which he lent to Franklin free of charge for use as the headquarters of the American commissioners at Passy, also took an active part in supplying the insurgent colonists, with results scarcely more rewarding than the efforts of Beaumarchais. Indeed, perhaps even less so; for while the latter's descendants did eventually obtain at least a fraction of the money due, Chaumont's son, who also made the journey to America and remained there for some years, was completely unable to extract any of the money owing to his father, and finally abandoned his attempts in despair.

In Beaumarchais' case, apart from the baleful influence of Lee, settlement of his account was of course obstructed from the beginning by the French Government's refusal to give any explanation regarding the missing million. It was clearly impossible, however, for the Government of Louis XVI to admit openly that they had been secretly financing the Americans before the official recognition of independence, and this attitude was maintained even during the period of the restored monarchy. The Duc de Richelieu, as Prime Minister in 1816, reiterates that, 'the French Government had no concern in the commercial transactions of M. de Beaumarchais with the United States...' and he finally concludes that, 'I am therefore warranted, after a fresh examination of the facts . . . in considering it a matter of certainty that the million paid on the 10 June was not applied to the purchase of shipments made to the United States at that period by M. de Beaumarchais.'

But it was a former American Minister to France, John Bigelow, who in 1870 gave what might be called a final summing up of America's debt to Beaumarchais:

To him more than any other person belongs the credit of making Louis XVI comprehend the political importance of aiding the colonies in their struggle with Great Britain; he planned and executed the ingenious scheme by which the aid was to be extended; he sent the first munitions of war and supplies which the colonists received from abroad and he sent them too, at a time when, humanly speaking, it was reasonably certain that without such aid from some quarter, the colonists must have succumbed.*

* Quoted by E. Kite, *Beaumarchais and the War of American Independence.* See Bibliography.

Chapter 13

AN ADVENTURE IN PUBLISHING

THE story of Beaumarchais' dealings with Congress, pursued to its unsatisfactory conclusion, has overtaken and passed other events in his life, and we must now return to the year 1775, when he was in London gathering information for his Government on the situation regarding America.

During his absence from Paris that spring, his father, then aged seventy-seven, had fallen into the hands of a designing woman who had persuaded the old man to marry her in the expectation that his son would provide her with the dowry which she had taken care to have included in the marriage contract. As she well knew, the elder Caron had no money of his own, what he had received from his second wife having been used to cover part of the loan made to him by his son who had furthermore provided him with an annuity. These matters had been regularized by a settlement which had been drawn up between father and son, but the stepmother who had established herself without the knowledge – or approval – of Beaumarchais was now threatening to contest it, counting no doubt upon the fact that a man in his situation, scarcely freed from the strangling mesh of the Goezman case, and with that of La Blache still outstanding, would scarcely be inclined to enter the lists for yet another contest. She was correct in her calculations: for the first time in his life Beaumarchais yielded to an adversary and bought her off for 6,000 francs. Fifty-four years later, when Loménie was going through Beaumarchais' papers, he found a bundle of documents relating to this incident, and written across them a sentence in Beaumarchais' own hand: 'Infamy of my father's widow pardoned.' For old Caron did not long survive his third plunge into matrimony, an event which had caused the only shadow of disagreement between father and son to be found in fifteen years of affectionate correspondence. But the last letter written (on 25 August 1775) by the old man as he was dying shows that the former good relations subsisting between them had been fully restored after this passing shadow; he asks Beaumarchais if possible to leave his London address with Janot de Miron, so that 'in case of accident' the father can send his last blessing to his beloved son. However, if Beaumarchais' family circle was thus sadly reduced, it was to be increased again in little more than a year: for in January 1777 Marie-Thérèse Willer-maula gave birth to a daughter, who was christened Eugénie.

The following few years were to see the climax of Beaumarchais' career: he was now at the height of his powers and his activities reached their greatest pitch of intensity and variety. As his correspondence shows, he was continuing to pursue actively his extraordinary role of unofficial adviser to the Government of Louis XVI on matters both of administration and finance. At Maurepas' request, for instance, he had many discussions with Vergennes about a plan for reorganizing the general system of tax-gathering; in one of his letters to Vergennes on this subject he writes that, 'I have given this statement of account in a very elementary manner, so that, when M. de Maurepas shows it to the King, his inexperience of such complicated affairs may not prevent him from understanding the details of it.' Later on, we find even the self-sufficient Necker consulting Beaumarchais, when problems arise over the distribution of the tobacco shipped from America, or of supplying the French troops which had been sent to America after the commencement of open hostilities between France and England in 1778. Yet until the late summer of that year this indispensable adviser to the King's Ministers was a man still under implication of being a forger! For it was not until July that the long-standing enemy La Blache was finally routed.

At the end of 1775, it is true, the Grand Council had annulled the judgment given against Beaumarchais in that case, and had referred the matter to a fresh hearing before the Parlement of Provence. But although La Blache had done his utmost to hurry the case on to a quick decision, Beaumarchais already had his hands sufficiently full with the necessity of clearing himself from the even more serious criminal charge involved in the Goezman case, as well as being in the very midst of organizing supplies for America. He therefore asked for a postpone-ment of the hearing, which he obtained through the support of Ver-gennes, to whom he was proving far too useful at this moment to be abandoned. The case was due for hearing at Aix-en-Provence in July; this suited Beaumarchais well enough, for he was obliged to visit Marseilles to superintend the despatch of two vessels to America. La Blache, meanwhile, had not been wasting his time; having surrounded himself with a squadron of no less than six legal advisers, he was busily preparing his campaign by the production of a pamphlet attacking his opponent. This he had distributed round the neighbourhood, where he was well known and had a certain amount of influence; but most unfortunately for him, his emissary inadvertently delivered one to the house where Beaumarchais and Gudin were lodging! Beaumarchais had already started his own defence with his usual weapon, his pen. The Aix pamphlets are on the whole not of the same quality as those against Goezman; possibly because the La Blache affair was lacking in those elements of drama and comedy which gave such scope in the Goezman case. The dispute with La Blache was indeed a dull enough legal wrangle, concerning itself with endless financial details, and the wearisome nature of the subject seems to have exercised a slightly blighting influence on Beaumarchais' usually exuberant wit. But the deliverance into his own hands of the enemy's missile gave him a superb opening of which he did not fail to take advantage in his second pamphlet. In it he describes how an excited messenger knocked at the door and thrust a pamphlet into his hands:

'M. le comte de la Blache begs you, sir, to interest yourself in his case.'
  'Eh! Do you know me, my friend?'
  'No, sir; but that doesn't matter at all; there are three of us running from door to door, and our instructions are not to forget even the convents and the shops.'
  'I am not curious, my friend, thank you.'
  'Ah, sir, accept it, I beg of you; I am so laden! So many people are refusing it.'
  'All right, then – and here are eight sous for your trouble and your present.'
  'Faith, sir, it's not worth that.'
He is still running, and I close my door.

If the La Blache pamphlets were not up to the standard of those on Goezman, they nevertheless fulfilled their purpose in ranging the public of Provence on Beaumarchais' side. But La Blache, finding that he was no match for Beaumarchais in a war of the pen, turned his efforts towards interviewing the judges, a procedure which, as Gudin says, Beaumarchais considered most improper. However, all the Count's moves availed him nothing when the case came up for hearing. The magistrates, after studying the matter in fifty-nine sittings, gave their verdict unanimously in favour of Beaumarchais. The agreement with Duverney was declared to be valid; La Blache was ordered to pay not only the costs but damages amounting to 12,000 livres for defamation of character, and his pamphlets were to be suppressed. Several of the judges were, however, heard by Gudin to remark that they would have awarded Beaumarchais even larger damages if they had not felt that he had already chastised his opponent sufficiently in his own pamphlets. Disapproving of the tone of these, they ordered him to give 1,000 écus to the poor of the town; whereupon Beaumarchais at once gave them 2,000, in order, he said 'to congratulate them on having such good and virtuous magistrates'.

The verdict was received in the town of Aix with the greatest rejoicing, the successful litigant being fêted with music and fireworks. Congratulation on his success was also to come to Beaumarchais from a wholly unexpected quarter. On their way back to Paris he and Gudin stopped in Lyon, 'to pay a few visits'. They were in process of calling on a certain countess when another visitor was announced: the Marquis d'Harrancourt, Chamberlain to Monsieur (the future Louis XVIII) and a brother of the Comte de la Blache. Even Beaumarchais' imperturbable assurance may have faltered at such a moment, but Gudin describes the surprising sequel:

He enters, perceives Beaumarchais, stops short, struck with astonishment, remains a few seconds without uttering a word, and then cries out: 'M. de Beaumarchais, I must either strangle you or embrace you.' And with these words, he casts himself into Beaumarchais' arms and presses him to his heart.

'You have just won your case, you have covered my brother with indelible ridicule, you have obliged me to change my name, for wherever anyone heard it spoken, when walking or on coming out of theatres, the crowd ran, and they would take me for your opponent; I would hear passages quoted from your pamphlets, and I would slip away as best I could. However, I cannot help doing you justice; the whole of our family condemned the Count's proceedings, but in his greed he would listen to nobody. We ourselves have been the victims of it.'

The spring of this same year 1778 saw the arrival in Paris of two celebrities who were each to have links with Beaumarchais' career. On 23 March the musical genius who eight years later would immortalize on the operatic stage Beaumarchais' second but as yet unborn comedy arrived with his mother in the city which he had last visited with his father and sister fifteen years before. But the Mozart of 1778 was no longer the child prodigy who in 1763 had provided the French capital with all the interest of amusing novelty, and although the little archduchess who had caressed him long ago at Schönbrunn was now Queen of France, she was at this time expecting her first child after eight years of unsatisfactory marriage, and had little thought to spare for her compatriot, whose very existence she had probably forgotten.

For his part, Mozart was now a serious young man of twenty-two, and conscious of his great gifts, which the frivolous society of Paris had not the capacity to appreciate. (What indeed was musical virtuosity but a slightly tiresome interference with that true function of the *salon*, the art of conversation?) The empty compliments showered on Mozart by polite society did not deceive him: 'They ask me to come on this or that day – I play, and then they say, "*O, c'est un prodige, c'est inconcevable, c'est étonnant*"–and then: "*Adieu*".' Baron Grimm, who had befriended the Mozarts on their previous visit, procured for Wolfgang an interview with the Duchesse de Bourbon; but the account he gives in a letter to his father of his reception by the Duchesse de Chabot shows the sort of treatment to be expected from the fashionable world of Paris – as well as giving a curious picture of conditions in the house of a great lady of France:

On my arrival I was ushered into a great room without any fire, and as cold as ice; and there I had to wait for half an hour until the Duchess came. At length she appeared, and very politely requested me to excuse the clavier, as not one in the house was in order, but said she would be very glad to hear me play. I replied that I should be most happy to play something, but that at present it was impossible, as I could not feel my fingers from cold, and I requested that she would have the goodness to let me go into a room in which there was a fire. *Oh oui, monsieur, vous avez raison* was the answer. She then sat down and began to draw, in company with several gentlemen, who all made a circle round a large table. This lasted for an hour, during which time I had the honour to be in attendance. The windows and doors were open, and my hands were not merely as cold as ice, but my feet and body too. . . . What most annoyed me was, that Madame and all the gentlemen pursued their drawing without a moment's cessation, and consequently I was obliged to play to the walls, chairs and tables.

Disappointment and frustration met Mozart at every turn in Paris, and not only as a performer on the clavier. Nearly all the compositions at which he worked so hard while in the French capital were either set aside on one excuse or another without being played or were produced by others as their own work. In July, a month of sweltering heat, his troubles were crowned by the death of his mother, who fell ill and died in the gloomy and unhealthy lodgings which she had endured for his sake. After her death Baron Grimm took Wolfgang into his own household; but this arrangement soon proved to be an embarrassment to Grimm, who was living with Mme d'Épinay at the time. Leopold Mozart's anxiety for his son to come home was a good excuse for the baron to rid himself of his guest, and he lost no time in arranging for Wolfgang's departure from Paris.

But the event which was the real sensation of the spring of 1778 was the reappearance of Voltaire, returning to Paris after thirty years of exile to supervise the production of his new tragedy, *Irène*, the last of his brain-children, begotten in his eighty-fourth year. It had taken some persuasion to induce the old sage to leave his sanctuary for the city where such fulminations had been hurled against him and his works; he could not forbear pointing out the possibility that forty thousand bigots would bless the chance of carrying forty thousand faggots to burn him at the stake. (Indeed, it had not been long since the question had been quite seriously asked why, when Voltaire's books had been publicly burned, their author should be allowed to escape.) However, he was told that he had eighty thousand friends in Paris 'who would all run to put out the fire, and, if it would amuse you, drown all the faggot-bearers'. He was also assured that he would be received with honour by the Court; but this proved to be wishful thinking, for the King's instant reaction was the terse enquiry: 'Has the order forbidding M. de Voltaire's return to Paris ever been annulled?' – even if subsequent enquiry revealed that in fact no such order had ever been issued! The old man was torn between a natural misgiving and his genuine wish to see old haunts and old friends once more before he died – or before they did, for many of them were older than he. (It does not seem to have occurred to anyone to wonder whether an octogenarian who for years had been in the frailest health would survive the long journey from Switzerland on eighteenth-century roads.) However, his longing to see Paris once more overcame his hesitations, and he set off from Ferney incognito on 3 February. But the incredibly lean old figure with the piercing eyes so full of fire and expression could not long remain unrecognized, and as he neared Paris his progress became more and more triumphal. On the afternoon of 10 February his carriage reached the Paris Customs barriers, and he was duly asked if there were anything to declare; to which the old sage could not resist replying that he thought there was nothing contraband except himself. His reception in Paris was delirious; even the dour Carlyle was to write of it later: 'Scarcely could the arrival of the Grand Lama of Tibet have excited greater ferment.' Despite the frosty official attitude of the Court, many of its members, as well as some of the Ministers, came to pay homage, and needless to say Beaumarchais was among the large number of admiring callers. Benjamin Franklin

even brought his grandson to see the eminent survivor of another
century and to receive his blessing: 'My child,' said the old philosopher
as he raised his hands over the boy's head, 'God and Liberty; remember
those two words.'

But all this, however gratifying it might be, was far too exhausting,
both physically and emotionally, for a fragile old man of eighty-four,
and when the time arrived for the first performance of *Irène* its author
was too ill to be present. Yet the acclamation which greeted the play
seemed to breathe new life into the dying embers, and Voltaire rallied
sufficiently to attend the sixth performance, remarking that he might
as well die in the theatre as in bed. On his way to the Théâtre Français
he visited the Academy, where he was treated to the unprecedented
honour of being received at the door by the entire body of acade-
micians, who unanimously elected him as their President. As he
remarked simply at the conclusion of this day: 'After so much honour,
it only remains for me to die.' But it was not until 25 May that the candle
which had been kept burning for so long by sheer will-power at last
flickered out. His body was smuggled out of Paris under cover of dark-
ness by his quick-witted nephew the Abbé Mignot, who gave it a proper
funeral at the Abbey of Sellières in Champagne; thereby foiling the
ecclesiastical fanatics who would have denied his uncle Christian burial.

At the time of Voltaire's death no complete edition of his works
existed, since a large number of them had been banned in France. The
bookseller Panckouche had been contemplating the production of one,
and Voltaire had been in process of correcting his works for this purpose at the time of his death; but after the author's exit Panckouche's
courage failed him, the venture appearing to him scarcely worth the
risks involved. According to Gudin's account the Empress Catherine
II of Russia proposed to Panckouche that his edition should be published in St Petersburg; Beaumarchais, having discovered this, hastened
to Versailles and pointed out to Maurepas what shame it would be for
France if she left it to the Russians to publish the works of the man who
had thrown such lustre on French literature. Maurepas saw this point,
but he also saw the perils threatening from Voltaire's two most irrecon-
cilable enemies, Church and magistracy. There was only one person,
he declared, who would be prepared to brave the risks of such an
enterprise: Beaumarchais himself. He promised royal protection for
the project if Beaumarchais would undertake it. This at least is Gudin's
version of the affair; but it was Gudin's habit to see the activities of his
friend through slightly rose-tinted spectacles. What is certain is that

Maurepas was a confirmed Voltairian who was probably not at all unwilling to support such a project on the quiet; while the patriotic aspect of the scheme as much as its undoubtedly grave difficulties and risks were just what would appeal to Beaumarchais. Here was something really big, far greater than the mere thirty-three volumes of Diderot's *Encyclopaedia*, far more worth while than supplying American insurgents. Beaumarchais, who was never one to do things by halves, threw himself into the project on a grand scale, with a reckless *panache* slightly startling in a careful man of business, especially one who was already so deeply committed in America.

As in the case of his American venture, he began by setting up a one-man concern, with a resounding title suitable to the nature of the work proposed: the *Société philosophique, littéraire et typographique*. He himself, the sole director, knew little about the technique of book production; but no matter, he would learn: 'In a craft whose details are less familiar to me than its principles, I take advice from everyone and then act according to my own results.' He sent an agent to Holland for the purpose of studying the manufacture of paper, another to England to purchase the Baskerville type, considered the best of its time, for 150,000 livres; then he set up three paper-mills in the Vosges. It was an essential condition of Maurepas' support that the actual printing should be done outside France, so Beaumarchais rented a disused fortress belonging to the Margrave of Baden at Kehl, and here set up his printing-works, which he put in charge of an able young man named Le Tellier. So far so good, even if costly enough. But now he began to run into difficulties; for book production turned out to be a far more complex affair than he had supposed. The text itself presented many complications: it required careful checking, so that any material of doubtful authenticity could be weeded out; selection had to be made of letters out of Voltaire's vast correspondence; commentaries and notes had to be added, which were done for the most part – rather indifferently, in the opinion of La Harpe – by Condorcet, Beaumarchais making only a few contributions here and there. Then the Margrave of Baden began to develop qualms about the publication of certain passages in *Candide* where Voltaire has his fun at the expense of German princelings, in his portrayal of the Baron de Thunder-ten-Tronckh ('one of the most powerful lords of Westphalia, for his *château* had a door and windows'), his Baroness, weighing 350 lbs., and their daughter, the fair Cunegonde. The Empress Catherine of Russia began to have even worse qualms about the publication of her correspondence with the old sage, and insisted upon its being segregated, so that a little discreet censorship could be exercised. At Kehl, Le Tellier, though efficient, turned out to be an arrogant and unpleasant character who soon antagonized those who worked under him, causing endless trouble with the printing staff. Beaumarchais had to try to instil in him some common sense and human understanding, in a letter which shows how much of these qualities he possessed himself:

The people of Kehl seem to me to be greatly incensed against you. It sometimes needs no more than this to spoil the best undertaking. I am sure you are always strictly in the right, but from where I stand, it seems to me that the rigidity of your arguments and the haughtiness of your bearing often alienate from you those whom a little more kindness would keep attached to you. . . . Just think: I have not received a single letter since you have been concerned with this Voltaire business which does not bring me some complaint about you, whether it comes from Paris, London, Deux-Ponts or Kehl! In short, I am being perpetually attacked from every quarter. It is impossible not to conclude that, with the best intentions in the world, you are isolating yourself by an immeasurable disdain which offends ordinary people, who always judge a man by external appearances. You will tell me it is not your fault if you are so badly served; but I reply that in the mass, people and workmen are the same everywhere, and that everywhere businesses are set up with agents worth no more than those you are employing, and that in general all the complaints made about you are founded on your air of disdainful superiority which offends everybody. This unbending haughtiness is what has just been the undoing of M. Necker. A man may have the very greatest talents, but from the moment he sells his superiority too dearly to those under him, he makes himself just so many enemies and everything goes to the devil without its being anybody's fault.

The size of the undertaking, as well as the difficulties arising, caused progress to be slow, and publication had not yet begun when in 1781 Maurepas died. His removal from the scene caused a resurgence of hostility towards Beaumarchais' project from both Church and Law, and an anonymous brochure was circulated denouncing it to the Parlement. But this peril was successfully stifled as Maurepas' successor Calonne continued his policy of support. Publication of the books, however, did not start until 1783, and before then, unfortunately for Beaumarchais' an edition of Voltaire's works appeared in Geneva. Moreover, the general financial situation in France was now growing so bad that people were less and less inclined to indulge in such an expensive purchase as a complete edition of Voltaire, who was in any case beginning to lose his vogue. Thus for the 15,000 copies of the edition printed, Beaumarchais received no more than 2,000 subscriptions, in spite of his efforts to stimulate sales by the offer of tickets in a 200,000 francs lottery to the first 400,000 subscribers. Complete publication was not finished until 1790, by which time Beaumarchais confessed to the Director-General of Posts, d'Oguy, who had been one of his secret supporters, conniving at the introduction of the prohibited volumes into France, that the business had cost him a loss of over a million livres; although he had used his establishment at Kehl for the publication of an edition of Rousseau, as well as several other works. The only concrete result of his speculation over Voltaire was to saddle him with mountainous piles of unsold print, which he was obliged to store in his new mansion in Paris, where in the dark days so soon to come they would be viewed with the deepest suspicion by red-bonneted representatives of the sovereign people.

Gudin says that Beaumarchais had a remarkable ability, when making sudden changes of occupation, to switch his whole attention as rapidly and completely on to the new object as it had been concentrated on the former one; a process which he himself described as 'shutting the drawer on a matter'. This is perhaps the key to his astonishing capacity for being able to deal with so many complicated affairs at the same time. We have seen him shipping arms to America, advising the French Government on its foreign policy and its domestic administration, conducting his own defence in the final round with La Blache. and embarking on a huge publishing venture; all of which were combined with a gay social life. But there was still time, at the beginning of 1779, for the descendant of the Calvinist watch-makers of Brie to take up his pen on behalf of the Protestant merchants of Bordeaux, who on account of their religion were being denied, by a policy of short-sighted bigotry, the right of admission to the Chamber of Commerce in that town. Beaumarchais writes to the Ministers:

A barbarous fanaticism debars Protestant merchants from entry to this Chamber, while in other more sensible towns such as Marseille and La Rochelle they pay so little attention to differences of religion in matters which have no bearing on it that at this moment the very deputy for the commerce of La Rochelle is a Protestant. When the English, much more embittered against Papists than we are against Anglicans, are today mitigating the lot of the unfortunate Catholics in the three kingdoms, and give us such a fine example of civil toleration; above all, when the King of France has deigned to confide the administration of finances to a man of genius who is neither French nor of the religion of the prince*; is it not the moment to present to his Council the request that I

* i.e. Necker, who was both Swiss and a Protestant.

am making unofficially on behalf of all the French merchants of the kingdom, for the honourable right to co-operate with Catholics in the benefit resulting from the institution and meetings of a Chamber of Commerce in each wealthy town?

Now even if it were not well known that, in our ports, Protestant commercial houses are the richest and most stable of all; even if it were not proved that nobody contributes more cheerfully, more abundantly and with a better grace to the relief of the unfortunate, to all taxes imposed to this end; even if it is not certain that on every occasion these houses give to the King's other subjects an example of devotion and patriotism: surely a simple process of reasoning would convince that these useful families, separated by difference of religion from everything which is offered to the ambition of a Catholic . . . must become in a little time the pillars of commerce and the firmest supporters of this honourable condition.

In our great towns, notably at Bordeaux, if one gathered together the property of all the Protestant merchants, one would find that the mass and extent of their business form an immense capital and that their industry considerably augments the revenues of the State. . . .

It is not then the well-known benevolence of His Majesty that I implore here for honest men who have not charged me to ask for it; it is the enlightened policy of his Council that I invoke, in order that the heads of Protestant houses may be attached more and more to their condition, to commerce and to the motherland, by being admitted to the Chamber of Commerce.

During these years, too, the man who described himself as 'the most cruel enemy of all that one calls lost time' was able to find yet another occupation for his pen. In the midst of his many other activities, he was writing the new comedy which would be the crowning achievement of his career as a dramatist.

Chapter 14

THE MARRIAGE OF FIGARO

WHEN *The Barber of Seville* had appeared in 1775, the Prince de Conti, declaring that the preface was even more amusing than the play itself, had challenged Beaumarchais to write a sequel. Within twelve months the creator of Figaro had produced the outline of a further set of adventures for his characters; although Gudin says that Beaumarchais had been planning this new play in his mind for a long time, 'and even at long intervals'.

In this sequel to his first comedy we meet the same three principal figures; but the Countess Almaviva now has a maid by the name of Suzanne, who is about to be married to Figaro, and the page Chérubin makes his appearance, as yet only a child in years but as precocious as his author at the same age, with a keenly awakening interest in the opposite sex. Count Almaviva, however, whose fancy wanders as frequently and incorrigibly as his author's, has already lost interest in the wife whom he won in the first comedy largely through the aid of the resourceful Figaro. As for that man of many trades, he is in the Count's service again, but now has to employ his keen wits in frustrating his master's strictly dishonourable intentions towards his own bride-to-be Suzanne. The Count's defeat is finally brought about and all ends happily after a breathless succession of the complicated intrigues, plots and counter-plots in which Beaumarchais revels in both his comedies. The first of these is in fact the better constructed of the two, since *The Marriage of Figaro* is unnecessarily drawn out, from the middle onwards, by incidents which hold up the action of the play, so that the final winding up of the plot is only reached at the end of five acts. Beaumarchais submitted his draft – under its first title of *La Folle Journée* – to the Prince de Conti at the beginning of 1776. But another four years were to elapse before its busy author could find the time to complete it, and yet another three before it was actually performed; for, as it was later said, more wit was needed to get *The Marriage of Figaro* produced than was ever required for the writing of it.

Having completed the play in 1780, Beaumarchais submitted the script to his old friends of the Comédie-Française, who received it, he says, with acclamation (no doubt they were now suitably chastened by their several years' battle with him over the question of authors' rights).

But all was not yet to be plain sailing:

> As soon as the actors had received with acclamation this poor *Marriage*, which
> has since had so many opponents, I begged M. Lenoir [the Lieutenant of Police]
> to appoint a censor, asking him as a special favour that the piece might not be
> read by any other person; which he readily promised. . . . Six weeks afterwards,
> I learned in society that my piece had been read in all the *soirées* of Versailles. . . .
> Well or ill read, or maliciously criticized, the piece was pronounced detestable,
> and without my knowing where I had sinned, because they expressed nothing
> in the usual way. . . . But as this proscription of the Court had only stirred up
> the curiosity of the town, I was condemned to readings without number. . . .

The disapproval of the Court to which Beaumarchais refers was no
less than that of the King, who had decided that he must form his own
opinion of the work by reading it himself. Mme Campan, whom we
have already met in attendance on Mesdames, the King's aunts, was
now Reader to the Queen, and she tells how she received a summons
one morning from Marie-Antoinette to present herself at 3 p.m. that
day. She was to have her dinner first, because she would be kept a
very long time. She continues:

> When I arrived in the inner room of Her Majesty, I found her alone with the
> King. A seat and a little table were already placed in front of them, and on the
> table was placed an enormous manuscript in several folders. 'It is Beaumarchais'
> comedy', said the King to me. 'You must read it to us; there will be some very
> difficult passages, on account of the erasures and references back; I have already
> run through it, but I want the Queen to be acquainted with this work. You
> will speak to no one of the reading you are about to give.'
>
> I began. The King often interrupted me by exclamations, always apposite,
> whether of praise or blame. Most frequently, he would cry out: 'This is bad
> taste. . .!' In Figaro's monologue, in which he attacks various parts of the ad-
> ministration, but particularly in the tirade against State prisons, the King
> jumped up with animation and declared: 'It is detestable! That shall never be
> played; it would be necessary to destroy the Bastille before the presentation
> of this play would not be a dangerous piece of inconsequence! This man mocks
> at everything which ought to be respected in a Government.'
>
> 'It will not be played, then?' said the Queen. 'No, certainly not,' replied
> Louis XVI, 'you can be sure of it!'

This first version of the play which Mme Campan read to the King
and Queen certainly underwent a number of amendments later on, at
the hands both of its author and of the censors, without whose approval
no play could be produced. The scene of the piece, for instance, was
first laid in France, at the *château* of Fraiche-Fontaine, which clearly
derived from that of Chanteloup, seat of the exiled Duc de Choiseul

and particularly familiar to Beaumarchais because close to the Forest of Chinon. The identity of the setting (complete with love-lorn page Petit Louis and the dog named Lindore) was perhaps too obvious; the scene was later discreetly transferred to Aguas-Frescas, near Seville, and Figaro's mention of the Bastille by name was cut out.

But a man so resourceful as Beaumarchais was not to be defeated by what he called 'the proscription of the Court'. He would fight back by deliberately stirring up public curiosity with constant readings of his play. In any case, the Court was far from being unanimously against him; even the Queen's close friend, the Princesse de Lamballe, sent the Duc de Fronsac, son of the old Duc de Richelieu, to Beaumarchais with the request that he would come and read his play to her at her house in Versailles. The King's youngest brother, the Comte d'Artois, having already embarked on the career of lifelong intrigue and opposition to his brothers, which would eventually end, as the wittiest of them said, in his finally intriguing against himself, must needs now come forward as the champion of Beaumarchais' play, since his brother had forbidden its performance. In St Petersburg, where *The Barber of Seville* had been given fifty performances, the Empress Catherine was all impatience for its sequel, and at the end of 1781 her Chamberlain sent a request to Beaumarchais through Daubcourt, a French actor at the Russian Court, begging him to let them have a copy of his new comedy as soon as possible. In the following spring, Paris was visited by the heir to the Russian throne, the Grand Duke Paul, and his wife, travelling under the name of the Count and Countess du Nord, and Baron Grimm, with a finger in every literary and social pie, undertook to inform Beaumarchais that they would like to hear him read his play; which he did, with great success.

Some of those who attended these readings have left us interesting glimpses of the scene. The usual sounds of *salon* life are suddenly stilled, as with a rustling of rich materials and the discreet clicking of dress swords a large circle is formed in which everyone takes his or her place: the young girls in their hoops, the women wearing the famous plumed headdress *à la Quesaco*, and behind their undulating seated ranks, the heads and shoulders of the men, with their enormous hair-bags sweeping their shoulders, their small tricorn hats in hand, and the scarlet coats with black buttons which open to display the dazzling hues of their waistcoats. Meanwhile, the author, enthroned on a raised stand, opens a red-ribboned manuscript, which he steadies with one hand while the other, upon which scintillates a large diamond ring, is used for expressive gestures. He begins with a prologue whose erasures, visible from afar, show what trouble he has taken to woo his listeners. He reads with great verve, occasionally pausing slightly to slip in some comment on his text. The latter, written in that blend of Rabelais and Voltaire which Beaumarchais himself described as his alliance of 'the old and free gaiety' with 'the light tone of our present-day wit', is evidently considered more than a little outspoken in places, even by so sophisticated an audience; for the Baronne d'Oberkirch notes that certain well-bred ladies, blushing under their powder and patches, take frequent refuge behind their fans. The men, however, standing on tiptoe in order to see over the heads of those in the front rows of the large gathering, punctuate with their laughter the cunningly timed pauses, or guffaw at the sallies which he launches in mordant tones while all the time keeping a watchful eye on the important members of his audience, to see how they are taking it. The reading finishes in a general outburst of laughter, and the audience crowds round Beaumarchais who does not fail to make mention of the difficulty into which he has been thrown by the ban laid upon his 'little work' ; written entirely, as he assures the Lieutenant of Police, for the amusement of the King and Queen.

This cleverly staged pantomime was repeated in numerous other houses of the great, who one by one were enlisted in Beaumarchais' cause. Emboldened by success and by the open support of a large section of the Court, headed by the Comte d'Artois, arrangements were now made on the quiet for production of the play at the royal theatre of the Menus-Plaisirs, which was used for operatic rehearsals, and tickets were distributed among a large number of aristocratic supporters. It seems to have been not until the morning of the appointed day that the plan leaked out, by which time the whole Court was talking of it. 'I do not know,' said the bewildered Lieutenant of Police, 'by whose permission they are giving M. Beaumarchais' play this evening at the Menus; but what I do know is that the King does not wish to have it performed.' He lost no time in seeing that Louis XVI was made aware of what was afoot, and soon after midday an order arrived from the King forbidding the performance. On the following day the Lieutenant of Police assembled the actors both of the Comédie-Française and the Comédie-Italienne and expressly forbade them, in the name of the King, to play Beaumarchais' comedy in any theatre or any place whatsoever.

The cancelling of the performance entailed an appreciable financial loss to its author, who in a flash of irritated defiance declared that his piece should be played even if the performance had to be in the choir of Notre-Dame; after which outburst, he removed himself to England on business. The unhappy King now found himself surrounded by a sullenly resentful Court muttering about 'oppression' and 'tyranny'. But as he was seldom able to maintain any firm decision for long in the face of determined opposition, he presently yielded to the pressure being brought to bear upon him by Marie-Antoinette and the Comte d'Artois, and consented to give permission for the banned play to be privately performed at the Duc de Fronsac's property of Gennevilliers. Beaumarchais, still in England, received a triumphant letter from Fronsac, dated 4 September 1783, and written with the duke's usual joyous disregard for spelling (illiteracy was the least of his failings):

I hope, Monsieur, that you will not object that I write to obtain your consent to have *The Marriage of Figaro* played at Gennevilliers. . . .

You know that I have for several years turned over my estate of Genne-villiers to M. de Vaudreuil. M. le Comte d'Artois comes there to hunt on the 18th, and Mme la Duchesse de Polignac with her society comes to supper. Vaudreuil has asked me to arrange a performance, for there is a good enough hall. I told him that there was nothing more charming than *The Marriage of Figaro*, but that we must have the consent of the King. *We have secured that* and I went running to find you, and was astonished and distressed to find that you were far away in the north.

Will you not give your consent that the piece should be played? I promise you that I will do my utmost to have it well done. M. le Comte d'Artois and his whole set are waiting with the greatest eagerness to see it, and certainly it will be a great step forward towards having it given at Fontainebleau and Paris. . . . I, in particular, have the greatest desire and I beg you to reply quickly, quickly. Let it be favourable, I beg you, and never doubt my gratitude and the esteem and friendship with which I shall always be, Monsieur, yours, etc. . . .

Beaumarchais hurried back to France instantly on receipt of this letter. But before the play could be presented, he insisted on a fresh censor-ship. This was a skilful move, since his purpose was to clear the ground for a public performance, and the time was well chosen when the piece was about to be played at a Court festivity; for who would dare to ban it at such a moment? Indeed, nobody did, least of all the historian Gaillard, who had been appointed censor and who passed the piece with only two small suggestions for amendment. But Beaumarchais was out to ensure that the price of agreement to the performance at

Gennevilliers should be the right of public performance in Paris; as he
wrote:

The piece being again approved, I took the precaution to warn that it must not
be played at the fête until I had the express promise from the magistrate that
the Comédie-Française might consider it as belonging to their theatre, and I
will certify that this assurance was given to me by M. Lenoir, who certainly
thought everything finished, as I might have thought myself.

So Beaumarchais' play was duly performed at Gennevilliers before
the assembled courtiers, who were enchanted to see themselves mocked
and held up to ridicule. On the very next day the author boldly applied
to the Lieutenant of Police for permission to have his play performed
in Paris. Louis XVI must have realized that his first line of defence had
now been carried, but he was not yet ready to admit total defeat. As
Beaumarchais noted, in the same memorandum:

Two months afterwards, the Lieutenant of Police told me that the King had
deigned to reply that *there were still things, he was told*, which should not remain
in the work; that one or two new censors should be named, and that the author
would be able to amend his piece the more easily as it was long. M. Lenoir had
the kindness to add that he looked upon this letter of the King as a raising of the
ban upon the playing of this piece, immediately after its examination by the
new censors.

The determined author was advancing inch by inch, consolidating his
position as he did so. But delay occurred over the appointment of the
third censor, and Beaumarchais in exasperation wrote once more to
Lenoir on 27 November 1783:

Sir – If the multiplicity of your occupations makes you forget that I also have
many, and that during the last three months I have gone fifty times from the
Marais to your hotel, without having been able to speak to you more than five
times, to obtain the most simple thing – a decision about a frivolous work –
you would perhaps have compassion on the pitiful part that I am forced to play
in this comedy. If you are required to load me with mortifications, I assure you
that I have drunk the cup to the very dregs; if it is a question of an absolute
prohibition of all that proceeds from my pen, why let me wait so long for the
order, and deny me all means of knowing what I am to do? . . .

This appeal resulted in the play getting as far as the third censor, who
duly passed it after a few modifications. Louis XVI, in slow and unwilling retreat, now demanded a fourth censor, who trimmed the
piece a little more and then passed it. The King demanded a fifth; this
one passed it without making any corrections at all. Yet a sixth was

appointed, one Suard, who at last did what was expected of him and banned it. But it was too late; neither he nor his royal master could now stem the flood of popular clamour (nor the increased pressure being applied by Marie-Antoinette and the Polignacs) for the public performance of the play, and since it was now being whispered in the King's ear that the piece would probably prove a disappointment after all the carefully fanned publicity, he decided that the simplest course was perhaps after all to allow its performance.

So at last, in March 1784, permission was given for *The Marriage of Figaro* to be played at the Comédie-Française, and its author lost no time in getting to work on rehearsals. The first performance was to take place on 27 April, and up to the last minute the King clung to the hope that the play would prove to be a flop. As the Marquis de Montesquiou was setting out for the theatre Louis asked him his opinion: 'Sire,' replied the Marquis, 'I hope that the piece will fail.' 'So do I,' was the King's heartfelt reply. But their hopes were doomed to the bitterest disappointment, for 'never', says Baron Grimm, 'did a piece attract such a concourse at the Théâtre Français. All Paris wished to see this famous *Marriage*, and the auditorium was filled almost from the moment the doors were opened to the public; scarcely half of those who had been besieging the theatre since eight o'clock in the morning were able to get seats; the greater part forced their way in, throwing their money to the door-keepers. . . . More than one duchess thought herself lucky that day to find a wretched little stool in the balconies where well-bred women would scarcely sit. . . .' The Duchesse de Bourbon sent her footmen to wait at the booking-office from eleven o'clock in the morning for the distribution of tickets which was not due to begin until 4 p.m. But some three hundred persons of quality took even more drastic measures, shutting themselves up in the players' dressing-rooms all day and eating there, in order to make sure of getting into the theatre that evening. The President of Parlement, Dupaty, to whom Beaumarchais had sent a ticket for a box, wrote blandly to enquire if the box in question could be exchanged for one on the ground floor where the occupants could not be seen, as he was proposing to take three ladies who did not approve of the piece and would not come unless their presence could be concealed. Beaumarchais' reply was trenchant:

I have no respect, M. le Président, for women who permit themselves to see a spectacle which they consider indelicate, provided they see it in secret. I do not lend myself to such whims. I have given my piece to the public for their amusement, not for their instruction; nor to offer prim fools the pleasure of thinking well of it inside a box, on condition of speaking ill of it in society. The pleasure of vice and the honours of virtue: such is the prudery of the day. My piece is not an ambiguous work; one must either take it or leave it.

I greet you, M. le Président, and keep my box.

La Harpe says that when the booking offices opened, the crush was so great that three persons were suffocated; that the performance was 'tumultuous', and so long that it was not over until ten o'clock, although there was no other piece on the programme, which was unusual.

'*The Marriage of Figaro*', says Grimm, 'had, from the very first performance, a prodigious success', and its triumphant progress continued, so that by the end of the eight months following its first performance on 27 April 1784 it had brought the Comédie-Française a gross profit of 346,197 livres, of which Beaumarchais' share as author was estimated at 41,499 livres. It is clear that by this time he must have been once more in prosperous financial circumstances after all his past troubles, for he now decided that the proceeds of the new play should be used to found a charitable institution for the benefit of poor nursing mothers: he wrote to the *Journal de Paris* announcing his scheme:

... At the risk of being again looked upon as a vain man, I will devote all my *Figaro* to this purpose; it is money which belongs to me, which I have gained by my labour in spite of torrents of printed and written abuse. Now when the actors have received 200,000 francs, my nurses will have 28,000; with the 30,000 from my friends I shall have a whole regiment of children fattening upon the maternal milk. All this compensates for a great many insults.

The Comédie-Française, not to be outdone in generosity by the man from whom they had themselves so greatly benefited, decided to devote the entire proceeds of the fiftieth performance of *The Marriage of Figaro* to its author's new project. But even when it was a question of a philanthropic undertaking, Beaumarchais met with the usual opposition from his enemies, who succeeded in stifling the scheme in Paris. However, the Archbishop of Lyon proved to be a prelate of more practical common sense, and in that city a flourishing Maternal Benevolent Institution came into being, created from the earnings of *Figaro*.

Baron Grimm said truly of this play that 'the author ... has put into the mouth of Figaro the greater part of the events which have made his own life so extraordinarily celebrated; he depicts, with an audacity to which we have so far had no parallel, the way of life, the ignorance and the baseness of the great; he dares to make fun of the Ministers, the Bastille, the liberty of the Press, the police, and even the censors. . . .' He also gives the magistrates their turn: in the court scene at the end of the third act, when the Count hopes to further his designs on Suzanne by compelling Figaro to marry Marceline, there is more than an echo of Beaumarchais' own lawsuits, in the characters of the judge, Don Guzman Brid'oison, and his clerk of the court, Double-Main. But it is in Figaro's monologue in Act V that the bitterness pent up inside his author, the accumulation of all that had happened to him during his career, really bursts forth, in his jibes at the *grand seigneur* who, with all his rank and fortune, has achieved no more in the world than to give himself the trouble to be born; whereas Figaro, 'lost in the obscure multitude', has had to employ 'more skill and calculation merely to subsist than has been put into governing all the dominions of Spain these hundred years'. As for the liberty of the Press: 'provided that I do not speak in my writings of the Government, religion, politics, public morals, people in office, respected public bodies, the Opera, other spectacles, nor of anyone connected with anything, I can publish every-thing freely, subject to the inspection of two or three censors.' Gambling and its devotees also receive attention: 'I set myself up as a banker at faro; then, good folks, I sup in town, and those supposed to be *comme il faut* politely throw open their houses to me, while hanging onto three-quarters of the profits for themselves.' No wonder that when Mme Campan read these lines to the King and Queen, even the easy-going Louis XVI sprang to his feet in indignation. For the shaft struck home: during the first years of his reign, Marie-Antoinette's passionate addiction to faro and her heavy losses in play had made a painful impression, particularly at a time when the Government was officially campaigning against gambling. As for the central character of Beaumarchais' piece, in this second comedy as in the first we can scarcely fail to recognize, in Figaro's description of himself, the portrait of his author: 'ardent in pleasure, working at all trades to make a living, ambitious by vanity, laborious by necessity, poet for relaxation, musician now and then, lover in mad bursts; I have seen everything, done everything, made use of everything'.

The Baronne d'Oberkirch went to see *The Marriage of Figaro* some little time after its first performance, though in order to get in she was still obliged to fight her way through the crowd ('it was even worse than at the Tuileries'). But while describing the piece as 'an immortal masterpiece, I would say, of impropriety' which would always amuse, she could yet see graver implications lying beneath its surface of light-hearted wit. 'It appears to me,' she writes, 'that the nobility showed a great want of tact in applauding it, which was nothing less than giving themselves a slap in the face. They laughed at their own expense, and, what was worse, they made others laugh too. They will repent it yet. The jokes that amused them were directed against themselves, and they do not see it. Their own caricature has been held up before them, and they reply: "That is it; it is very like." What inexplicable blindness!' She adds that on leaving the theatre 'my heart was oppressed by what I had seen' and that she was enraged against herself for having been amused.

But the fact that *The Marriage of Figaro* had its first public perform-ance only five years before the beginning of the French Revolution is probably what has contributed most to giving it a political significance far beyond its author's intention, or beyond what most of its contem-porary audiences saw in it. (Though Danton was later to declare that 'Figaro killed the nobility'.) Beaumarchais' first aim was to amuse, and if in doing so he seized the opportunity to hit back with the weapon of ridicule against those at whose hands he had suffered, who can blame him? But because he was always a rebel against privilege and the arbit-rary use of power, that is not to say that he was a full-blown revolu-tionary of the type so soon to become familiar. He had now at last reached a position of fame and affluence, in which he would have everything to lose and nothing to gain by a great social upheaval, and he was not the man to throw away what he had achieved only after years of uphill struggle. For a dramatist to pillory society and to make the small laugh at the expense of the great was, after all, no new thing; Molière and many others had done it, and society had survived their onslaughts. Strange as it may seem to us now, looking back from the distance of nearly two centuries across the panorama of succeeding events, there were many people in the Paris of 1784 who were still serenely unaware how near was the edge of the precipice towards which the *ancien régime* was inexorably sliding. These people could enjoy seeing their friends mocked on the stage (the ridicule could not, of course, include themselves) with a happy detachment which sur-prised even the author of the play: 'There is something more outrage-ous than my piece, and that is its success.' There can be no doubt that Beaumarchais' comedy caught the spirit of the hour (Figaro has been called the personification of the Third Estate), but to see in it a direct cause of the French Revolution is surely to take little account of such far more important and long-standing factors as an antiquated administrative system and a social structure based on relics of feudalism, both of which were finally to collapse under the pressure of acute economic stress.

But Beaumarchais' enemies, led by Suard, the only censor who had banned his play, continued their attacks upon him, enraged as it would seem by the comedy's very success. Suard was secretly supported by the Comte de Provence (the future Louis XVIII), who, having attended the first performance of *The Marriage of Figaro*, had been greatly incensed by it. Beaumarchais bore the attacks, which appeared in the *Journal de Paris*, with good humour at first; but as they grew more and more venomous he at last wrote to the editors, on 6 March 1785, concluding his letter with the rather strangely expressed sentence: 'When I have had to overcome lions and tigers to get a comedy played, do you think to reduce me, after its success, like a Dutch maidservant, to beat out every morning the vile insect of the night?' (Suard, it may be mentioned, was very small.) But unfortunately for Beaumarchais, it was not only Suard with whom he had to deal: behind the small form of the 'insect' there stood the portly figure of the Comte de Provence, who now insinuated to his royal brother that the 'lions and tigers' represented the sovereigns of France. Although it would scarcely be possible to imagine anyone less like either of those fierce beasts than Louis XVI, he had already been so severely tried with Beaumarchais that his long-suffering patience gave way. He was sitting playing cards at the time, and in a sudden burst of exasperated fury quite out of keeping with his usual good nature he wrote on one of the cards – a seven of spades – the order that Beaumarchais should be arrested and taken to St Lazare prison. Now this place of confinement was then used only for young delinquents, and when the news spread on the following morning that the fifty-three-year-old author of *The Marriage of Figaro* had been treated like an unruly adolescent all Paris sniggered. But by the following day people were beginning to demand to know why Beaumarchais had been arrested; a question to which the Government was not in a position to give any reply. The public mutterings grew louder, and by the fourth day had grown into a clamour of general protest against what was considered to be an act of arbitrary tyranny. 'People are enquiring,' said the writer of an anonymous pamphlet, 'whether anyone can be sure of sleeping tonight in his own bed.' Meanwhile Beaumarchais' hand had as usual flown to his pen, and he had written a letter to the King, in which he explained away, as best he could, the phrasing of his unfortunate remark; his purpose, he declared, being merely to illustrate two extremes in the scale of comparison. 'But should anyone persist in thinking there could exist any being in France so completely mad as to wish to offend the King, in a letter submitted to the censorship, and published in a newspaper, have I up to now given signs of such a madness that people should hazard such an accusation against me without proof?' By this time the King's natural good humour and sense of justice had reasserted themselves; probably too he was not a little dismayed at the the storm which his hasty action had aroused. Calonne was therefore instructed to write to Beaumarchais informing him that the King accepted his explanation and would be pleased to take every opportunity of demonstrating his good-will. No time was lost in releasing the prisoner from St Lazare; though the aggrieved victim of the royal wrath would have been prepared to remain in the prison until a charge had been brought against him in the proper form. Baron Grimm says that the performance of *The Marriage of Figaro* which was given immediately after Beaumarchais came out of prison was a particularly brilliant one, that nearly all the Ministers were present, and that they were thus able to witness the frenzied applause which greeted Figaro's statement in his monologue that 'not being able to disparage intellect, they avenge themselves by persecuting it'.

The King now gave visible signs of his renewed favour by allowing a performance of *The Barber of Seville* to be given in the theatre of the Petit Trianon, to which the author was invited, to see the Queen playing the part of Rosine and the Comte d'Artois that of Figaro. There were further, and even more substantial signs of the royal favour: Beaumarchais received payment of 800,000 francs in respect of the loss he had suffered over his ships when Admiral d'Estaing had conscripted the *Fier Roderigue* before engaging the British fleet. This was actually the third instalment of a sum which now amounted to a total of 2,275,625 livres paid to Beaumarchais as compensation in this affair, and it gives some idea of the large scale of the financial operations undertaken by the former pupil of Pâris-Duverney.

The Marriage of Figaro marks the triumphant climax of its author's career, both as a dramatist and as a man of business. But it was also in another respect an important landmark in Beaumarchais' life. For from now onward his star, which had scintillated so brilliantly in the Parisian firmament, would gradually begin to wane; as surely as the society he had satirized would itself presently crumble into ruins around him, in the tumult and blood of revolution.

Chapter 15

OPERATIC INTERLUDE

WHILE Beaumarchais was engaged on his long struggle to get *The Marriage of Figaro* publicly performed on the stage of the Théâtre Français, a new career was developing for his characters, which was to bring them even more widespread and enduring fame.

The Court of St Petersburg had been a stronghold of Italian opera ever since the Empress Anne had imported an Italian company in 1734, and for the rest of the eighteenth century many prominent Italian composers of the day visited St Petersburg from time to time. The Empress Catherine II, a keen patroness of the arts, had carried on this tradition, and in 1776 had invited to her Court for a period as Music Director the composer Giovanni Paisiello, who had begun his career in Naples and had subsequently acquired European fame as a composer of comic operas; *opera buffa*, as it was called, providing a welcome and exhilarating change of diet from the rather awful solemnity of *opera seria*, which, steeped in the gloomy legends of classical antiquity, had been reigning undisputed for some fifty years. Beaumarchais' comedy *The Barber of Seville* had had a great success at the Russian Court, and it now occured to Paisiello to make it into an opera, using the libretto of his compatriot Giuseppe Petrosellini, who made a 'dramatic comedy' of two acts out of Beaumarchais' four. Petrosellini follows the plot of the original fairly closely, though he gives more importance to the character of the old guardian, Dr Bartholo, who is made the embodiment of staid conservatism, than he does to Figaro, who is no more than a comic. But Paisiello's music is only a tentative beginning of what Mozart was soon afterwards to bring into full flower; written in the conventional language of the eighteenth century, it is full of beautiful themes, which however, are never fully developed, but, as Stendhal said, are merely repeated in variations, each one of which is more graceful than the other. Nevertheless, Paisiello's *Barber* had a great success in its day, and indeed was to remain for the next thirty years one of the most popular works in the repertoire of European opera. Its first performance took place in St Petersburg on 15 September 1782 (though unfortunately no one who was present has left us any account of the occasion) and exactly two years later it was performed at Versailles.

In the same year, 1784, the period of his appointment in Russia having come to an end, Paisiello left St Petersburg to return to Naples, a rich as well as a successful man. For during his stay at the Russian Court he had continued to receive the substantial salary paid to him by the King of Naples, in addition to the large one with which the Empress Catherine had enticed him into making the long journey north to St Petersburg. On his way south he paused in Vienna, where several works he had been commissioned to write for the Emperor Joseph were about to be produced. The famous musicologist Dr Burney, who had visited Vienna a few years before, on his tour of European music centres, wrote that the city 'is so rich in composers, and encloses within its walls such a number of musicians of superior merit, that it is but just to allow it to be, among German cities, the imperial seat of music, as well as of power'. The Emperor Joseph II, who was now ruling alone since the death of his mother, Maria Theresa, in 1780, was a keen musician who frequently took part himself in the daily concerts given at Court, playing either the 'cello or harpsichord, or singing operatic arias in a pleasing bass voice. In Vienna, as in St Petersburg, Italian opera held the stage at this period, for although the Emperor had tried to promote a revival of German opera (which like much else in Germany had been trampled out of existence during the Thirty Years War) by making the imperial theatre a national institution, the results had disappointed him. Certainly Mozart had written his *Entführung aus dem Serail*, which had had a favourable reception by the public, but it had not altogether met with the imperial approval. ('Too fine for our ears, and an immense number of notes, my dear Mozart'!) Finding, however, that the massive Teutonic masterpieces he awaited did not appear at his order, the Emperor evidently considered that he had done his duty by German music, and reverted to his own preference by returning the use of his theatre to the Italians, who gave performances of opera three times a week, while the remaining four days were devoted to German plays. The Irish tenor Michael Kelly (whose name, for professional purposes, was Italianized as Signor Ochelli) has left in his memoirs an entertaining account of his career in Vienna. He says that while he was still in Venice he received a message to call upon the Austrian Ambassador, 'who informed me that he had received a letter from Prince Rosenberg, Grand Chamberlain of His Majesty Joseph II, Emperor of Germany, directing him to engage a company of Italian singers for a comic opera, to be given at the Court of Vienna; that no expense was to be spared, so that the artists were of the first order; that no secondary talent would be received amongst them, and that characters were to be filled by those engaged, without distinction, according to their abilities, and the will of the director appointed by the Emperor'. (The will of the director was in fact that of the Emperor himself, for he not only supervised the choice of works to be produced, but also the cast, and even sometimes details of production.) So Michael Kelly was duly engaged to come and sing in Vienna, his contract to include the provision of lodging and fuel, plus an allowance of four wax candles per day. The Director of the Italian opera was the composer Antonio Salieri, who not only occupied that post but since 1774 had also been Court Composer. He was thus firmly entrenched across the path of Mozart, who, having finally severed his connection with the Archbishop of Salzburg in 1781, was now entirely dependent on his own efforts for a livelihood. Although Mozart was at the height of his career as a concert pianist and as a teacher at this time, a definite Court appointment would have given him the security which he now needed more than ever, when in spite of his father's opposition he had just married his Constanze.

It was at the home of one of his most gifted pupils, Babette von Ployer, that Mozart renewed his acquaintance with Paisiello, whom he had met some years previously in Naples, and the two soon became on very friendly terms. Paisiello's opera *The Barber of Seville* was being performed in Vienna with great success, and this seems to have stirred in Mozart's mind the idea of writing an opera round Beaumarchais' second comedy. The official Theatre Poet to the Italian opera company was the Venetian Jew, Lorenzo da Ponte; but his first attempt at a libretto, for Salieri's *Il ricco d'un giorno*, had not been very successful and though the failure of the work was as much the fault of Salieri as of his librettist the irate composer swore that he would write no more music for Da Ponte, who had therefore to turn elsewhere. "I went to Mozart," he says, "and asked him if he would like to compose the music for a play I would write for him. 'I would do so most willingly,' he answered at once, 'but I'm sure I shan't get it accepted.' . . . When we were talking about it one day, he asked me if I could easily adapt Beaumarchais' comedy *The Marriage of Figaro*. The proposal pleased me very

well, and I promised to do as he wished. But there was a great difficulty
to be overcome. Only a few days before, the Emperor had forbidden
the company at the German theatre to act this same comedy, as it was,
he said, too outspoken for a polite audience. . . ." However, the wily
Da Ponte suggested that they should write the opera on the quiet, and
bide their time, waiting for a favourable opportunity to bring it forward. This was done; Da Ponte declares that they completed the opera
in six weeks, in the spring of 1786, and that as he wrote the words
Mozart composed the music for them. The finale of the second act is
said to have taken two nights and a day of non-stop work to produce;
no wonder that Mozart collapsed on the second night, when there
were still a few pages to be completed – especially as he was composing
two piano concertos at this same time! 'As Mozart's good luck would
have it,' continues Da Ponte, 'they were in need of a new work at the
theatre. So I seized the opportunity and without saying anything to
anybody, I went to the Emperor himself and offered him *Figaro*.
"What!" he said. "Don't you know that Mozart, though excellent at
instrumental music, has only written one opera, and that nothing very
great? . . . I've forbidden this *Marriage of Figaro* to the German company." "Yes," I said, "but as I was writing a play to be set to music, and
not a comedy, I have had to leave out a good many scenes and shorten
a great many more, and I have left out and shortened whatever might
offend the refinement and decorum of an entertainment at which Your
Majesty presides. And as for the music, as far as I can judge, it is
extraordinarily fine." "Very well," he answered, "if that is so, I'll trust
your taste as to the music, and your discretion as to the morals. Have
the score sent to the copyist" '. So says Da Ponte; but we must take
this last statement with a grain of salt, for, as we shall see, the Emperor
intended to make his own decision. 'I hastened at once to Mozart,' says
Da Ponte, 'and had not finished telling him the good news when one
of the Emperor's lackeys came with a note requesting him to go to the
palace at once with the score. He obeyed the royal command and had
various pieces performed before the Emperor, who liked them wonder-
fully well and was, without exaggeration, amazed by them. He had
excellent taste in music, as indeed in all the fine arts, and the great success which this piece achieved throughout the world showed clearly
that he was not mistaken in his judgment.'

But Mozart and Da Ponte were not yet out of the wood, for there
were two rival operas competing for production in the imperial
theatre. One was by Regini, and the other, *The Grotto of Trophonius*, by

Mozart's persistent rival Salieri. 'These three pieces,' says Michael
Kelly, 'were nearly ready for representation at the same time, and each
composer claimed the right of producing his opera for the first. The
contest raised much discord, and parties were formed. . . . Mozart was
as touchy as gunpowder, and swore he would put the score of his
opera into the fire if it was not produced first; his claim was backed
by a strong party. On the contrary, Regini was working like a mole in
the dark to get precedence. The third candidate was Maestro di
Cappella to the Court, a clever, shrewd man, possessed of what Bacon
called crooked wisdom, and his claims were backed by three of the
principal performers, who formed a cabal not easily put down. Every
one of the opera company took part in the contest. . .' From which it
will be clear that Figaro's marriage had as great a struggle to get on to
the operatic stage as ever it did on to that of the Théâtre Français.
Indeed, things would probably have gone hardly for Mozart in such a
morass of intrigue, had it not been for the personal intervention of the
Emperor, who put a stop to the wrangling by ordering *The Marriage
of Figaro* to be put into rehearsal without more delay.

Michael Kelly, who was to sing the parts of Don Basilio and Don
Curzio in the first performance, had by now become very friendly
with Mozart, whom he describes as 'a remarkably small man, very
thin and pale, with a profusion of fine fair hair', and he was of course
present at the rehearsals, of which he has left us an interesting picture.
'All the original performers had the advantage of the instruction of the
composer,' he says, 'who transfused into their minds his inspired
meaning. I shall never forget his little animated countenance, when
lighted up with the glowing rays of genius. . . . I remember at the first
rehearsal of the full band, Mozart was on the stage with his crimson
pelisse and gold-laced cocked hat, giving the time of the music to the
orchestra. Figaro's song *Non più andrai, farfallone amoroso* Bennuci gave,
with the greatest animation and power of voice. I was standing close to
Mozart who, *sotto voce*, was repeating "*Bravo! Bravo! Bennuci!*" and
when Bennuci came to the fine passage *Cherubino, alla vittoria, alla
gloria militar*, which he gave out with stentorian lungs, the effect was
electricity itself, for the whole of the performers on the stage, and those
in the orchestra, vociferated, "*Bravo! Bravo, Maestro! Viva! Viva,
grande Mozart!*" Those in the orchestra I thought would never cease
applauding, by beating the bows of their violins against the music
desks. The little man acknowledged, by repeated obeisances, his thanks
for the distinguished mark of enthusiastic applause bestowed upon

him.' Da Ponte tells us that at the final rehearsal the Emperor came, 'and with him half the nobility of Vienna'.

The actual first performance was a success, in spite of the efforts of Mozart's rivals and the misgivings of his father, who on 18 April had written anxiously to Nannerl, telling her that the first stage rehearsal of *The Marriage of Figaro* was to take place on the 28th:

It will be very significant if the opera succeeds, for I know there are astonishingly strong cabals against it. Salieri and all his tribe will move heaven and earth to put it down.

They moved heaven and earth to such purpose that the first performance was in danger of being wrecked by a number of the singers, who either sang flat or pretended to have forgotten their parts. In great agitation Mozart appealed to the Emperor between the first and second acts, and Joseph II personally intervened, ordering the culprits to behave themselves and sing properly, or they should leave his service that very night.

Da Ponte's discreet rendering of Beaumarchais' text into a piece suitable for 'the refinement and decorum' of an entertainment presided over by the Emperor had reduced it to four acts, instead of the comedy's five, and this had the advantage of cutting out much padding which had slowed down the action of the original. Political satire is now removed: the judge Don Gusman Brid'oison and his venal henchman Double-Main give place to the stuttering Don Curzio who in the opera makes only the briefest appearance in a short scene in the third act; while Figaro's long monologue in the last act of the comedy, with the bitter jibes at government and society which caused Louis XVI to ban the play, is also cut out, though its opening sentence has clearly been the inspiration of Figaro's operatic aria on the deceitfulness of women. As for the music: 'at the end,' says Kelly, 'I thought the audience would never have done applauding and calling for Mozart. Almost every piece was encored, which prolonged it nearly to the length of two operas, and induced the Emperor to issue an order on the second representation, that no piece of music should be encored.'

Yet in spite of this opening triumph, and the fact that the opera was performed nine times that season, interest in it soon began to wane, as the composer's rivals produced other works, and it was not until *Don Giovanni* appeared, to remind the fickle public of Mozart's capabilities in opera, that *The Marriage of Figaro* was revived. But if the Viennese were slow to appreciate what was for them a new type of operatic spectacle – a comedy set to music, rather than *opera buffa* in its usual pattern – there was no such hesitation in Prague, which Mozart visited in January 1787, and where he conducted performances of *Figaro* in person. In the capital of Bohemia his triumph was complete, and he was able to write delightedly that

Here, they talk of nothing else but – *Figaro!*. They play, they sing, they whistle nothing but – *Figaro!*. No other opera draws except *Figaro*, always *Figaro* – truly a great honour for me!

The music of *Figaro* became so popular, in fact, that it was arranged in all manner of forms – for the piano, as chamber music, and even for German dances; though Mozart got no financial profit from the performances in Prague, since no law of copyright existed in those days.

It is astonishing, however, even in view of political conditions, to find that Mozart's *Figaro* never reached Paris until the spring of 1793, at the height of the Terror. But it is scarcely surprising that it should then have had little success, since Beaumarchais had the unfortunate idea of sandwiching into Da Ponte's operatic libretto the greater part of his own text. 'It is a good idea', he writes cheerfully to the performers at the Opera, 'to mix the two kinds, to increase the receipts – grand opera and opera which is spoken and sung.' The indigestible and interminably drawn-out result of this unhappy amalgam did justice neither to the comedy nor to the opera and must indeed have been enough to make the composer of the latter turn in his grave. (Mozart had died at the end of 1791.) In Beaumarchais' letter to 'the assembled Actors of the Opera', written, as he tells them, with 'the sole wish to be useful to your stage, which made me overcome the repugnance I had to busy myself about anything but beating all the dogs who bark at me', he airs some of his ideas on the subject of opera, from the viewpoint of the French dramatist for whom the spoken word is of primary importance: 'The habit of constant singing injures the delivery of comedy, and the length spoils the effect, especially in light comedy.' But he has presently to admit that 'as every act begins with words, there is nothing so chilling as to go on the stage and talk while the public is getting weary', and that there must be 'grand and fine orchestral music' to make a variety. He suggests that 'a splendid ballet for the wedding will be a good end to *The Marriage*' (no French opera was complete without a ballet, which, indeed, had been the original starting-point of opera in France). But not all these suggestions could avail to prolong the life of the production, which was taken off again after only five performances. This was partly, no doubt, owing to the political circumstances of those stormy times; Mozart's *Figaro* did not reappear in Paris until 1807, and it was not until 1812 that it reached London, when it was given in the original Italian at the Haymarket Theatre.

But in 1787, the year following the original production of *Figaro* in Vienna, Beaumarchais was to produce an opera of his own in Paris. It was derived mainly from a Persian tale, *Sadak and Kalasrade*, though the title, *Tarare*, was taken from the chief character in Hamilton's *Fleur d'Épine*, apparently for no other reason than that Beaumarchais thought the name unusual and arresting. Since philosophy and natural sciences were very much the craze of the day, his opera starts with a Prologue, in which the Genius of Nature combines with the Genius of Fire ('which presides over the sun, Nature's lover') to conjure up a crowd of shades who are fashioned into the characters of the piece, to the accompaniment of a scientific dialogue between the genii! They select two particular shades, one of them is made 'the Emperor Atar, despot of Asia, reigning in the palace of Ormus'. The other is the soldier Tarare, of unknown parentage, but of virtue and wit, who will struggle against all manner of difficulties and overcome them by his ingenuity, thus representing the triumph of worth and intelligence over the gifts of birth and chance: in other words, Figaro once more, but in an Eastern setting. The Prologue opens with a ballet of 'Winds unleashed, which in whirling about, perform the most violently agitated dances', and concludes with the ascent of the two genii into the clouds, to the accompaniment of a chorus of ethereal spirits. Even the devoted Gudin, whose loyalty to, and admiration for, his friend is his most shining characteristic, has to confess that, 'I did not conceal from him that I considered it impossible to set this Prologue to music'. In the following acts (five of them) we see how Figaro-Tarare defends his beloved, here called Astasia, from the nefarious designs of the tyrant Atar; all this seems very familiar, but in this opera the hero goes even farther than at his last appearance; for after having surmounted every obstacle in his path, he raises himself to such heights of public favour that he is acclaimed as the occupant of the imperial throne in place of Atar, who conveniently stabs himself in sheer vexation. After this satisfactory climax the two Genii of Nature and Fire reappear, and sing ('majestically', according to their author's directions) an elevating verse which informs 'mortal man, whether prince, Brahmin or soldier' that

> Thy greatness on earth
> Pertains not to thy calling;
> 'Tis all in thy character.

Beaumarchais' first idea had been to write his opera in prose, but, carried away no doubt by the magnitude of his theme, he decided that verse could be the only worthy vehicle for such a sublime concept ('The dignity of man is the moral issue of which I wish to treat, the theme which I have set myself'). Unfortunately, as had been only too clearly shown by his first attempt to write *The Barber of Seville* as a comic opera, he was no true poet, and French critics have agreed as to the poor quality of his verse in *Tarare*.

The first draft of his libretto, in its prose form, was completed as early as 1775; perhaps stimulated by the production, in the previous year, of *Iphigénie en Aulide*, the first of Gluck's operas to be produced in Paris (amid the usual hostility of rival factions, and only after the personal intervention of Marie-Antoinette, who had been one of Gluck's pupils in Vienna). The German composer had been in Paris since 1773, and Beaumarchais was strongly influenced by his views. For some years Gluck had been in rebellion against the absurd conventions ruling Italian opera, which, although it held undisputed sway in the principal cities of Europe, had become no more than a rigidly stereotyped medium for vocal acrobatics. Gluck's aim, as he explains in the preface to his *Alceste*, was to 'bring back music to its true function, that of supporting poetry, in order to strengthen the expression of feeling and the interest of dramatic situations, without interrupting the action and chilling it by superfluous ornaments'. His ideas met with considerable favour in Paris, all the more so as in French opera, still clinging to the traditions of Lully and Rameau, music had always had to take second place to declamatory recitative. Operatic circles in the French capital were now divided into two camps: those who, like Gluck, wished to see opera restored to its earlier form of music drama, and those still supporting the Italians, who set up Piccini as Gluck's rather unwilling rival (for the two were on friendly terms). In his preface to *Tarare* Beaumarchais shows how much he supports Gluck's views: 'I consider that the music of opera is, like its poetry, only a new artifice for embellishing the spoken word, and one which must not be abused.' Music, he declares, 'is to opera what verses are to tragedy ... merely a stronger way of presenting feeling or thought; let us keep ourselves from abusing this distinction by putting too much profusion into this style of representation'. But in his true French veneration of the spoken word Beaumarchais goes beyond Gluck to the point of absurdity when he declares that 'there is too much music in our opera; it is overloaded with it'.

However, when he had completed his libretto, the question next arose as to who should write the music for his strange compound of philosophy, natural science, drama, comedy and ballet. Gluck himself was naturally Beaumarchais' first preference, but that experienced veteran professed himself to be too old to undertake the task, and suggested that approach should be made to Salieri, who had been one of his most brilliant pupils and had already several operas to his credit. Salieri was therefore persuaded to come from Vienna, and was lodged in Beaumarchais' own house, while he tackled the task of setting the formidable epic to music. It is perhaps hardly surprising if he failed to do himself full justice, when his music had to be subordinated to the claims of indifferent verse, and he was persuaded to renounce some of his finest musical inspirations 'because they prolonged the scene and slowed down the action'. It is to be hoped, however, that he felt suitably rewarded later, when, although an unkind critic had observed that the music of *Tarare* added nothing to its composer's reputation, the author of the libretto wrote to Salieri that 'you have helped me, my friend, to give the French an idea of the ancient Greek spectacle such as I have always conceived it'. Certainly, Beaumarchais spared no pains to make his piece a striking production; it was superbly staged – the French had always excelled in that direction – with an Oriental splendour of scenes and costume worthy of a more inspired cause, and which alone cost its author some 50,000 francs.

The first performance took place on 8 June 1787. 'Never before,' said an eye-witness, 'did any of our theatres see such a crowd as that which besieged all the avenues of the opera on the day of the first representation of *Tarare*. Barriers raised expressly for the purpose, and protected by a guard of four hundred men, scarcely sufficed to hold it in check.' From which it will be clear that Beaumarchais had not yet lost his power of becoming the focus of general interest. The public reaction to his work, however, seems to have been one of surprise rather than of admiration. Yet *Tarare* did achieve a considerable measure of success; as one critic wrote diplomatically: 'The author will always have the merit of having introduced in this opera an action, the progress of which resembles no other. . . .' By 15 August Beaumarchais was writing triumphantly to Salieri, who was on his way back to Vienna:

It is now, my dear Salieri, that I owe you the account of your great success. *Tarare* has only been played on the 3rd of this month; the Opera has put it on with enormous care, the public has enjoyed it as a sublime work on the part of the musician. So there you are at the head of your calling! The Opera, which in the previous year made five or six hundred livres, has made six thousand four hundred the second. . . . The actors, returning severely to my principle of regarding singing as an accessory of the acting, have been for the first time counted among the greatest talents of the theatre, and the public cried: '*There is music!* not one note over-emphasized; everything moves towards the great effects of the dramatic action.' What pleasure for me, my friend, to see you being at last rendered this great justice, and that they name you in chorus as *the worthy successor of Gluck*.

A week or two later he writes again to Salieri that

we have reached the eighteenth representation without the public ceasing for one moment to hurry in crowds to hear it. On the 8th day of this month [September], the great day at St Cloud, you drew 4,200 francs, and last year on the same day, an excellent work only produced 600 francs. Bravo, dear Salieri! Remember me to the giant named Gluck.

In December Baron Grimm noted that the public was still flocking to the piece, as on the first night. 'The spectators', said one observer cryptically, 'who arrive in fresh crowds at each representation of this opera, listen to it with a silence and a kind of wonder, of which there has been no previous example at any theatre.'

The theme of the overthrow of tyranny and the triumph of the common man was of course exactly to the taste of the time, and *Tarare* continued to be revived at intervals throughout the period of the Revolution, with slight amendments each time to suit the rapidly veering changes of the political weather-vane. Thus in 1790 the tyrant Atar became a constitutional monarch; but by 1795, when kings of any kind were completely out of currency, Tarare was overthrowing the tyrant in order to restore liberty to the people; philosophy, however, had become too indigestible a topic for popular taste, and to the author's great distress the whole of the Prologue was cut out. Having thus skilfully weathered the storms of revolution, *Tarare* actually survived into the period of the restored monarchy, reappearing in 1815 with suitable amendments. Atar, instead of killing himself at the end, now becomes a respectable constitutional monarch who appoints Tarare to command his army; while Tarare, prostrating himself at his sovereign's feet, swears fidelity to him, and the army does likewise. The work seems, in fact, to have lingered on until about 1819, a total span of thirty-two years; which is a remarkable record for a piece whose verse and music were admittedly of no very high order. But even if *Tarare* did not fulfil the author's hope of conveying 'a great philosophical idea', or of making its mark as an opera, it obviously succeeded in catching the popular fancy as an original and dramatic spectacle, of vivid colour and ingenious construction.

Chapter 16

BEAUMARCHAIS IN FRESH TROUBLE

SOME few years before the events related in the previous chapter, Beaumarchais had been approached by two engineers, the Perrier brothers, who sought his financial support for a scheme they had devised to supply Paris with water from the Seine by means of a steam pump to be installed on the hill of Chaillot. This was just the sort of useful undertaking to appeal to Beaumarchais and which would in fact perform a much needed public service, since hitherto householders in Paris, as Mercier tells us, had been dependent on twenty thousand water-carriers, with two buckets on a yoke, who besides mounting 'from the first to the seventh floor in some houses' would 'sometimes make upwards of thirty of these journeys from the riverside in one day.'

Beaumarchais threw himself into the project with his usual enthusiasm and not only financed the scheme but became one of its directors and chief shareholders in the company which he set up – the Compagnie des Eaux de Paris. For the first few years the shares remained well below par, but suddenly in 1785 the concern sprang into life and the shares began to rise rapidly. Now Beaumarchais, with the formation of his company, had already put several spokes into the wheels of certain financiers who had planned to bring the waters of the Yvette to Paris, and the rise in the shares of his undertaking gravely impeded the activities of two bankers who had been charged by Calonne, the Controller-General of Finance, with the launching of a Treasury loan. It was thus to the interest of a number of people in financial circles that the growing prosperity of the water company should be halted, and a ready instrument came to their hands in the person of the notorious Mirabeau, the dissolute younger son of an aristocratic but violently quarrelsome family. He had already acquired an infamous reputation by his scurrilous writings as well as by his disreputable life, and his quarrels with his own father had resulted in several terms of imprisonment under *lettres de cachet*. He had at this time just emerged from such seclusion, and being in his usual financial straits was ready to sell his vitriolic pen for the use of any promising bidder. He was now offered, and accepted with alacrity, the congenial task of blackening the water company and setting out to prove that the undertaking was not to the public interest. Beaumarchais replied to his attack with a pamphlet written in what were, for him, unusually mild terms; but he could not resist ending by comparing Mirabeau's attacks with the Philippics of classical times: 'Perhaps, in the future, some wit will call the present ones by the pretty name of Mirabelles, as derived from the Comte de Mirabeau, who *mirabilia fecit*.' This shaft, together with certain doubts cast on Mirabeau's disinterestedness in the case, roused the latter to full fury, and in his next pamphlet, brushing aside the affairs of the water company, he made the most scurrilous personal attack on 'the mountebank Beaumarchais' – which came well indeed from a man with the reputation of Mirabeau. But Gudin has another explanation for Mirabeau's attack. 'The Comte de Mirabeau,' he says, 'lived almost entirely by what he borrowed. He came to see Beaumarchais; they only knew one another by repute, and the conversation between them was lively, animated and witty. At last the Count, with the levity customary with borrowers of quality, asked Beaumarchais to lend him the sum of *twelve thousand francs*. Beaumarchais refused, with that original gaiety characteristic of him. "But you could easily lend me that amount," said the Count. "Without doubt," replied Beaumarchais, "but, M. le Comte, as I should have to break with you when the day of payment arrived, I would rather do so straight away; I gain twelve thousand francs by it." '

But whatever the true cause of Mirabeau's attack on Beaumarchais, there could be no doubt of its scurrilous venom, and all Paris waited for the victim's reply, from that redoubtable pen which had crushed so many adversaries in the past. But no answer came; Beaumarchais remained silent. It is now known that Calonne was putting pressure upon him, begging him not to make any reply; but the result was very unfortunate as far as Beaumarchais was concerned, and it marks a step in the gradual decline of his fortunes. For it was not long before other enemies began to take courage from his silence in face of Mirabeau's onslaught, and were emboldened, like so many waiting wolves, to close in for the attack.

Yet his passage of arms with Mirabeau was to have a happy sequel four years later, when the wounds of the past were healed in a correspondence which passed between them and which throws a pleasing and very different light on both men. Mirabeau, of the luridly disreputable past, had now become the great orator-statesman of the Constituent Assembly, in which he had at last found an outlet for his talents. But he was obviously growing weary of his life of storm and stress, and on 17 September 1790 he wrote unexpectedly to Beaumarchais:

As my writing cannot displease you, Sir, when it is accompanied by behaviour of which you will not disapprove, I have determined to address myself to you, rather than to intermediaries, in order to be enlightened upon a point concerning you.

Having almost reached that age, and, above all, that mental disposition, in which I also wish to think only of my books and my garden, I had in looking over the national estates cast my eyes upon the Minims* in the Bois de Vincennes. I hear that your thoughts are turned in that direction; it is even said that you have made the highest bid. There can be no doubt that if you desire this pleasing residence, you will give much more for it than I should, because you are much more able to do so, and that being settled, I should think it very disobliging of me to send up, to your disadvantage, the price of a thing to which I should no longer be able to aspire. Please tell me then if I have been correctly informed, if you are very anxious to make this purchase, and from that moment I withdraw my offers. If, on the contrary, you have only a slight inclination to possess it, or merely a desire to encourage these sales for the good of the State, reserving to yourself to get rid, at a subsequent period, of an estate which is probably too near your present beautiful habitation for you to intend to make it your country house, I am persuaded you will behave to me as I do to you, and that you will not compete to send up the price.

After what had passed between them a few years before, Beaumarchais might surely have been forgiven if his response had been chilly. But he wrote in reply:

I am about to reply to your letter, Sir, with frankness and freedom. I have long been seeking an opportunity of revenging myself on you. You now offer it to me yourself, and I seize it with joy.

All the motives you mention did indeed influence me in wishing to make the purchase. Another more powerful one was added to them, and although it may appear strange, it was nevertheless the one which decided me. At the age of twelve, when about to make my first communion (you laugh?), I was taken to the Minims; a large picture of the Last Judgment, which was in their vestry, made such an impression on my mind, that I returned to see it very often. An old monk, of much wit, thereupon undertook to tear me away from the world. He gave me a sermon, every time I saw him, on the large picture, accompanying

* The monastery of the Minims (an order of St François de Paule), which had now became national property.

his sermon with refreshments. I had become very fond of his retreat and his moral lessons, and I went there every holiday. Since this time, I have always taken a pleasure in visiting this cloister, and as soon as the estates of our poor shorn ones were offered for sale, I gave directions to outbid all comers for this one. So many motives combined make this acquisition dear to me; but my vengeance is still more so, and I am no longer so good-natured as I was in my childhood. You desire my cloister, I give it up to you, and resign all claims upon it, too happy to place my enemy at last between four walls. There is only I who can do it, now that there are no more bastilles.

If in your anger you are still sufficiently generous not to interfere with the salvation of my soul, reserve for me, Sir, the great picture of the Last Judgment. My last judgment upon it is that it is a very fine piece, and made to honour my chapel. You will thus have your revenge on me, as I have my revenge on you. If you have need of good information, or even of my assistance, to facilitate your purchase, speak, and I will do whatever you wish in the matter. For if, Sir, I am the most implacable of all your enemies, my friends say laughingly that I am the best of all ill-natured men.

Mirabeau's reply shows that he was really touched by this letter:

I must have been beside myself with joy, yesterday, as in fact I was, Sir, not to have replied at once to your kind letter. The candour of the age you recall is shown in it, no less than its gaiety and cunning; and never did more engaging form accompany kinder conduct.

Yes, certainly, the picture which has remained so vividly impressed on your imagination in the course of a life which must necessarily have somewhat distracted your attention from the Last Judgment is yours, if I become the owner of this cloister; and to my ambition in this respect is added a prayer – it is that you will come yourself to seek your souvenir of the vestry, and admit that no faults are inexpiable and no anger eternal.

This is indeed a different side of Mirabeau, and the correspondence ends with an equally graceful reply from Beaumarchais:

I am more touched, Sir, with your letter than I dare confess. Allow me to send to you the good man whom I had entrusted with the settlement of this affair. He was formerly one of the brokers of the municipality; he will explain to you what value your purchase possesses, and what you can do with it. This will enable you to judge, if you do not already know, to what amount you can bid.

Since my joking did not displease you, receive now my most sincere assurance that the past has been totally forgotten. Turn my old vestry into a dining-room and I will accept with joy a civic and frugal repast. Thanks to the Revolution, no one feels humiliated now at offering only one of such a kind, and we have all become rich from the diminution it has caused in vain expenses which made us poor without giving us any real pleasure. Have good workmen, and let them be good enough to finish their work quickly. . . .

But Mirabeau did not live to enjoy the country retreat he was preparing for himself. Prematurely worn out by his excesses, he died the following spring; while as for Beaumarchais, the march of political events soon put an end to any question of his acquiring more property.

Even before the episode of the Compagnie des Eaux, he had become entangled in an affair which was to have far more serious repercussions on his career. It had had its beginning as far back as October 1781, when he had been dining with the Prince and Princess of Nassau-Siegen. They had unfolded to him the melancholy tale of a certain Mme Kornman, a wealthy orphan of Swiss extraction who at the age of fifteen had been married against her will to an Alsatian banker. They had had two children, but the marriage had not been a success; according to the Baronne d'Oberkirch, Kornman was 'of very un-prepossessing appearance', little calculated to attract a young girl. The inevitable soon happened. There was in Strasbourg an elegant, witty young man named Daudet de Jossan, who held the important post of Syndic-Royal and was a grandson of Marshal Saxe and the great tragedienne Adrienne Lecouvreur. Mme Kornman became his mistress, and was now expecting a third child, of which he was the father. Korn-man, it appeared, had been perfectly well aware of this liaison for some time, but it had suited him to turn a blind eye towards it, since Daudet de Jossan was under the powerful protection of the Minister of War, the Prince de Monbarey, and moreover was extremely useful to Kornman over financial speculations. But suddenly there had been a change in the Ministry for War (Monbarey's amiable inefficiency could no longer be tolerated when Maurepas had gone) and Daudet had lost not only his patron but his appointment. At once, Kornman became conscious of his wife's affair, and as she refused to hand over her dowry of 360,000 francs to bolster up her husband's finances, declaring that she wished it to go to her children, he had her imprisoned under a *lettre de cachet*, and, although pregnant, she was shut up in a place of detention reserved for prostitutes and lunatics. She was now claiming the right to have her case heard in a proper court of law, and not to be left to have her child in her present horrible surroundings. Beaumarchais was shown letters written by Kornman to the wife's lover, clearly showing the husband's previous knowledge of the situation and his tolerance of it; he was also introduced to Daudet, a personal friend of the Prince of Nassau-Siegen. Beaumarchais, from the depths of his own experience as well as from an instinctive good nature, was always ready at any time to answer an appeal for help from a person unjustly imprisoned, and most of all if that person happened to be a woman ('I should be indeed ungrateful to refuse help in my old age to a member of the beloved sex which made my youth so happy!'). He took up the case of Mme Kornman with his usual energy, although he did not know her personally at that time, and since he still possessed a good deal of influence with the King's Ministers he was able not only to get the *lettre de cachet* revoked, but also to obtain an order in the King's name authorizing the Lieutenant of Police, Lenoir, to escort Mme Kornman to the house of an accoucheur, where she would be able to have her child and also attend to business in connection with her husband. No less than five years of negotiation now dragged on between the couple, in vain attempts to settle their differences and arrange a separation; during this time Kornman's financial affairs went from bad to worse, as he continued his unavailing efforts to get possession of his wife's money.

Then, unfortunately for Beaumarchais, Kornman made the acquaintance of an unknown but ambitious, forceful and quite unscrupulous young advocate named Bergasse, who saw in the affair an unparalleled opportunity of focusing public attention on himself by attacking Beaumarchais, who had been continuing during this time to help Mme Kornman with his advice. He could hardly have done less, after taking up her case. But Beaumarchais' fatal silence in face of the onslaught of Mirabeau was now to cost him dearly; for Bergasse gives away the true mainspring of his own attack when he speaks of Beaumarchais as a man who, 'when dragged publicly through the mud by a famous writer whom he had had the impudence to insult, did not dare to raise his head before him, and by his guilty silence justified the opprobrium with which he was covered'. Bergasse decided to conduct a war of pamphlets, to be circulated in their thousands all over Paris, exactly as Beaumarchais himself had done against Goezman; with the difference, however, that it was now Beaumarchais who was the villain of the piece, whose machinations were alleged to be responsible for the continued estrangement of Kornman and his wife. The first of these pamphlets, which appeared under Kornman's name in February 1787, when Beaumarchais was in the middle of rehearsals of *Tarare*, was a curiously muddled document, in which the real author was so busy hurling his envenomed darts at Beaumarchais that he let slip some extraordinary statements regarding his client Kornman, who, for instance, was reported as saying that the reason why he had waited six years before taking this action was because the Lieutenant of Police – whom he now accused of being one of his wife's lovers – had promised him a post in 'the Indies'!

Beaumarchais replied to this document by the publication of Kornman's letters to Daudet; letters which showed that at the very time when, according to Bergasse's pamphlet, Kornman had been filled with righteous indignation at Daudet's relations with his wife, he had in fact been maintaining the most friendly, close and confidential correspondence with the young man. Kornman was thus shown to be, as Daudet's advocate put it when the case came to court, 'either the most atrocious of libellers, or the vilest of husbands'. Bergasse now threw aside all pretence of writing under Kornman's name, and continued the war under his own, and with increasing violence of language against Beaumarchais, 'a man whose sacrilegious existence attests in so disgraceful and flagrant a manner the degree of profound depravity to which we have arrived'.

Beaumarchais then cited both Kornman and Bergasse before the Parlement for defamation of character. But unfortunately political events were now marching rapidly towards the explosion so soon to come, and, with the suspension of Parlement a few months after the fall of Calonne, the administration of justice was interrupted, so that Beaumarchais' case remained undecided for nearly two years. During this time, Bergasse continued to press home his attacks with increasing effect, shifting his ground gradually away from the Kornmans and more exclusively on to Beaumarchais; while certain enemies of the latter, who never failed to stir into activity when he was in trouble, now once more reared their heads. These were the Aubertins, the brother and sisters of Beaumarchais' first wife. They had harassed him with years of unnecessary litigation over her estate, and when judgment was finally given against them, declaring them to be Beaumarchais' debtors to an extent greater than their total assets, their attitude changed to one of whining excuses that they had been misled about him, and appeals to his generosity, larded with references to his 'well-known kindness of heart' and the fact that their sister had been his wife. In spite of all that he had suffered from them Beaumarchais with his usual good nature agreed that the one surviving sister – the other had just died – and her brother should have the use, for their lifetime, of the money which they owed him. 'It is thus that I take revenge for ten years' persecution, during which my goods, my income, my furniture, have been seized ten times.' The Aubertins now showed their gratitude for this indulgence by handing over to Beaumarchais' arch-enemy letters and confidential papers he had written to his first wife thirty-three years before. In addition to possessing this material, Bergasse was displaying diabolical skill in linking Beaumarchais to the political events of the hour. The crafty young advocate was now setting himself up as the champion of the people against the man who, he declared, was in league with the aristocrats, sold to the Ministers, and was finally crowning his iniquities by cornering grain – that most deadly of all charges in a time of poor harvest and food riots.

During the course of these fatal two years nearly four hundred pamphlets poured from Bergasse's poison pen; while Beaumarchais, that once inveterate writer of pamphlets, now wrote only three in reply, and these much below the standard of those against Goezman. But he had fought so many battles in his long career – he was getting on in years – and it seemed particularly hard that the one in which above all he could feel that he had acted rightly should yet have brought down upon him such trouble. 'Great God!' he cries in the first of his replies to Bergasse's attacks. 'What is my destiny! I have never done any good action which has not caused me anguish, and I only owe all my success – shall I say the word? – to follies!' Yet his friends could not make Beaumarchais realize that his usual light satiric style was of no avail in dealing with a man who was now covering himself with the heavy armour-plate of public morality and who therefore needed to be met with a serious vigour equal to his own. Certainly, when at last the case came up before Parlement, Bergasse's pamphlets were denounced as 'false, insulting and calumnious' and their author condemned to pay Beaumarchais 1,000 livres' damages, with a warning of 'exemplary punishment' for any repetition of the offence. But the damage had been done. Popular opinion had been completely swung round against Beaumarchais. It was Bergasse who had become the hero of the hour, the victim of Parlement, while his opponent received nothing but a rain of anonymous letters, and was once even attacked in the street. There could scarcely indeed have been a more unfortunate moment for Beaumarchais to find himself thus covered with the mud of Bergasse's vilification. For the moving finger of time had now reached the spring of 1789, and the sands of the world he had known were fast running out.

Chapter 17

THE FACE OF REVOLUTION

YET, like many of his contemporaries, Beaumarchais was little conscious of the nearness of catastrophe; so little, in fact, that in this very year 1789 he was in process of having a large mansion built, for the site of which he had chosen, of all places, a plot of land right opposite the Bastille and the road leading out of the city to the Faubourg Saint-Antoine, cradle of revolution! Since the Bergasse-Kornman affair he had been keeping himself as much as possible out of the limelight of public attention; but he had welcomed the summoning of the States-General, hoping, as so many did, that it heralded the establishment of a constitutional Government and the ending of the worst abuses of the old régime. He was, indeed, far more sanguine in this respect than Gudin, and rebuked his friend's distrust of coming developments. 'Do not alarm', said he, 'those minds that can be sustained by the firm hope of a great improvement, in the astonishing course of events which is opening before us.'

Beaumarchais' daughter Eugénie, whom he idolized, was fast growing up, and it may well have been for her sake as much as for his own that he was now setting about the consolidation of his position as a man of substance. La Harpe declares that at this stage in his career Beaumarchais was richer than Voltaire and Buffon together, and both of these were wealthy men, Buffon by inheritance and Voltaire, following the advice of old Pâris-Duverney, by judicious management. Beaumarchais' first step had been to make an honest woman of his Marie-Thérèse, Eugénie's mother, whom he had at last married in March 1786. At that time he was living in the Veille Rue du Temple; but in June of the following year, as *Tarare* was being successfully launched, he bought a large plot of land, the site of a former rampart, at the corner of the Rue Amelot and of the boulevard which today bears his name, facing on to the present-day Place de la Bastille. Here he began the construction of a mansion and gardens which are estimated to have cost him, by the end of two years, the colossal sum of 1,663,000 francs.

For Beaumarchais, characteristically, wished to have 'a house that will be talked about', and his desire was undoubtedly fulfilled (though what was actually said about it is another matter; Napoleon later described it as 'a folly'). But it was certainly one of the sights of Paris. The visitor approaching it from the boulevard was confronted by a wall crowned by a terrace like that in the Tuileries gardens, ornamented with trees. At the end of the terrace, in the midst of the trees, stood a round temple dedicated to Voltaire, with a globe upon its domed roof, and across it a large gilt pen quill which acted as a weather vane. The entrance to the main building was reached across a large circular court-yard in the centre of which stood on a rock the figure of a gladiator. The frontage of the house was semicircular, with an impressive colon-nade and some two hundred windows; while the interior was on an equally grandiose scale, its large and ornate apartments being reached by a spiral staircase of mahogany, underneath which were kitchens and cellars. The most remarkable rooms on the reception floor were an enormous circular *salon* with a thirty-foot high dome and mosaic floor of the choicest woods, and a billiards-room with a gallery for spec-tators. The furnishing was as opulent as the rooms themselves: in Beaumarchais' study his writing-desk was entirely decorated with inlaid mosaics of landscape scenes, and was estimated to be worth at least 30,000 francs.

The garden was, if possible, even more remarkable than the house. It was, in the first place, laid out with considerable cunning to appear much larger than the rather limited space it actually occupied, and it was adorned with every contrivance dear to the eighteenth-century heart: ornamental sheets of water, with cascades falling from the inevitable rocks, a Bacchic temple, an assortment of statuary peppered about the groves at every turn, with edifying inscriptions on their bases; among them a bust of Pâris-Duverney, inscribed, very fittingly,

> *Il m'instruisit par ses travaux:*
> *Je lui dois le peu que je vaux,*

and a statue of Cupid, on whose base a doting parent had had carved:

> *O toi qui mets le trouble en plus d'une famille,*
> *Je te demande, Amour, le bonheur de ma fille.*

There were also caverns, tunnels, an arcade (which opened into the Rue

Amelot), and last but not least a Chinese bridge, complete with accompaniment of bells. It took two years to complete all these breathtaking marvels, and as the proud owner was not yet inhabiting his creation himself he threw it open to the public, inaugurating the proceedings with a musical fête under the presidency of the Duc d'Orléans. So great was the number of people who wished to be present that special tickets of admission were printed.

In 1789 the builders' scaffolding was still up round the house; but already that spring there were ominous rumblings of the coming storm, as Paris began to be swept with the extraordinary wave of hysteria known as the Great Fear. The Ile-de-France, the densely wooded country surrounding the city, had always been the haunt of bandits and undesirable characters, and now persistent rumours were circulating that they were beginning to force their way into the suburbs of the capital, that they had even in some places got through the city gates into Paris itself, and were pillaging and burning. In April two mansions in the neighbourhood of Beaumarchais' new house, one belonging to the industrialist Rebeillon, had been sacked and burnt, Rebeillon's because it was said – quite wrongly – that he had suggested reducing wages. Ugly threats were now being muttered that Beaumarchais' turn would come next. He had himself been a horrified witness of the burning of his neighbours' houses, and reported in May to the Lieutenant of Police that

All the workmen of buildings meet on certain days at a fixed time; when they are seen assembling in the evening in unfrequented places, something is being prepared. I have observed this, several evenings; in one of these groups, I heard these words: 'A good many more will be killed before next week.' A friend of mine heard the words: 'We must work in the night.'

The fisherwomen in the cemetery of Saint-Jacques were speaking aloud in the open market, a few days ago, of my houses as *marked places*.

An infamous fellow named Michelin lodges in this market. . . . This man, who played the part of a false witness in my last lawsuit, paid by my enemies, and justly suspected of having placarded my doors and broken my bas-reliefs, is one of those who incite the mob against me.

July 1789 was a month of sweltering heat, and the tension of already overheated brains rose to boiling-point when the news leaked out on the 12th of Necker's dismissal. In the gardens of the Palais Royal the excited demagogue Camille Desmoulins made his frenzied call to arms: 'Not a moment must be lost! M. Necker's dismissal sounds the tocsin of the St Bartholomew of patriots! Tonight all the Swiss and

German battalions in the Champ de Mars will turn out and slaughter us!' As night fell, the great bell of the Hôtel de Ville began to send forth its message of terror, and by dawn on the following morning a large mob had assembled in front of the building, having already done an appreciable amount of successful looting on their way. During the course of the day the wildest rumours circulated about the town, while Camille Desmoulins continued to rant that 'the beast has fallen into the snare: let us strike it down! Never have victors been offered a richer prey! Forty thousand palaces, town houses and country mansions will be the reward of valour!' No wonder that when the Duc d'Orléans signified his intention of visiting Beaumarchais' famous mansion its owner wrote to him: 'Make haste, Monseigneur, for my garden has already narrowly escaped being destroyed these ten times. I do not know what is in store for me.'

The night of 13 July has been likened, in its atmosphere of tension, to the eve of St Bartholomew. Houses in Paris were lit up, their owners either fearing attack or being occupied in manufacturing arms (50,000 pikes were made in thirty-six hours), while groups of armed men silently patrolled the streets. On the following morning, the 14th, the mob attacked the Invalides, and, brushing aside the Governor's attempts to play for time while he sent to Versailles for instructions, they seized 27 guns, a mortar and 32,000 muskets. Then the cry went up: 'To the Bastille!' The fortress which symbolized royal power stood apparently impregnable behind its double moat, though the outer courts had been left unguarded by its meagre garrison. These were soon reached by the agility of two men who slid off an adjoining roof on to a wall, whence they were able to jump down into the court, and they were followed by two ex-soldiers who cut the chains of the draw-bridge with axes. But when the multitude tried to rush the bridge leading to the inner court, the garrison opened fire upon them, inflicting considerable casualties and filling the attackers with blind rage, since it was thought that the emptiness of the outer courts had been a deliberate trap to lure them on. The battle now raged with fury; in addition to reinforcements streaming to the attack from the Faubourg Saint-Antoine, the insurgents received further support from a group arriving with five cannon seized at the Invalides; these were trained on the main gate. But the mob had no settled plan of attack and after five hours of struggle the garrison had sustained only one casualty, while the attackers had lost over eighty of their number killed and a slightly greater total wounded. The rather inept Governor, the Marquis de Launay, seems, however, to have been torn between that part of his garrison from the Invalides who were in favour of giving up the struggle, and the tougher Swiss troops, who were for continuing resistance since the fortress and its defenders were still practically intact. But in the end weaker counsels prevailed, and de Launay agreed to cease further resistance and surrender the fortress on the promise, for himself and his garrison, of a safe conduct – which lasted for just so far as the gates, after which the head of the Governor and those of most of his troops ended up on top of pikes. Beaumarchais, from the terrace where he was superintending the putting of the final touches to his house, had a front-row view of these happenings; little did he know that at one moment the Governor of the Bastille had nearly decided to blow the whole building sky-high. But since he was President of the district of Blancs-Manteaux (a post he had not thought it wise to decline) Beaumarchais was able in his official capacity to save the lives of several unfortunate soldiers who had been disarmed by the mob. A letter exists which he wrote to a captain of the Salis-Allemand Regiment the following day:

In returning to my house, Sir, I add to the good I have been happy enough to accomplish, that of preventing your soldier from setting out in broad day; he would be torn to pieces. I have had given to him a great-coat and a hat belonging to one of my people, which you will return to me. I have also made him take off his gaiters, that nothing may cause him to be recognized. A grenadier of the Garde Française, full of humanity, promises me to protect him to the barrier.

God save the King, and restore him to his people, who, in the midst of their fury, have not lost a religious respect for this sacred name. Everything else is broken up.

At his own request Beaumarchais was deputed by the Mayor of Paris to supervise the demolition of the Bastille, so as to ensure that no damage should be done to neighbouring houses or to the great sewer which ran close by. He was also made a member of the municipality. But all these efforts would avail him little in the stormy times now beginning; accusations and denunciations soon began to assail him, which he tried in vain to disarm by throwing open his property to public view, in order to refute statements that he was hoarding either grain or arms, and by giving a lead in various charitable projects. But his new mansion, flaunting itself in the face of the Faubourg Saint-Antoine, was by its very existence a provocation to austere 'patriots'; so was his manner of living, when at last he took up residence in it with his wife and daughter, his sister Julie and the faithful Gudin; not to mention his dog, an English greyhound, who bore upon her collar the inscription: 'I am Mademoiselle Follette. Beaumarchais belongs to me. We live on the boulevard.' Gudin's mother had just died at the age of eighty-three. 'Beaumarchais at once came to me,' he says, 'offered me all the consolations of friendship and reclaimed the promise which we had given one another long ago, to unite the rest of the days which nature reserved to us. It is thus that I found in the family of my friend all those attentions which could sweeten the irreparable loss of the tenderest mother and one whom I had almost never quitted.'

In his resplendent new abode, Beaumarchais lived in a style befitting his surroundings, with as many as ten horses in his stables, keeping open house and receiving distinguished members of the political, literary and artistic worlds in nightly assemblies over which Mme de Beaumarchais presided with grace and tact. Every evening guests were entertained with music and gambling, though the host did not take any part in the latter; instead, he would give readings of his works. His contemporary Arnault has pictured the scene for us: it is laid in the 'great circular *salon*, partly ornamented with mirrors, partly with landscapes of vast dimensions, and half of it occupied by seats for the auditors. Upon a stage furnished with a desk stood the armchair. There, as in a theatre, Beaumarchais read, or rather played, his dramas; because it is to play, if one delivers a piece in as many different inflexions of the voice as there are different personages in the action; because it is to play if one gives to each one of the personages the pantomime which should characterize him.'

But Beaumarchais had not yet come to the end of his career as a dramatist; he was even now busy writing his last work, *The Guilty Mother*, which was to form the final part of the trilogy commenced by his two comedies.

Chapter 18

DRAMATIST'S SWAN SONG

THE agitating events of 1789 were followed by a year of comparative quiet, while the Constituent Assembly set about the task of framing a constitution. Once again, optimists began to hope that the worst of the Revolution (which had scarcely yet begun) was over, and that all was now set for the rosy future of liberty and enlightened government that Wordsworth had in mind when he carolled,

> Bliss was it in that dawn to be alive,
> But to be young was very Heaven!

During this relatively peaceful interregnum, as misleading in its false calm as the 'phoney war' of our own day, Beaumarchais completed the writing of *The Guilty Mother*, in which the author takes farewell of the four chief characters of his comedies, though in a very different atmosphere. Gone is the exuberant gaiety of the two first plays; this one, as befits the darkening times in which it was written, is a drama. We meet the Count and Countess Almaviva again after the lapse of twenty years; though, since the scene is laid in the Paris of 1790, the Count has dropped his title. They are still served by Figaro and his wife Suzanne, but Figaro has changed with the passing of time, for like his creator he has lost all his bubbling gaiety, though not his resourcefulness and sharp wits. The Almavivas have suffered a cruel bereavement by the death in a duel of their son and heir, but there are now two other young people in the household: Florestine, an illegitimate daughter of the Count, who passes her off as his ward, and Léon, a natural son of the Countess. For that virtuous and long-suffering wife, neglected as usual over the years by her husband, has had a momentary lapse during the time he was away for three years as Viceroy of Mexico, and has had a son by Léon d'Astorga, who is none other than their former page Chérubin. When d'Astorga went off to the wars, the Countess wrote him a letter telling him of her condition, but also of her firm decision that they must never see each other again. He had replied – most conveniently on the same sheet of paper – that there was nothing left for him to do but to get himself killed, and a postscript was added at the bottom 'written in his own blood', saying that he was mortally wounded, and bidding her farewell. This document, it is scarcely necessary to say, has been carefully preserved in the double bottom of the Countess's jewel-case, all ready for discovery by the villain of the piece, one Bégearss, Almaviva's former secretary, alleged to be an Irishman (Beaumarchais' knowledge of the English language, in spite of many visits to England, seems never to have progressed very far beyond the strange word 'God-dam'). It is of little moment, however, what the villain's nationality was supposed to be, since obviously his name is the most thinly veiled variant of that of the author's recent enemy. Bégearss, a scheming scoundrel of the first water, has insinuated himself into the good graces of Almaviva and designs to marry Florestine, and through her gain possession of Almaviva's money, Léon being disinherited and the Countess to be disposed of by a divorce. The fact that Florestine is in love with Léon and he with her is merely a small obstacle to be rapidly disposed of, and the first step in Bégearss's plans is to get possession of the letters out of the jewel-case, which he passes on to Almaviva. The latter furiously confronts his wife with the document in a scene (largely inspired by *Tartuffe*) in the fourth act which was much criticized as improbable and offending public taste, where, as Almaviva storms at her, Rosine prays aloud, and finally, seeing the spectre of Chérubin rising before her eyes, collapses fainting to the floor. But all ends well, thanks to the sharp wits of Figaro, who as usual saves the situation and unmasks the machinations of Bégearss. The Almavivas are reconciled, and the two young people are each recognized as full members of the family by their respective 'step-parents'. As for Figaro, when the delighted Almaviva offers to reward him with the 2,000 louis which Bégearss was about to pocket, the faithful servitor proudly refuses the money:

No, if it please you; shall I spoil by a vile salary, the good service I have rendered! My reward will be to die among you. . . .

In his preface to the play, which as usual had a double title, *L'Autre Tartuffe, ou La Mère coupable*. Beaumarchais says that his intention was to present the whole story of the Almaviva family in three consecutive performances: 'After having laughed heartily, on the first day, in *The Barber of Seville*, at the turbulent youth of Count Almaviva, which is practically that of all men; after having, on the second day, gaily considered, in the *Folle Journée* [*The Marriage of Figaro*] the faults of his maturity, which are only too often our own; come and be convinced with us, by the picture of his old age in *The Guilty Mother*, that every man who is not born appallingly wicked, always finishes by being kind, when the age of passions passes, and above all, when he has tasted the sweet happiness of being a father. That is the moral aim of the piece.' (Like a true man of the eighteenth century, Beaumarchais in his plays had always to have a moral purpose – whatever impression to the contrary they might give to a deliciously scandalized public.) His two comedies, he declares, were only a preparation for this third play. 'When I wrote my other pieces, I was for a long time outrageously attacked for having dared to put on the stage this young Figaro, whom since then you have liked. I too was young; I laughed at it. But in growing old, the spirit saddens, the character becomes gloomy. I have tried in vain; I no longer laugh when an ill-natured person or a rogue insults me on account of my works; one is not master of that.'

Many French critics have condemned as the purest melodrama what one has described as *cette Mère trop coupable*, and do not consider the piece to be one of Beaumarchais' best efforts. Professor Eugène Lintilhac thought that this was at least partly owing to the speed at which the author wrote it, compared with the patient care and numerous retouchings given to his other works, and that this haste, rather than any decline of his powers, was the true explanation of the more absurd passages in it. Yet, melodramatic though it undoubtedly is in its treatment and often improbable in some of its situations, the play was very much to the taste of its day, and indeed to that of many years afterwards. Napoleon was impressed with it, and even in the middle of the nineteenth century Loménie could still speak of the plot as 'a conception which does not lack either elevation or interest'.

The play was finished in January 1791, and was read to, and accepted by, the Théâtre Français in February. It so happened that the widow of Prince Charles Edward Stuart was in Paris at the time under the name of the Countess of Albany, and she asked Beaumarchais to give a reading of his new work at her house. His reply to her was amusingly typical of his style:

Mme la Comtesse – Since you wish absolutely to hear my very severe work, I cannot object to it; but note one point: when I wish laughter, it must be in shouts; if you weep, it must be in sobs. I know of nothing in between but boredom.

Admit then whom you will to Tuesday's reading, but keep away the worn-out hearts, those dried-up souls who view with pity the emotions that we find so delicious. Those people are only good for talking of revolution. Have some sensitive women, and men to whom the heart is not an illusion, and then we can weep in full spate. I promise you this sorrowful pleasure, and am, with respect, Mme la Comtesse . . . etc.

No doubt the author was very gratified to know that women were frequently overcome on attending the play. But it was not yet to appear at the national theatre. The battle between Beaumarchais and the players over authors' rights was still going on with increasing intensity, and relations between the two sides had reached breaking-point. Meanwhile, a new theatre had just been started in the Marais, near to Beaumarchais' new mansion, and as he had acquired a controlling financial interest in it *The Guilty Mother* was transferred there, and the first performance took place on 6 June 1792. It was not, however, very well played by the new company, and in any case the moment was an unfortunate one for a new theatrical venture. For who could care for the unrealities of stage melodrama now that, after the false calm of the preceding eighteen months, the Revolution had unleashed itself again in full fury? With France at war against the threat of Austro-Prussian invasion, events in Paris boiled up, on 10 August, into the attack on the Tuileries. It was not to be until five years later, in the time of the Directory, that *The Guilty Mother* achieved real success, when the play returned to its true home, the Théâtre Français, and was properly produced there in May 1797.

It is curious to think, however, that it might, like its two predecessors, have been set to music, if circumstances had been more favourable; for André Grétry, composer of more than sixty operas, who had settled in Paris since 1767, wrote to Beaumarchais:

I dream only of *The Guilty Mother*. I have remarked that music is never so well placed, or has so good an effect, as when it occurs rarely. Would you like me to choose twelve places where you will rhyme your prose? That will be enough. I will answer for it that if you consent to my request, people will speak one day of the anger of Almaviva as they now speak of the anger of Achilles. If you give the piece to the Italian company, it could have fifty successive representations; if you add to it twelve or fifteen pieces of music in different styles – it ought to have a hundred – I shall have composed music upon a masterpiece worthy of old Grétry.

Whatever might have resulted from Grétry's suggestions, however, nothing further came of them, owing probably to the increasing disruption caused by political events and the consequent preoccupations of the author. Yet although Beaumarchais' drama would assuredly not appeal to modern taste, it is an interesting speculation to wonder, in view of the play's favourable reception from 1797 onwards, whether, if times had been happier, *The Guilty Mother* might not have joined the other two plays of the trilogy on the operatic stage.

But in the dark days of tumult and bloodshed now at hand Beaumarchais was to have no more time for writing plays. During the next four years he would have need of all Figaro's resource and ingenuity to keep his own head safely on his shoulders, and to do what little he could do to ensure the safety of his family. His daughter Eugénie, now aged fifteen, was being educated at a convent, but her father, becoming uneasy at increasing signs of anti-clericalism in the political climate, took her away and brought her home. A pleasing light is thrown on Beaumarchais by a letter which he wrote to the prioress of his daughter's convent at about this time, concerning a school-fellow of Eugénie who was too poor to be able to pay for further schooling:

I send you, madame, a note for 200 livres for your unfortunate scholar. Now her year is paid for. I shall have the honour to give to you, or her, the first time I go to the convent, 3 louis in money, which will be 6 francs a month, the same that I give my daughter. But I entreat you, madame, that this assistance may not be used to force or urge her vocation. I should be deeply grieved if she were to be in the least constrained as to the future. I have not the honour of knowing her; the good you told me of her was what determined me. Let her be free and less unhappy; these are the only thanks I ask. Keep my secret; I am surrounded by violent enemies.

Beaumarchais was frequently accused of trumpeting his good deeds abroad; yet this is not the only case of his doing good by stealth.

But he was now about to become involved in the last secret mission of his career, which would once more bring him to the brink of financial ruin and was to land him in a greater mass of troubles and difficulties than any of those he had undertaken in his early life.

Chapter 19

IN PURSUIT OF

SIXTY THOUSAND MUSKETS

AT the beginning of 1792 a Belgian approached Beaumarchais with the offer of 60,000 muskets, which had been collected by Austria during the disarmament of the Low Countries and had been deposited in Holland. Foreseeing war with France, however, the Austrian Government had stipulated that any purchaser of the arms must not re-sell them in Europe. France being now faced with a war deliberately brought about by her revolutionary politicians in order to rally popular support round themselves, she was certainly in desperate need of weapons. But the undertaking would be a risky affair, even for a man like Beaumarchais for whom difficulty and danger always added spice to an enterprise. Gudin, however, in his comments on the subject, has probably pinpointed the crux of the matter when he says: 'I told him [Beaumarchais] that a wise man in revolutionary times does not trade in arms or corn. But my prudence was misplaced; in these times of disorder and arrest they would have made it a crime on his part to have refused to acquire the arms which were offered to him. His refusal would have been held to be ill-will; he had only a choice of dangers: he exposed himself to the peril of being useful to his country.' So the unfortunate Beaumarchais, far from being able to relax and enjoy the fruits of his long labours, now found himself, at the age of sixty and troubled by a progressively increasing deafness ('like a sepulchral urn' as he put it himself), committed willy-nilly to the most difficult and complicated of any of the missions he had undertaken – although it was probably the means of saving his life in the end, since it took him out of France during the worst phase of the Terror.

He duly transmitted the Belgian's proposal to the Minister of War, de Grave, who charged him with the task of bringing the muskets secretly into France, at an agreed price; he was advanced 500,000 francs in assignats, the miserable paper money issued in 1789, which had already fallen to 47 per cent of its face value, so that the actual worth of the amount was only 235,000 francs. At the same time the Minister required Beaumarchais to deposit securities to the amount of 745,000 francs guaranteed by the city of Paris. He was promised, however, that if he needed more money for transport of the arms the Government would remit to him part of the amount left on deposit, and they would do their best to overcome the resistance of the Dutch Government, which, fearing to become embroiled with Austria, was holding up the arms at Tervuren, a port of Zeeland.

It was soon after this, however, that France had declared her general 'war against kings', and apart from other agitating events of this year Ministers succeeded one another in bewildering sequence, while Beaumarchais exhausted himself in vain efforts to obtain their support in putting pressure on the Dutch Government (Holland being one of the few countries with which France was still at peace); 'I have tired out in a few months fourteen or fifteen of them', said he. Nor could he obtain the promised money out of his deposit for the transport of the muskets. Meanwhile, in an atmosphere of rapidly mounting public hysteria, his enemies busied themselves spreading tales that he had the muskets safely in his own cellars and was keeping them there to use for the slaughter of patriots; he was denounced by a member of the Legislative Assembly on a charge of concealing arms. On the very day after the attack on the Tuileries and the massacre of the Swiss Guard the mob descended on Beaumarchais' new house, in order to search it from top to bottom. He had already sent his wife and daughter away for safety to Le Havre, and a long letter which he wrote to Eugénie on 12 August gives a graphic picture of his experiences (which must have been those of many other people, if only too often with a different ending):

On Saturday the 11th, towards eight in the morning, a man came to warn me that the women of the Porte Saint-Paul were going to lead all the people, spurred on by a false rumour that there were arms in my house, into the *alleged vaults* that they have got into their heads so many times, and about which three or four visits have not yet been able to destroy their suspicions – there, my child, you have the fruits of calumny. . . .

Upon receipt of this warning, I opened everything in the house, writing-desks, cupboards, rooms and studies, all in fact, being determined to yield up my person and my house to the severe inquisition of all comers. But when the mob arrived, the noise and their shouts were so loud that my agitated friends would not allow me to go downstairs, and all advised me to save at least my person. As they were fighting to open my gates, I was obliged to get away through the upper end of my garden; but they had put a man on guard, who cried out: 'There he is, making off!' although I was walking slowly. He ran along the boulevard to warn all the people assembled at my main gate; I only doubled my steps, but the women, a hundred times more cruel than the men in their horrible abandonment, all gave chase to me. It is certain, my Eugénie, that your unfortunate father would have been torn to pieces by them, if he had not been well ahead of them; for the search not yet having been made, nothing could have got it out of their heads that I was escaping because of my guilt. . . .

I entered the house of a friend whose door was shut after me, in a street which, making an angle with that along which the cruel women were running, caused them to lose track of me, though I could hear their cries. You will pardon me, my dearest child, if at this moment of peril I had conceived a horror of all your sex. . . .

While I was shut up in an impregnable refuge, thirty thousand souls were in my house, where, from the lofts to the cellars, locksmiths opened all the cupboards, or masons excavated in the vaults, probing everywhere . . . and making holes in the walls, while others in the garden dug right down to virgin soil, all going through the apartments twenty times, but some of them saying, to the great regret of the bandits who had gathered there in their hundreds: 'If we find nothing here relating to our search, the first one who pilfers the smallest piece of furniture, even a ring, will be hanged without mercy, then axed into pieces by us.' . . .

At last, after seven hours of the most stringent search, the mob withdrew, at the orders of I know not what chief. My people have swept up more than an ounce and a half of dust; *but not the smallest item lost.* Children raided the green fruit; I only wish it had been riper. . . . A woman in the garden picked a gilli-flower; she was repaid with twenty blows; they wanted to duck her in the poplar pool.

I returned home. They had carried their attentions to the point of drawing up a report garlanded with 100 signatures testifying that they had found nothing suspect in my possession. . . . I dined at home as if nothing had happened, and my people, who had all behaved marvellously and as faithful servitors, told me all the details: 'Monsieur, they have been thirty times in the cellars and not one glass of wine sniffed.' . . . 'They ransacked all the linen cupboards, and not a duster is missing'; another one: 'One of them came to warn me that your watch was beside your bed; there it is, Monsieur! there it is! Your spectacles, your pencils were on the writing table, and nothing has been disturbed.'

But there was one member of the household who was found to be missing after all these happenings: Mlle Follette had disappeared and was never seen again. Probably her nerves had been unequal to the strain of that terrible day, and she had bolted out of house and grounds into the unknown world outside.

Now that the affair was presumably over, it was suggested to Beaumarchais that there would be no harm in his spending the night in his house again; but he thought otherwise, in view of the warning he had received about bandits who were operating by mixing with the mob, and who had undoubtedly been inside his house that very day. He therefore decided to go round and spend the night at the house of a friend in the Rue des Trois-Pavilions, a quiet street in the Marais quarter. He duly set off after supper, and, snugly dug in there, with the front door securely fastened and only one of his friend's servants in the house with him, he prepared for a good night's rest. But

at midnight, the valet in his shirt, terrified, entered the room where I was: 'Monsieur, get up; the mob has come to look for you, they are hammering enough to break in the door; they have betrayed you at your house; the place is going to be pillaged.' . . . Scarcely awakened, the man's terror communicated itself to me. 'One moment,' I said, 'fright damages judgment.' I put on my overcoat, forgetting my jacket, and with my slippers on my feet, I said to him, 'Is there any exit by which one can get out of here?' 'None, monsieur, but hasten, for they are about to break in the door. Ah, what will my master say?' 'He will say nothing, my friend, for I am going to remove my person in order that they may respect his house. Open the door to them, I am coming down with you.'

Beaumarchais now starts to come downstairs with the terrified valet; on his way down he can see through a shutter that the street is full of people, which at once extinguishes the fleeting thought that had crossed his mind to jump from a window. Then, near the kitchen, his eye falls on a china cupboard whose large folding doors happen at that moment to be wide open. He continues his account to Eugénie:

For all asylum and last refuge, your poor father, my child, placed himself behind one of the doors, standing upright, supported on his cane, the door of this little closet strangely bulging in a manner impossible to describe; and the search began. Through the little windows giving on to the courtyard, I saw the candles moving about, going up, coming down, running through the rooms. They marched over my head, the court was guarded, the street door open, and I, standing on tiptoe and holding my breath . . . recovered my sang-froid. I had two pistols in my pocket and had considered for some time whether I ought or ought not to use them; my conclusion was that if I used them, I should be axed on the spot and should advance my death by an hour, while taking away the last chance of crying for help and perhaps obtaining it by giving my name, on the way to the Hôtel de Ville.

In this unpleasant situation Beaumarchais remained for over four hours, until rescued at last by no less a person than his friend Gudin, who appeared solemnly arrayed in the uniform of a National Guard, complete with musket and accompanied by several other persons! Gudin explained to him that he had been invited for his own safety to join forces with a patrol of the National Guard, but had presently found to his horror that they were on their way to surround and search for arms the very house where, as he knew, Beaumarchais was spending the night.

Such were the topsy-turvy conditions of life in Paris during those terrible days. Beaumarchais took great care to publish everywhere the fact that nothing had been found after the extensive search of his house, but it would not avail to save him from further trouble. 'On 23 August,' says Gudin, 'upon awakening, I perceived armed men in the streets, sentinels at the doors and under the windows. I hastened to my friend's apartment; I found him surrounded by sinister men occupied in searching his papers and putting his effects under seal. Calm in the midst of everything, he directed their operations. When they were finished, they took him with them, and I was left alone in that vast place, guarded by *sans-culottes* whose aspect made me doubt whether they were there to conserve the property or to give the signal for pillage. Beaumarchais had been carried off to the Mairie, where he defended himself so perfectly that his denouncers were confounded and were about to release him when Marat denounced him anew. . . .'

He was now taken to the Abbaye prison; here he would have remained, to lose his life in the September Massacres, but for an episode out of his past which was now to stand him in good stead. In December 1778, soon after his triumphant victory over La Blache at Aix, he had received the first of a series of long letters from a young girl of seventeen, signing herself simply as 'Ninon', in which she sought his advice about her love-life, having just been abandoned by the man to whom she declared she had sacrificed herself. In a letter of vast length she sought to prove, with a wealth of detail, that, as Loménie puts it, 'she was as virtuous in intention as she had been unvirtuous in fact'. Beaumarchais, in spite of all his preoccupations at that moment, was never one to refuse help to a woman, especially a young one, and he replied kindly, asking for further particulars that he might the better advise her in the light of his own not inconsiderable experience. The further particulars had been only too readily forthcoming; in short, he had drawn upon himself an avalanche of correspondence, to which he soon ceased to reply, having his hands more than full by that time with his American business. But he had not been forgotten by his correspondent, and one day in 1789 he had received a visit in person from 'Ninon', now a woman of twenty-eight and Comtesse de la Marinaie. Her morals had not improved with the passing years, but she was evidently attractive, and the susceptible Beaumarchais was soon captivated by her charms. Fortunately for him, by 1792 she had become the mistress of the Procurator of the Commune, one Manuel, and she was now able to use her influence to obtain Beaumarchais' release. It was in the nick of time: forty-eight hours later the general massacre of prisoners began.

Beaumarchais now went into hiding outside Paris during the day, but with obstinate courage he would come back into the city by night, picking his way in across the fields, in order to continue his chivvying of Ministers to fulfil their part of the bargain over the muskets. His action was partly due to his suspicion that the Minister Lebrun was trying to double-cross him by conducting the business on the quiet to his own profit. He even tackled the formidable Danton on the subject, who, at first exasperated by his persistence, was finally struck with the grim humour of the situation and burst out laughing. But in the end Beaumarchais' pertinacity had its reward: a commission of the Legislative Assembly, calling itself the 'Commission of Arms', declared that he had deserved well of the nation, and Lebrun was obliged to give him a passport to Holland, with the promise to remit to him at the Hague the money necessary to raise the embargo laid by the Dutch on the weapons; he was further assured that the French Ambassador there would give him every assistance.

Beaumarchais now set off for the Hague, *via* Le Havre and London. In the French seaport he was able to see his wife and daughter, and when he was safely gone to England Mme de Beaumarchais returned to Paris to look after his interests. In London he borrowed a large sum of money from an English merchant with whom he had dealings. But when he reached the Dutch capital he found obstruction at every turn: there was none of the promised money, and the French Ambassador had received no instructions. Letters to Lebrun produced, at first, evasive answers, and finally the outright declaration that the French Ministry no longer wanted the weapons.

For the Revolution was marching on, and the Legislative Assembly had given place to the Convention. On 1 December 1792 Beaumarchais at The Hague had the pleasure of reading in the newspaper that he was accused of conspiracy, of secret correspondence with Louis XVI, and that, once more, seals had been put on his house. His friends wrote at the same time, warning him of proposals to have him seized in Holland and brought back to Paris, and they begged him to return to England, which he did. But in London he read the account of his denunciation by Lecointre before the Convention, in which he was described as 'an essentially vicious man, corrupt by inclination, who has reduced immorality to a principle and villainy to a system'. Beaumarchais in obstinate fury was making plans to return to Paris and plead his cause in person – which would have been suicidal – when fortunately the English merchant from whom he had borrowed money on his previous visit had the presence of mind to devise an effective way of stopping him: he had Beaumarchais arrested for debt. However, the latter had also to think of his family in the clutches of the Convention, and, while Gudin set to work procuring funds to pay off the English debt, Beaumarchais with a flash of the old spirit wrote a long pamphlet to the Convention. As soon as his debt was cleared, in March 1793, he returned to Paris and had 6,000 copies of his pamphlet printed and distributed. To the ex-brewer Santerre, then Commandant of the National Guard, he wrote boldly: 'I have come to offer my head to the sword of justice if I cannot prove I am a great citizen. Save me, Citizen Commandant, from pillage and the dagger, and I shall again be of service to my country.' His pamphlet to the Convention is couched in such astonishingly plain-spoken terms that the wonder is that he preserved his head on his shoulders. 'I would defy the devil', he says, 'to advance any business, in this frightful time of disorder that they call liberty.' He dares to describe Marat as 'a little man with black hair, snub nose, a frightful countenance' and finishes up: 'O my country in tears! O unhappy French! What use will it have been to you to have thrown down bastilles, if robbers dance upon them and slaughter us on their ruins! True friends of liberty! know that its first executioners are licence and anarchy. . . .'

With all his daring speech, however, Beaumarchais proved his case: that his inability to supply the arms as agreed was owing to the Government's complete failure to give him the promised support. The upshot of the matter was that he was summoned before the Committee of Public Safety and required – the alternative being, of course, condemnation – to go again to Holland and fetch the muskets. The task had now become infinitely more difficult, firstly because Holland had joined the anti-French coalition and secondly because Lecointre's denunciation of Beaumarchais had drawn the attention of the British Government to the affair and they now had their eyes on the arms. Beaumarchais had tried to balance this by getting his English merchant friend to hold them at Tervuren as his own property, an expedient which would answer for the time being at least. But as Beaumarchais now insisted that he would need more money, and the French need of the weapons had become very great, the Committee allowed him another 618,000 francs in assignats (representing in actual money about 200,000 francs). They also bestowed upon him the high-sounding title of 'Commissioner of the Republic'.

So in June 1793 the former secret agent of Louis XV, now in his sixty-second year, set out again under the name of Pierre Charron in search of the muskets. His subsequent adventures were as complicated in intrigue as the plot of one of his own plays, and entailed journeys from Amsterdam to Basel, from Basel to Hamburg, from Hamburg to London – where, however, this time he was given three days to quit – while he used all manner of ruses, including the fictitious sale of the arms at one stage to an American merchant, to prevent their being seized by the Dutch or British Government. At the same time he was urging the Committee of Public Safety to settle the matter for good by ordering Pichegru to advance and seize the guns. But the wolves in power in Paris were now too busy devouring one another to pursue any coherent policy, and the only notice they took of their 'Commissioner' was to place his name on the list of *émigrés*, seize his property, stop his money and imprison his family. Upon the vigorous protest of Mme de Beaumarchais, however, the Committee thought again, and pronounced that 'the citizen Beaumarchais was fulfilling a secret mission and should not be treated as an *émigré*'. The seals were then removed from his property. But three months later, when a fresh set of thugs were in power, the order of the Committee of Public Safety was annulled, Beaumarchais was once more declared an *émigré*, his income was stopped, and seals were again set on his estate. His wife and eighteen-year-old daughter and his sister Julie were now imprisoned in the former convent of Port Royal, which was being used as a prison; they had the grim experience of arriving there just as a party was setting off on their last journey in the tumbrels, and of being put into the cells just vacated by these unfortunates. But, mercifully, Beaumarchais' family was saved by the fall of Robespierre, which at last brought to an end the blood bath which was sickening all but the most sadistic fanatics. In one of the very last of the carts to set out on the journey of no return there rode, alongside the luckless poet André Chenier, a certain Valentin Goezman, one-time Councillor of the Parlement Maupeou, and now condemned, in the terse words of the Public Prosecutor Fouquier-Tinville, as 'an agent and slave of despotism'.

But Beaumarchais probably did not hear of the fate of his old enemy. He was by this time a refugee in Hamburg, where a large number of prominent people had sought asylum, among them Talleyrand, just returned from America but still a proscribed *émigré*, and Joseph Louis, the future Minister of Louis XVIII, whose brilliant financial talent was well appreciated by Beaumarchais. But he was now without any news at all of his family, for, in her efforts to save their daughter, Marie-Thérèse had for the time being ceased to write to him and had resumed her family name, since, as the wife of an *émigré*, she had been required to divorce him. This she had duly done, to comply with the law, but she declared to the Committee: 'Your decrees oblige me to demand a divorce; I obey, although my husband, charged with a commission, is not an *émigré*, and never thought of being one. I attest it, and I know his heart. He will justify himself of this accusation, as he has of all the rest, and I shall have the satisfaction of marrying him a second time, according to your new laws.' But in the meantime the unhappy Beaumarchais, without any news of his family, was a prey to the greatest agony of mind. 'I sometimes wonder', he wrote at this time, 'if I am not mad; but on seeing . . . the succession of ideas by which I endeavour to ward off everything, I think I cannot be. But where am I to write to you?' he asks his wife. 'Under what name? Where do you live?'

And in the following spring all his work in the affair of the muskets was rendered vain. For in the midst of the wrangling which followed the fall of Robespierre the matter came up for discussion once more, and the wretched Lecointre not only reiterated his assertions of Beaumarchais' complicity with the Ministers of the late King but now added fresh accusations of similar connivance with those lately of the Committee of Public Safety; in short, Beaumarchais was accused of having defrauded the State from beginning to end. The uproar in the tribune once more attracted the attention of the British Government, and this time they delayed no longer in taking action: the arms were seized by them and carried off to Plymouth, for valuation by an arbitrator if they were found not to be French property. Beaumarchais was now in danger of losing all the money he had expended in the affair, with the added prospect of having to reimburse to his own Government the sum total of the assignats which had been advanced to him on his deposit of 750,000 livres. Fortunately, however, in June 1795 the British Government agreed to pay him, as the purported owner of the arms, at least a proportion of the money, and so, as far as Beaumarchais was concerned, the whole miserable business at last came to an end.

But he was still a proscribed *émigré*, and though his wife worked with unceasing persistence to try to get his name off the list, the difficulties were heartbreaking in the chaotic state of political affairs. As she wrote to him at this time:

A law is made today; four days after, it is repealed. Thus they took away from the Legislative Committee the power of striking off the names of *émigrés*; now they have given it back. In the interval, we have lost our *rapporteur*, who has left the Committee of Public Safety in his turn and has set out on a mission. It has been necessary to speak to his successor, to instruct him, stir him up, etc. In virtue of this new decree, we thought that the committees could decide alone on our affair. Not at all: at the Legislative Committee, they told us that it was to the Committee of Public Safety that we must go at once, since it was already in possession of the affair. We went there . . . they told us the Convention was taken by surprise, the affair could only be terminated by a decree, and not by a resolution; it was a Government matter, quite a special case. . . .

Although the fall of Robespierre had delivered Beaumarchais' family from the imminent menace of the guillotine, their position in other respects was hardly any better than his own. For under the law relating to *émigrés* his personal property and income were confiscated, all claims for debts passing into the hands of the Treasury, while his own debtors hastened to discharge themselves by paying in worthless assignats to the State. Thus the fortune which Beaumarchais had spent so much labour in building up was in ruins; while the famous mansion, now labelled 'National Property', was threatened with sale. Eugénie had conceived a horror of the place, after all the scenes with which it had been associated, and had persuaded her mother to rent a house in the Rue de Paradis-Poissonière. But it was necessary that some member of the family should inhabit the mansion, if it were not to go entirely, and it was Julie, now sixty years of age but with her gay courage quite unquenched by her recent experiences, who went to live in the great empty building with one aged servant. She writes to her sister-in-law, Mme de Beaumarchais, a letter which shows that she can still laugh through the trials of the hard struggle to live:

Morbleu! my child. . . . Here are the fruits, as they were last year, brought into requisition; the cherries being ripe, they are going to gather and sell them to-morrow, and the other things in time, and then close the garden to the profane and gluttonous. Is it not delightful to occupy this solitary house for six months, and to eat none of its fruit except the stones, and they will sell even them with the rest. It is for the birds I speak; for as for myself, I never thought, considering the price at which these things sell, that there would be much left for us, even though the garden is ours. However, it is a pity the agency have put their noses in here this year. The gardener from that authority came yesterday; they are going to have a sale one of these days; see whether you will bid, or rather prevent this robbery by some decisive act towards the agency; and since they have suspended the inventory, why will they not also leave our fruit suspended on the trees? On my honour, I believe we shall never get out of this state of things. What times!

Here is a pound of veal they bring me for 28 francs and yet it is cheap; it is worth 30. Rage! Fury! Curses! How can one live ruining oneself, and spending three times one's fortune? How happy are those who have gone before me! They do not feel the beatings of my head, the tears that are in my eyes, nor my devouring fever, nor my teeth, sharpened to eat 28 francs' worth of veal; they feel nothing of our misfortunes.

For with the rapidly continuing depreciation of the wretched assignats, the price and scarcity of food were bringing something very near famine conditions. A friend of Mme de Beaumarchais tramped the suburbs of Paris trying to find her some bread; he wrote to her from Soizy on 5 June 1795 that

they say here that at Briare one can have flour; if it were so, I would bargain with a safe man in this neighbourhood, who would take it to your house by the passage boat which goes from Briare to Paris; but all that very much increases the price. You will let me know what you think of it; in the meantime I do not despair of getting hold of some rolls. Ah! if I had the gift of miracles, I would shower on you, not manna from heaven, but some good and very white bread.

But all things, even the most unpleasant, must have their end, and for Beaumarchais this was to come at the close of the year, when at last the Convention fell and was succeeded by the Directory. His wife and their friends now renewed their efforts to get the proscription lifted from his name. In the summer of 1796 they were successful, and on 5 July Beaumarchais was able at last to return to Paris, to be reunited with his family and to set about trying to rebuild his ruined fortune.

Chapter 20

LAST YEARS

It was indeed a strange new world to which Beaumarchais returned in 1796. In the violent reaction from the régime of terror and blood which had just been overthrown people thought of nothing but eating, drinking and enjoyment. Society was ruled by the Director Barras' mistress, Mme Tallien, who queened it at the Luxembourg and set the fashions, which ran up and down the scale of exoticism from Oriental turbans and scarves to diaphanous Greek and Roman draperies when the sculptor David made classical times the vogue. Society itself was the oddest mixture, where the wives of *émigrés* and regicides mingled together, and the men, for the most part contractors and speculators, were either kings of the financial world or on the way to becoming so; the wars which enriched them, and which were now to go on almost continuously for the next twenty years, having taken out of France most other able-bodied males. In this strangely assorted and tasteless society there reigned a fevered activity. There was dancing everywhere, even on the site where the guillotine had so recently stood, and sons of the victims could sometimes be seen dancing with daughters of the men who had sent their parents to execution. But family life, which had been so powerful an influence under the old régime, had been practically destroyed; divorce had been made so easy that any husband or wife could take a new partner if the original one had been away for six months – a startling state of affairs for many a man returning to his home from the wars.

In Beaumarchais' own family there were two matrimonial affairs which required immediate attention: the first was to remarry his own wife, and the second to get his daughter suitably settled. While Eugénie had been still at the convent, was known to be a rich heiress and was considered to be nearing marriageable age, her father had received numerous offers from ingenuous persons who either wished to marry her themselves or wished her to be reserved for a son still at school. But a certain young man named André-Toussaint Delarue, who in

1789 had been aide-de-camp to Lafayette and who was to continue a long career of honourable service under the succeeding régimes, had always been a faithful admirer of Eugénie. Beaumarchais, in a letter to Gudin, describes Delarue as 'a good young man, who persisted in wishing to marry her, when it was thought I possessed nothing. She, her mother and I considered we ought to reward this generous attachment. Five days after my arrival I made him this handsome present.'

But when these family matters were settled there still remained to Beaumarchais the task of rebuilding, as far as he could, his shattered fortune, and he spent the next two years trying to obtain a settlement from the Government. Acknowledgment was finally made of the State's debt to him of 998,875 francs (which included his deposit of 745,000 francs); this was less than he had claimed, but it was no small achievement to have obtained an acknowledgment even of this amount, which at least would enable him to satisfy his most pressing creditors. But it was too good to be true; a short time afterwards a fresh commission was deputed to reconsider the case, and its decision was to annul the conclusion reached by the first. The history of the whole affair is painfully reminiscent of Beaumarchais' dealings with the American Congress, with whom he was of course still arguing his case. The new commission, calmly passing over the financial loss incurred by Beaumarchais under his unjust proscription while he was absent on the State's business, and the money expended by him in keeping the muskets at Tervuren, not only denied that the State owed him any money, but declared him to be its debtor to the amount of 500,000 francs. Apart from the injustice of this decision it provided great encouragement to Beaumarchais' creditors, who became ever more pressing in their demands. He was still saddled with his great white elephant of a mansion on the boulevard, which he could neither sell nor let, and yet had to find money for the taxes on its two hundred windows and four iron gates. Yet he did not cease the uphill struggle, drawing up pamphlets in his usual style and besieging the Ministers, and that his efforts were not in the end entirely unsuccessful, in spite of all the difficulties, becomes evident when Gudin's brother, who acted as Beaumarchais' book-keeper and cashier, was able to report by 1809 to Eugénie and her mother that their fortune had risen once more to very near the million mark – and that in spite of the fact that the money owing from America was still outstanding.

Gudin himself had taken refuge in the country at the height of the Terror, and one of the first things which Beaumarchais did on his return was to write to his friend and beg him to come back. Gudin, however, was in such financial straits that he could not even raise the money for the journey until Beaumarchais made him an advance. But he writes of their meeting: 'I came from the depths of my retreat to embrace my friend. Meeting after so many years, after so many atrocious events, was it not to be saved from the perils of shipwreck and to find ourselves on the rock? It was in a way like escaping from the tomb, to embrace each other among the dead, after an unhoped-for resurrection.' Yet he would not at first consent to rejoin Beaumarchais' household, feeling that, in their state of financial stringency, he would only be a burden to them. But later, when the money affairs of both had become more settled, Gudin returned to live with his friend.

Beaumarchais meanwhile had lost none of his interest in the world around him, and in the midst of all his financial worries could still find time and energy to pour out a stream of letters and pamphlets: now expressing his indignation at the shameful negligence which permitted the body of the great Turenne to be left lying about among animal skeletons in the Jardin des Plantes; now saluting in verse a wondrous motor called the *vélocifère*, or expressing his keen interest in the beginnings of aeronautics. Before the Revolution two balloon flights across Paris, at which Beaumarchais and Gudin had both been present, had caused the greatest interest and excitement; in 1798 Beaumarchais writes to the Minister of the Interior that

One of the most majestic ideas in discovery which have honoured our century is certainly *the ascension of heavy bodies in the light fluid of the air*; but our nation, which is only momentarily infatuated with the finest of discoveries, has soon made nothing but child's play out of the one calculated to change the face of the globe more than that of the compass, if people would seriously occupy themselves with raising the idea to the point of aerial navigation. . . . Can spherical bodies be directed? An enlightened thinker communicated to me an idea which he had conceived for directing in the atmosphere ships without weight, but under the elongated form of fish, to which the aeronaut is to be assimilated. Scientific men contested the possibility of this direction being given, with the thoughtless objection that there is no supporting point in the air; although everyone sees birds of all size rise, support themselves, direct themselves, and travel through the air in every way, notwithstanding their weight. . . . This reasoning, worthy of a musketeer, irritated me with our savants; but while they were discouraging the aeronaut, Monsieur Scott, I encouraged him myself by printing what he had written. . . .

The Revolution came; I lost sight of Monsieur Scott, and thought he had been swallowed up by it; as for myself, proscribed during four years, I abandoned the idea of navigating in the air, forced as I was to drag myself along the miry roads of the north of Upper Germany.

Finally, recalled to my post by the justice of the Government, chance made me find my aerial navigator again. . . . His ideas were ripened by years of reflection; they appeared to me worthy of being offered to the first authorities. . . .

Ah! citizen, let us not always allow ideas which germinate with us to be perfected by usurping Englishmen; let us profit by this one ourselves; let it do honour to your Ministry; its author, with a modesty worthy of your benevolence, solicits a commission; appoint the members according to your choice. . . .

But not all Beaumarchais' letters were dealing with the practical affairs of everyday life; he could even find time for a dissertation on the hereafter, setting forth his views in a letter to the shady Morande, of all people, written about 1799:

I do not like your considering the dissolution of the body in your philosophical reflections as the fate which is exclusively destined for us. This body is not us; it will doubtless perish, but the Maker of such a splendid edifice would have made a work unworthy of His power if He reserved nothing of that great faculty which He has allowed to reach to a knowledge of Himself. My brother, my friend, my Gudin, often converses with me about this uncertain future, and our conclusion is always: let us at least deserve that it may be good; if it be so, we shall have made an excellent calculation; if we are to be mistaken in such a consoling view, this reflection on ourselves, preparing us for an irreproachable life, has very great comfort.

He had not, of course, lost his interest in affairs of the stage; he continued his struggle with the Comédie-Française over the question of author's rights – in the middle of which he was supervising a fresh production of *The Guilty Mother* in the national theatre; where it appeared, with an appreciable measure of success, in May 1797.

In January of that same year, however, a much more important event occurred in Beaumarchais' family circle: he became a grandfather. His beloved Eugénie, now Mme Delarue, gave birth to the first of her three children, a daughter (she was later to have two sons, who both had distinguished careers). But less than twelve months after this joyful event the family circle was to be reduced again by the loss of one of its original members; for in May 1798 Julie died at the age of sixty-two. In the last years of her life Julie had become very devout, but this had in no way damped her gay spirit; nor had six years of revolution, or the months she had spent in prison under the shadow of the guillotine, been able to undermine her well-balanced serenity of mind. Gay and courageous to the last, she could still compose and sing, as she lay dying, the rhymed couplets which her brother not inappropriately described as her 'swan song'.

Beaumarchais' own health had by this time begun to show some ominous signs of wear and tear; the year before Julie's death he had written to Eugénie that during the night of 6-7 April he had had a long period of unconsciousness, 'which was the second warning nature has given me in five weeks'. The passport which had been issued to him in Hamburg at the time of his return to France described him as being stout and of florid complexion, and Beaumarchais' own description of himself at about this time was *un bon veillard grand, gris, gros, gras*. However, he assured Eugénie that his condition was better, and as time rolled on into the last year of the century he seemed to be again in good health, and certainly in excellent spirits.

On 18 May 1799, says Gudin, Beaumarchais and he

had spent the day together in the midst of his family, with one of his oldest friends. He had been very gay, and had recalled in the conversation several events of his youth, which he recounted with pleasing charm, and which carried back our memories to the happiest days of the monarchy. I left him at ten o'clock in the evening. He retired at eleven, after embracing his wife. She was slightly indisposed, and he recommended her to take some precautions for her health; his own seemed perfect. He went to bed giving orders that he should be awakened early. He fell asleep and woke no more. He was found next morning in the same position as that in which he had placed himself on getting into bed; there was no disturbance to indicate that he had suffered in any way. The doctors and surgeons who were summoned declared that he had died of a severe apoplexy; that the blood was carried to the brain and had deepened his sleep instead of disturbing it; that he had gone out of life as he had entered it, without suffering and without having any idea of what had happened to him. He had often said to me that he would like to finish that way. But we could hardly believe that he was dead. His son-in-law and his wife showered attentions on him in vain. His daughter was pregnant; it was necessary to conceal from her the unexpected loss she had suffered, and she had to be prepared for it by degrees.

Yet even after Beaumarchais' death the tongues of spiteful gossip were not stilled. Because he had died so suddenly, there were not wanting those who declared that he had committed suicide – on no better grounds, apparently, than that he had sometimes discussed the ethics of the matter with Lemercier. But apart from the fact that the doctors who attended Beaumarchais were unanimous in declaring that he had died from perfectly natural causes (of which, as we have seen, he had already had warning), his son-in-law Delarue wrote personally to Loménie in 1849, refuting the tale of his father-in-law's suicide, and giving an account of his end which tallies exactly with Gudin's version:

Beaumarchais after passing with his family a most lively evening, during which his wit had never been more free or more brilliant, was struck with apoplexy. His valet, on coming into his room in the morning, found him in the same position in which he had left him when he had put him to bed, with a calm face and apparently asleep. I was informed of it by the cries of despair uttered by the valet. I hurried to my father-in-law's room, when I discovered that he had suffered a sudden and tranquil death; my only subsequent care was to save his daughter, who really worshipped her father, the anguish of hearing news which might have been fatal to her if it had been communicated without preparation. This, Sir, is the exact truth.

Moreover, at the time of his death, Beaumarchais had been engaged in combating the iniquitous decision of the commission which had reversed the verdict of its predecessor by making him the State's debtor by 500,000 francs instead of its creditor to the amount of 997,000 francs. Only ten days before his death he had written to Talleyrand, with whom he was on friendly terms:

It is against this murderous commission, *which I shall deal with separately* . . . that I now appear before the Minister of Finance; I at once place my just claims before him in a light as clear as the sun, and this is the time for you to speak in my favour.

So it is clear that at the very moment of his death Beaumarchais was engaged in yet another of those battles against injustice which had occupied so much of his career; scarcely a time when he would have been likely to commit suicide.

They buried him in a little grove in the corner of his garden, which he had selected for that very purpose. 'It was there that we placed him,' says Gudin, 'it was there that his son-in-law, his relatives, his friends and a few men of letters who loved him paid their last respects, and that Collin d'Harleville read a discourse which I had composed in my overflowing sorrow, but which I was in no state to deliver.' But Beaumarchais was not to rest there for very long. His house and garden were acquired by the municipality of Paris in 1818 as part of an improvement scheme, and in 1822 his remains were removed to the cemetery of Père Lachaise. Today the site of his fabulous mansion and garden lies under the surface of the Boulevard Beaumarchais.

It has often been asked why Beaumarchais should have been throughout his career the object of such savage attacks by so many bitter enemies. He seems to have pondered over this question himself, for Loménie found among his papers a curious document written in Beaumarchais' hand which is at once an attempted explanation and a concise summary of his career:

From the period of my thoughtless youth I have played every instrument, but I belonged to no body of musicians; the professors of the art detested me.

I have invented some good machines; but I did not belong to the body of engineers and they spoke ill of me.

I composed verses, songs; but who would recognize me as a poet? I was the son of a watch-maker.

Not caring about the game of Loto, I wrote some pieces for the stage, but people said: 'What is he interfering with? He is not an author, for he has immense speculations, and enterprises without number.'

Unable to meet anyone who would undertake my defence, I printed long pamphlets, in order to gain actions which had been brought against me, and which may be called atrocious; but people said: 'You see very well that these are not like those our advocates produce; he does not tire you to death. Will such a man be allowed to prove without us that he is in the right?'

I have treated with Ministers on the subject of great points of reform of which our finances were in need; but people said: 'What is he interfering in? This man is not a financier.'

Struggling against all the powers, I have raised the art of printing in France by my superb editions of Voltaire – the enterprise having been regarded as beyond the capabilities of one individual; but I was not a printer, and they said the devil about me. I had constructed at the same time the first establishments of three or four paper factories without being a manufacturer; I had the manufacturers and dealers for my adversaries.

I have traded in the four quarters of the globe; but I was not a regular merchant. I had forty ships at sea at one time, but I was not a ship-owner, and I was calumniated in all our seaports.

A ship of war of fifty-two guns belonging to me had the honour of fighting in line with those of His Majesty at the taking of Grenada. Notwithstanding the pride of the Navy, they gave the cross to the captain of my vessel, and military rewards to my other officers, and what I, who was looked upon as an intruder, gained was the loss of my flotilla, which this vessel was convoying.

And nevertheless, of all Frenchmen. . . . I am the one who has done the most for the liberty of America, the begetter of our own; for I was the only person who dared to form the plan and commence its execution, in spite of England, Spain, and even France; but I did not belong to the class of negotiators, and I was a stranger in the bureaux of the Ministers.

Weary of seeing our uniform habitations, and our gardens without poetry, I built a house which is spoken of; but I did not belong to the arts.

What was I, then? I was nothing but myself, and myself I have remained, free in the midst of fetters, calm in the greatest of dangers, making head against all storms, directing speculations with one hand, and war with the other; as lazy as an ass, and always working; the object of a thousand calumnies, but happy in my home, having never belonged to any set, either literary or political or mystical; having never paid court to anyone, and yet repelled by all.

This is not, of course, the whole explanation of the enmity which Beaumarchais aroused. It will have been already sufficiently apparent that modesty was not one of his characteristics. His failings were mainly those of the parvenu: he was boastful and ostentatious, with a brazen self-assurance which was frequently taken for insolence. He must always be in the limelight and be talked about, not only over the house that he built but even in regard to his most intimate family affairs: when he at last married the woman who had been his mistress for twelve years he must needs trumpet the fact in a public announcement expressed in a manner which was considered the height of bad taste. Moving in a society in which money-making was still looked upon as a distinctly low occupation (in the time of Francis I the nobility had been forbidden to engage in trade, on pain of losing their hereditary status) and it was not unusual for a nobleman to load himself with a mountain of debt which he could have no hope – or intention – of paying off, Beaumarchais could yet never rid himself of his instinct to see everything in terms of money. It is not inappropriate when in the first act of the *Marriage* Suzanne tells Figaro: '*De l'intrigue et de l'argent, te voilà dans ta sphère.*' The Comte de Vaudreuil, who had been instrumental in getting *The Marriage of Figaro* performed at Gennevilliers, drew his income from the French West Indies, which meant that his source of supply was cut off during the war in America; but since he was the lover of Mme de Polignac, the Queen's most intimate friend, he had been provided with an allowance from the royal treasury. Beaumarchais came to see him one morning at Versailles, at such an early hour that the Count was scarcely out of bed, and, eagerly outlining to him a new financial project he had just conceived, suggested that if de Vaudreuil would give his support to the scheme it would be made well worth his while. 'M de Beaumarchais,' was that haughty nobleman's reply, 'you could not have arrived at a luckier time; for I have passed a good night, my digestion is in excellent condition and I never felt better in my life. Had you come to me yesterday with such a proposal, I should have thrown you out of the window.' It was indeed Beaumarchais' financial operations which probably did more than anything else to earn him public distrust, in an age when bitter experience had taught that great wealth was seldom honestly acquired, and large-scale financial projects were therefore looked upon with misgiving. In Beaumarchais' case distrust was deepened by the mystery which shrouded so many of his dealings with Pâris-Duverney, while his adventures in connection with the various diplomatic missions of his early career had unfortunately shown that he was by no means scrupulous in the methods he employed. Public opinion echoed only too well the reproach which Almaviva levels at Figaro in the *Marriage*: 'Why must there always be something shady in what you do?' It was in any case difficult to take the Bohemian writer of frivolous and distinctly Rabelaisian comedy as a serious financier and man of business, while Beaumarchais undoubtedly dissipated his many-sided talents by trying to do too many things at the same time. His work for the theatre suffered from this, no less than his other activities: there is not in his plays the steady and progressive improvement in quality such as is to be found, for instance, in those of Molière.

Yet those who disliked or even detested Beaumarchais were usually the people who did not really know him. The contemporary dramatist Arnault was an old friend and a frequent visitor to the house on the boulevard. He says:

I went to visit him there from time to time, and I saw nothing which did not confirm me in the first opinion I had formed of him. This man, so terrible when irritated, was in fact a very kindly soul. Full of domestic affection, adored by the family he in turn worshipped, he looked like a retired old soldier, an old soldier who is resting, although he is still in a condition to take up arms. Of all the authors then in repute, Beaumarchais was the one who most encouraged young people.

Gudin, who probably knew him more closely than any other of his friends, declares that it was impossible to know Beaumarchais well without becoming fond of him, and that he had been loved passionately by all three of his wives and by his mistresses. Certainly his widow (who was to survive him until 1816) wrote, a few days after his death:

Our loss is irreparable. The companion of twenty-five years of my life has disappeared, and leaves me nothing but useless regrets, a frightful solitude, and memories that nothing can efface. He forgave with a good grace, willingly forgot injuries and bad turns. He was a good father, a zealous and useful friend, and the natural defender of all the absent who were attacked in front of him. He was above the petty jealousies so common among men of letters, he advised and encouraged all, and served them both with his purse and his counsels.

As for his affairs with other women, it may be doubted whether these were, on his side, much more than an expression of his abounding vitality. He was a man of his time and environment: '*Toute femme en vaut un homage,*' he once declared, '*bien peu sont dignes de regrets.*'
But there can be no doubt that he was a good son to his old father and a good brother to all his sisters; he provided dowries for those who married, and also for his niece, the only child of Tonton, Mme de Miron. To Julie, who never married, he made an annuity of 4,000 francs, and in her will, after distributing her few possessions among her friends and asking for their prayers on her behalf, she concludes:

As for you, my excellent brother, you from whom I hold everything, and to whom I can only give everlasting thanks for all the good you have done to me: if it is true, as I do not doubt, that one survives the tomb with the noblest part of one's being, then my grateful and devoted soul will not cease to love you in the infinite duration of the centuries.

The son of his elder sister, Mme Lepine, who went to serve in America and was subsequently killed there, wrote to Beaumarchais before going into action:

Your nephew, my very dear Uncle, may perhaps lose his life, but he will never do a deed unworthy of one who has the honour of belonging to you. This is as certain as the tenderness which he will always have for the best of uncles.

Beaumarchais' papers and correspondence also give evidence of many lifelong friendships extending over thirty or forty years, some even going back to the days when he was a young clock-maker. He was by nature a kind man, when not lashed by the attacks of vitriolic enemies, and if, with his craving for self-advertisement, he often took care to publicize his larger benefactions to charity, there were many other individual cases which remained unknown until after his death. 'The inventory which is made at a man's death,' says Gudin, 'often reveals the secrets of his life. That of Beaumarchais showed us that to succour families in distress, artists, men of letters, men of quality, he had advanced more than 900,000 francs without hope that these sums would ever be repaid. If one adds to these, sums that he had lavished without leaving the smallest trace, one would be convinced that he had expended more than 2,000,000 francs in benevolences.' Gudin even declares that Mme Goezman, whose perjured testimony so nearly sent Beaumarchais to the galleys, was among those helped by him when she had fallen into poverty and distress.

Even those who had only known Beaumarchais slightly were often captivated by his charm. The Baronne d'Oberkirch, who met him at the time of the production of *The Marriage of Figaro*, and had been prejudiced against him beforehand by hearing of his reputation, has to admit that 'I admired M. de Beaumarchais very much; he had a handsome, open, intellectual countenance, with perhaps an expression a little too bold. He was in every way a remarkable man. It is said that he loved his daughter with the greatest affection, and I do not believe it possible that a good father could be a bad man. M. de Beaumarchais' conversation is quite as witty and agreeable as his writings. . . . The intelligence and determination of this man are almost miraculous. "When I undertake anything, Madame, I always succeed, because I make it the sole object of my thoughts and every act and word of mine has reference to it. I only think of how soon it may be accomplished and in the end I have the double satisfaction of conquering a difficulty and obtaining what I wish." '

After Beaumarchais's death Gudin proposed to produce a full-scale biography of his friend; for although La Harpe had written about him at some length in his *Cours de littérature* it was felt that he had not given sufficient account of Beaumarchais' struggles and adventures in relation to the history of his time. Gudin therefore produced a 419-page manuscript which he intended to place at the beginning of an edition of Beaumarchais' works which he published in 1809. It was not, however, a very accurate account of the early life of its subject, and Beaumarchais' widow, after having read it through, was unwilling to have it published, since Gudin had given vent to certain views on the subject of religion which were current in the century of Voltaire but quite out of place in the changed intellectual climate of 1809. She feared that the publication of these would injure not only his own reputation but that of her late husband as well. As this was of course very far from being Gudin's intention, he bowed to her wishes and his manuscript went into retirement alongside his unpublished history of France. It was not until 1888 that it was rescued from the recesses of the

Bibliothèque Nationale and published by Maurice Tourneux, who had already edited the voluminous correspondence of Baron Grimm. By that time both Loménie and Lintilhac had published their detailed studies of Beaumarchais based on papers and correspondence in the archives of his family, of the Bibliothèque Nationale and of the Comédie-Française.

ROSSINI:

THE BARBER OF SEVILLE REBORN

BEAUMARCHAIS, like Mozart, had not outlived the century of which they were both so essentially a part. But the characters created by Beaumarchais had not yet reached the full extent of their operatic career.

On 29 February 1792, less than two months after Mozart's death, the wife of the town-crier of Pesaro, on the Adriatic coast of Northern Italy, gave birth to a son, while in the next room her frenzied spouse was engaged in demolishing with a stick the statuettes of the saints whom he considered had failed him by ignoring his frantic pleas for the shortening of his wife's labour. Only St James survived the holocaust, for at the very moment when doom was about to descend upon him also, the unmistakable wail of a newly born infant was heard coming from the next room. Thus did Gioacchino Rossini make his agitating appearance into a world which he would one day delight with the music of the thirty-eight operas he was to compose before he had lived as many years.

By the fateful summer of 1815, which saw the final overthrow of Napoleon, the young Rossini, who, as noted by a contemporary French musician, was 'making a devil of a fine reputation for himself just now in Italy', had reached Naples, that operatic Mecca of the period, where the aged Paisiello, fifty-two years older than he, was living in retirement – though jealously watchful of any new star rising in the operatic firmament. Rossini, however, stayed in Naples only long enough to present an opera on Elizabeth I of England, which was well received, for he had already been invited to go to Rome. On his arrival there, to produce his latest work, *Torvaldo e Dorliska*, he was approached by the director of the Argentina Theatre, the Duke Francesco Sforza-Cesarini, who was searching for a suitable *opera buffa* libretto which Rossini might set to music for the theatre. The composer himself had the idea of approaching the poet Sterbini, his librettist for

Torvaldo, with the proposal that he should make a new libretto out of Beaumarchais' *Barber of Seville*. Sterbini agreed to do so, and on 26 December 1815, the very day of the first performance of *Torvaldo*, Rossini signed a contract with Sforza-Cesarini in which he undertook to provide the score of the new opera by the following 20 January – a period of little more than three weeks.

There was obviously no time to be lost; poet and composer came to live under the same roof and set to work. Sterbini began by reading Beaumarchais' play to Rossini. Then as he wrote the lines of the libretto Rossini set it to music, throwing the sheets as they were completed to copyists who were sitting in the room with them. Rossini worked at such speed that he sometimes found himself ahead of the librettist, and it was then he who would suggest verses for the music he was already carrying in his head. Although the main framework of Beaumarchais' plot is reproduced in both settings of the opera, Sterbini carefully avoided using the same distribution of scenes as Paisiello. (The production of a libretto from Beaumarchais' comedy was of course made easier by the fact that the original play had first been intended by its author as a comic opera, and had been already interspersed with songs based on airs he had brought from Spain.) As regards the music, however, where Paisiello would have employed the recitative characteristic of his day, Rossini replaced it with dialogue sustained by the orchestra, in accordance with his usual practice of using the orchestra to emphasize vocal expression in a continuously flowing current of melody. There is no truth in Stendhal's tale that Rossini wrote to ask Paisiello's permission to re-set the opera; for it was not in the least unusual, in those days, for composers to use plots which had already been made into operas. But when the libretto went to press he did try to ward off possible trouble by changing its title to *Almaviva* and by prefacing it with the following notice:

ADVERTISEMENT TO THE PUBLIC

Beaumarchais' comedy, entitled *The Barber of Seville, or the Useless Precaution*, is presented at Rome in the form of a comic drama, under the title of *Almaviva, or the Useless Precaution*, in order that the Public may be fully convinced of the sentiments of respect and veneration by which the author of the music of this drama is animated with regard to the celebrated Paisiello, who has already treated the subject under its original title.

Himself invited to undertake this difficult task, the *maestro* Gioacchino Rossini, in order to avoid the reproach of entering rashly into rivalry with the immortal author who preceded him, expressly required that *The Barber of Seville* should be versified entirely anew, and also that new situations should be added for the musical pieces, which, moreover, are required by the modern theatrical taste, entirely changed since the time when the renowned Paisiello wrote his work. . . .

This may have disarmed Paisiello, but it did not disarm his supporters in Rome, who would have to be confronted at the first performance of the opera, the score of which was ready early in February. Roman audiences had at any time the reputation of being tough; Michael Kelly said of them that they 'assume that they are the most sapient critics in the world; they are certainly the most severe. They have no medium: all is delight or disgust. . . . It is customary for the composer of an opera to preside at the pianoforte the first three nights of its performance, and a precious time he has of it in Rome. Should any passage in the music strike the audience as similar to one of another composer, they cry, "Bravo, thief!" or, "Bravo, Paisiello! Bravo, Sacchini!" if they suppose the passage stolen from them, "the curse of God light on him who first put a pen into your hand to write music!" This I heard said, in the Teatro del Altiberti, to the celebrated composer Gazzaniga, who was obliged to sit patiently at the pianoforte to hear the flattering commendation.'

In addition to this well-known ferocity of Roman audiences, Rossini had also to contend with supporters of the rival Teatro Valle; the latter seem to have been chiefly responsible for the virtual wrecking of the performance of the opera at its first presentation on 20 February 1816. Mme Giorgi-Righetti, who sang the part of Rosina, has left an account of that disastrous evening. The overture was played to the accompaniment of a general murmuring from the audience. The part of Almaviva was sung by the Spanish tenor Garcia, and 'the composer was weak enough to allow him to sing beneath Rosina's balcony a Spanish melody of his own arrangement. Unfortunately, Garcia forgot to tune his guitar; he began the operation in the presence of the public; a string broke, the vocalist proceeded to replace it, but before he could do so, laughter and hisses were heard from all parts of the house. When Zamboni [Figaro] entered, with another guitar in his hand, a loud laugh was set up, and not a phrase of *"Largo al Factotum"* was heard. . . . The duet between Almaviva and Figaro was accompanied throughout with hissing and shouting. . . .' Mme Giorgi-Righetti was herself a great favourite in Rome, so that when she came on her singing was listened to and received with great applause; but when the unfortunate Basilio appeared there was fresh trouble. 'A small trapdoor had been left open on the stage' – almost certainly not by accident – 'at which he stumbled and fell. The singer bruised his face terribly and began his admirably dramatic air with his handkerchief to his nose. . . .' As the finale of the first act began a cat appeared – or more probably was deliberately let loose – on the stage: Figaro drove it one way, Bartholo another, and in trying to avoid Basilio it became entangled in Rosina's skirts; the act ended amid laughter, howls and piercing whistles. During the second act the uproar became even worse, in the midst of which the unhappy composer sat at the piano, outwardly unmoved. But he was unable to face the prospect of undergoing a similar ordeal for the second time on the following night, and he became conveniently indisposed. On the second night, however, musical appreciation began to get the better of factional prejudice, and the Romans decided at last to give the work a hearing, even applauding some portions of it. With each succeeding performance their approval gradually increased, and the opera finally achieved great success throughout Italy. Paisiello having died four months after its first performance, it was put on at Bologna later in the same year under the original title of *The Barber of Seville*, which it has retained ever since. It reached London in 1818, where it was performed both at the Haymarket Theatre and at Covent Garden; while in Vienna it was received from the first with rapture. In Paris, however, it had a chilly reception, and rival factions promptly put on Paisiello's version; but the public soon showed their preference for Rossini's opera.

There could, indeed, be little comparison between the old-fashioned, if graceful, simplicity of Paisiello's work – which in fact had been already going out of favour before the appearance of its rival – and the exuberant vitality of Rossini's *Barber*, fully orchestrated (where Paisiello had used only strings) with a brilliance only equalled up to then by Mozart. Rossini, moreover, had in his own character a good deal in common with Beaumarchais, so that the gay Bohemianism and mocking wit which he contrives to infuse into his music make his *Barber* far nearer to the spirit of its original author than the previous operatic settings of either of the comedies.

There is perhaps a gentle irony in the thought that Beaumarchais, so firmly convinced that the function of operatic music was merely one of supporting and embellishing the spoken word, should yet owe the full extent of his fame to that same music. For in the words of the French literary critic Dr André Hallays: 'It is Mozart and Rossini who have spread the glory of Beaumarchais beyond the narrow limits of a literature; it is they who have assured to Figaro that world-wide fame which only masterpieces of music can give to the characters of fiction.'

BIBLIOGRAPHY

UNPUBLISHED MANUSCRIPT MATERIAL

PUBLIC RECORD OFFICE State Papers: SP 78 France, 295-306 (1775-78).
BRITISH MUSEUM MS Egerton 16. Folios 60, 62, 64, 66 (1778-98).

PUBLISHED MATERIAL

ARNAULT, A.V., *Souvenirs d'un sexagénaire*, Vol. IV. Paris, 1833.

D'ARNETH, A. and GEOFFROY, A. (ed.), *Correspondance secrète entre Marie-Thérèse et le Cte de Mercy-Argenteau. Lettres de Marie-Thérèse et de Marie Antoinette.* 3 vols.
Paris, 1874-5 (2nd edition).

BAILLY, A., *Beaumarchais*. Paris, 1945.

BARBIER, E.J.F., *Chronique de la Régence et du règne de Louis XV*. Paris, 1885. 8 vols.

BEAUMARCHAIS, CARON DE, *Œuvres complètes*. ed. Saint-Marc Girardin. Paris, 1872.
Clavijo. Paris, 1880.
Mémoires dans l'affaire Goezman. Paris, 1873.

BLANC, L., *Histoire de la Révolution*, Vol. II. Paris, 1847.

BONNEVILLE DE MARSAGNY, L., *Mme de Beaumarchais*. Paris, 1890.

BOUTARIC, E., *Correspondance secrète inédite de Louis XV sur la politique étrangère avec le comte de Broglie*. 2 vols. Paris, 1866.

CAMPAN, MME, *Mémoires sur la vie privée de Marie-Antoinette*. 3 vols. Paris, 1823.

CLARK, G.L., *Silas Deane*. London, 1913.

CLUNN, H., *The Face of Paris*. London, 1933.

COLLÉ, CHARLES, *Journal et Mémoires*, Vol. III. Paris, 1868.

DA PONTE, LORENZO, *Memoirs*. London, 1929.

DEFFAND, MARQUISE DU, *Lettres à Horace Walpole, Voltaire*, etc. (and some of Walpole's letters to her) 4 vols. Paris, 1824.

DENT, E. J., *Mozart's Operas*. London, 1913.

DERWENT, LORD, *Rossini*. London, 1934.

DONIOL, H., *Histoire de la participation de la France à l'établissement des Etats-Unis d'Amérique*. 5 vols. Paris, 1886.

DOUGLAS, JOHN, 'Journal of a Tour through Germany, Holland and France, 1748-9', *Select Works* (ed. W. Macdonald), Salisbury, 1820.

DUCROS, L., *French Society in the Eighteenth Century*. London, 1926.

EDWARDS, H. SUTHERLAND, *Life of Rossini.* London, 1869.

EINSTEIN, A., *Mozart.* London, 1946.

FERNAN-NUÑEZ, COUNT OF, *Vida de Carlos III.* Madrid, 1898. 2 vols.

FLEURY, J.A.B., *Mémoires.* 3 vols. Paris, 1836-8.

GAILLARDET, F., *Mémoires sur la Chevalière d'Éon, et 12 lettres inédites de Beaumarchais.* Paris, 1866.

GOOCH, G.P., *Louis XV.* London, 1956.

GREEN, F.C., *Eighteenth-century France.* London, 1929.

GRIMM, BARON F.M., *Correspondance littéraire, philosophique et critique.* 16 vols. Paris, 1877-82.

GUDIN DE LA BRENELLERIE, *Histoire de Beaumarchais.* Paris, 1888.

HALLAYS, A., *Beaumarchais (Les Grands Écrivains Français).* Paris, 1897.

HOLMES, E., *Life of Mozart.* London, 1845.

HUSSEY, DYNELY, *Mozart.* London, 1928.

IMBERT DE ST ARMAND, *Les dernières années de Louis XV.* Paris, 1876.
Les beaux jours de Marie-Antoinette. Paris, 1879.
La fin de l'ancien régime. Paris, 1891.

KANY, CHARLES, *Life and Manners in Madrid, 1750-1800.* Berkeley, Cal., U.S.A., 1932.

KELLY, MICHAEL, *Reminiscences.* London, 1826.

KITE, E.S., *Beaumarchais and the War of American Independence (Studies in American History).* 2 vols. Boston, Mass., 1918.

LA HARPE, J.F. DE, *Cours de littérature ancienne et moderne.* Vol. XIII. Paris, 1825.

LIGNE, PRINCE DE, *Mémoires et mélanges historiques et littéraires.* 5 vols. Paris, 1827-9.

LINTILHAC, E., *Beaumarchais et ses œuvres.* Paris, 1887.

LOEWENBERG, A., *Annals of Opera, 1597-1940.* Geneva, 1955.

LOMÉNIE, L. DE, *Beaumarchais et son temps.* 2 vols. Paris, 1878 (3rd edition.)

LOOMIS, S., *Du Barry.* London, 1960.

MADELIN, L., *The French Revolution (National History of France.)* London, 1928.

MARSAN, JULES, *Beaumarchais et les affaires d'Amérique; lettres inédites.* Paris, 1919.

MAXWELL, C., *The English Traveller in France, 1698-1815.* London, 1928.

MERCIER, L.S., *Le Tableau de Paris.* 2 vols. London, 1802.

D'OBERKIRCH, BARONNE, *Mémoires.* 2 vols. Paris, 1853.

PERKINS, J.B., *France in the American Revolution.* London, 1911.

POMEAU, RENÉ, *Beaumarchais: l'homme et l'œuvre.* Paris, 1956.

RICHARD, PIERRE, *La vie privée de Beaumarchais.* Paris, 1951.

RIVERS, JOHN, *Figaro: the Life of Beaumarchais.* London, 1922.

SAINTE-BEUVE, C.A., *Causeries du Lundi.* Vol. VI. Paris, 1853.

SCHENK, E., *Mozart and his Times.* London, 1960.

SCHOLES, P., *Dr. Burney's Musical Tours in Europe.* 2 vols. London, 1959.

Ségur, Cte de, *Mémoires*. Paris, 1859.

Telfer, J.B., *The Strange Career of the Chevalier d'Éon*. London, 1885.

Thicknesse, P., *A Year's Journey through France and Part of Spain*. 2 vols. London, 1789 (3rd edition).

Vigée Le Brun, Mme, *Souvenirs*. 2 vols. London, 1879.

Villefosse, René H. de, *Histoire de Paris*. Paris, 1955.

Voltaire, *Œuvres complètes*.
 Vol. 23. Mélanges II. Paris, 1879.
 Vol. 48. Corresp. XVI. 1772-4. Paris, 1882.

Walpole, Horace (Earl of Orford) *Letters* (ed. by Mrs P. Toynbee). Vols. IX, XIII, XIV. London, 1903-5.

Wharton, F. *The Revolutionary Diplomatic Correspondence of the United States*. 25 vols. Washington, 1889.

Young, A., *Travels in France, 1787-9*. Cambridge, 1950.

INDEX